Tony Thomps

Tony Thompson is the crime correspondent of the *Observer*. He is also the author of *Gangland Britain*, published by Hodder.

Also by Tony Thompson
Gangland Britain

GANGS

TONY THOMPSON

A JOURNEY INTO THE HEART
OF THE BRITISH UNDERWORLD

HODDER

Copyright © 2004 by Tony Thompson

First published in Great Britain in 2004 by Hodder and Stoughton
A division of Hodder Headline
This edition published in 2005

The right of Tony Thompson to be identified as the Author
of the Work has been asserted by him in accordance with the
Copyright, Designs and Patents Act 1988

A Hodder paperback

20

A CIP catalogue record for this title
is available from the British Library

ISBN 978-0-340-83053-6

Typeset in Sabon by Hewer Text Ltd, Edinburgh
Printed and bound by Clays Ltd, St Ives plc

Hodder Headline's policy is to use papers that are natural,
renewable and recyclable products and made from wood grown in
sustainable forests. The logging and manufacturing processes are expected
to conform to the environmental regulations of the country of origin.

Hodder and Stoughton Ltd
A division of Hodder Headline
338 Euston Road
London NW1 3BH

For Harriet

CONTENTS

INTRODUCTION

In the ten years since the publication of *Gangland Britain* the nature of organised crime has changed almost beyond recognition. It used to be the case that both the criminals and the commodities they dealt with could be neatly isolated, most often along ethnic lines: one gang dealt crack, another smuggled cocaine, another heroin and so on. This is no longer the case.

Though the individual ethnic gangs are still there, the lines between have become increasingly blurred. The members of a gang that falls under the umbrella of 'Yardies' are just as likely to have been born in the UK and will be as active in fields like fraud, prostitution and heroin as they are in crack cocaine.

The very nature of criminal activities has changed too. A decade ago crimes like people-smuggling, identity theft and even money-laundering were in their infancy in the UK and virtually unknown to a wider public. They are now staple gang activities. Before 1999 there had never been a case of kidnap in the Greater Manchester area. Then, in a single weekend, the police force there found itself dealing with three all at once. Kidnap is now one of Britain's fastest-growing crimes and the trend looks set to continue.

With this and other trends in mind, the philosophy behind the writing of *Gangs* has been a simple one: despite the best intentions of police and law-enforcement agencies in Britain and around the world, the only people who truly know exactly what is going on in the world of crime are the criminals themselves.

To this end in the course of writing this book I have socialised with robbers, thugs, killers and thieves the length and breadth of the country, propositioned prostitutes of multiple nationalities, bought

1

guns, been threatened with knives and sampled two of the most dangerous drugs known to man.

Many of those who assisted me on my journey are too shy to be mentioned by name; others made it clear that if I indicated in any way I had ever spoken to them I would not live long enough to regret it. A few agreed to speak only after I handed over my full address and that of my parents so that they might more easily seek retribution should I ever betray them.

There have been some memorable encounters: the fearsome gangland hitman who asked me not to leave the bar where I had interviewed him until I had written up my notes and read out my piece to him. When I told him that simply would not be possible he explained that if I didn't he'd break my legs. Suitably inspired, I spent ten minutes transcribing my notes, then gave a fifteen-minute presentation of the man's life and times, thick with puff and praise.

'That was lovely,' he said. 'Just wait there one minute.' He left the room and returned with a group of burly friends. 'Now,' he said, taking a seat, 'read it again so this lot can hear it.' It took more than three hours of multiple readings before he finally let me go.

Then there was the time when I naïvely agreed to meet a notorious villain at his home so that he could 'put me straight' on some facts he felt I had got wrong in a magazine article. 'Ron' and his minder Chris – a man so tall that he had to stoop to avoid his head bashing on the ceiling of Ron's south London home – installed me in the back of a large silver Mercedes and set off at speed.

For more than ten minutes neither man said a word to me or one another and I grew increasingly uncomfortable. Then finally Chris turned to Ron. 'What do you want to do with him?' he grunted.

Ron briefly glanced at me in the rear-view mirror then turned to Chris. 'Let's take him down the docks.'

It's a cliché, I know, but my life really did flash before my eyes. How could I have been so stupid and put myself into such a sticky situation? I had a chilling vision of my lifeless body floating down the Thames.

INTRODUCTION

My mind was racing but so was the Merc. I wondered how badly hurt I would be if I threw myself from the car at speed, what the chances of being hit by the vehicle behind were. The panic started rising. I could feel my chest tightening, my throat getting dry, my heart pounding against the walls of my chest. This is it, I thought. I'm going to die.

All this and more was running through my mind as the car suddenly turned left and pulled into a small car park. One minute I was in fear of my life, the next I was laughing hysterically. They had taken me to the docks all right, their local pub – the Dockers Arms.

But not all my encounters ended well. In particular there was the time I travelled to Cambridge to meet a retired career criminal by the name of Jeremy Earls, who insisted he had information about widespread corruption and drug-dealing by members of Lincolnshire's police force.

For more than two hours I sat in his car and listened patiently to Earls's increasingly paranoid and gun-obsessed explanation of what he believed was going on. When he had finished he insisted I take away reams of statements, papers and tape-recordings that he said would support his claims. More than anything, Earls was convinced that his life was in danger, that he would be murdered and that his killers would attempt to make his death look like an accident or that he had committed suicide.

A few days later his name caught my eye as I flicked through some local news bulletins. Earls was dead. Soon after our meeting he had brutally murdered two young brothers, then shot himself in the head, all with an Uzi submachine-gun that he kept under the passenger seat of his car at all times. The same seat in which I had sat during our initial meeting.

A slightly surreal inquest later concluded that Earls was severely mentally ill and had committed suicide after deliberately laying a false trail to make it appear he had been murdered.

Despite such experiences, the lasting impression I have come away with is just how ordinary most of those involved in the world of organised crime truly are. Sure, there are a fair few psychopaths out there but even the people who are known to be as violent and ruthless as they come generally have families, a sense of humour and go through the same stresses and strains as the rest of us. Just because they manage to put it to one side when they are 'working' doesn't mean it isn't there.

'It's like that bit in *Pulp Fiction*,' one gang member told me, 'when the two hitmen are on their way to a job and they're talking about different burger chains around the world. Then before they go into the house one says to the other: "Let's get into character." It's just like that. When it's time to go to work, you go into a different mindset.'

It is this same mindset that *Gangs* seeks to explain.

Tony Thompson London 2004

ARMED ROBBERY

CHAPTER ONE

Jimmy Tippett Jnr throws open the door to his Humberside home and demands to know who the hell I am and what the fuck I want.

The stocky thirty-two-year-old, once jailed for beating a man senseless with a baseball bat and who famously fought as an unlicensed boxer under the sponsorship of Reggie Kray, is in no mood for visitors and cannot contain his anger at my arrival.

I stutter and stumble over my words as I try to explain the reason for my visit – to find out whether he's willing to talk about his alleged friendship with a long-dead drugs baron – but I manage only a few garbled phrases before a mobile phone bursts into life and Tippett rushes off to answer it.

The door is open so I step forward gingerly into the hallway as Tippett takes the call in his kitchen. I can make out a few snippets of conversation and soon realise that he's talking about the death of George Francis, a notorious south London gangster gunned down in an apparent contract killing just a few days earlier.

It was the second time that Francis, strongly suspected of helping dispose of gold bullion from the £26 million Brinks Mat robbery, had been the target of an assassination attempt. In May 1985, just two years after the Brinks Mat job, a hooded man ran into his Kent pub, singled him out and fired a volley of shots, one of which hit him in the shoulder.

Eighteen years later nothing was left to chance. As sixty-three-year-old Francis arrived at the office of his Bermondsey courier company, his killer emerged from hiding and pumped four bullets into his head and chest at point-blank range.

His death echoed that of another south London 'face', Brian Perry, also sixty-three and linked to the Brinks Mat raid, who had been shot dead in almost identical circumstances seventeen months earlier as he, too, arrived for work. Perry had died just a few hundred yards from where Francis had been shot but nobody had been convicted for the murder and there was an immediate suspicion that the same hitman was responsible for both deaths.

Tippett finishes his call and returns to the hallway, surprised to find me still waiting there. He motions towards the door and explains that I'll have to leave as he has some urgent business to attend to.

'Has something happened with the Francis murder?' I ask.

Tippett eyes me suspiciously. 'What do you know about it?'

I quickly tell him everything I've heard about it from other gangsters, journalists and police contacts, and he listens intently. I also take the opportunity to reiterate the reason for my visit, talk about the book I plan to write and also manage to mention the name of the well-respected criminal who provided me with Tippett's address. When I've finished, Tippett seems much calmer and the earlier hostility has almost gone.

'So, what's happening with the Francis case?' I ask again.

'The police have pulled in a seventy-two-year-old for questioning.'

'Anyone you know?'

'It's my dad.'

For a moment I am struck dumb with shock. Then a question falls out of my mouth before I have a chance to stop it: 'Do you think he did it?'

There is a long pause, then Tippett shrugs his shoulders and moves to one side. 'Perhaps you'd better come in after all.'

Jimmy Tippett Jnr was introduced to the gangster life at an early age. His father, a hugely successful boxer in the early fifties and once the leading contender for the British Lightweight crown, had been an honorary member of London's underworld almost from the moment he stepped into the ring.

With a reputation as a fearsome puncher – twenty-three of his twenty-four professional wins were by knockout – Tippett Snr earned the respect and friendship of the top villains of the day who then, as now, were big fans of the fight game. The links became even stronger when his sister, Julie, married notorious armed robber Freddie Sewell, who sparked a massive police hunt when he shot dead a police officer in Blackpool after a botched raid on a jeweller's.

After an unexpectedly early retirement from the fight game – he lost his licence after a brawl with six police officers – Tippett Snr used the power of his name to gain work as a celebrity minder and movie stuntman, associating with the top villains of his day along the way.

In the mid-1960s he opened a club, the El Partido in south London, which was closed down by Drugs Squad officers after a High Court judge labelled it: 'the biggest narcotics distribution centre in England'.

Since then, Tippett Snr's name has cropped up in connection with everything from the Brighton bombing to a multi-million pound diamond robbery, as well as a number of contract killings. But because none of the allegations against him have ever been proved in a court of law, Tippett's name has failed to appear in any of the many books that chronicle what is now regarded as the golden era of organised crime.

As we sit in his kitchen drinking coffee, Jimmy Tippett Jnr's respect and admiration for his father is unmistakable, and he feels it is high time more people were aware of his unsung status among the criminal élite, particularly as his father is often reluctant to talk about it.

'The problem,' Tippett tells me softly, 'is that the only people who anyone ever gets to hear about are the ones that get caught. If you're doing the business and you make a good living but then you retire without going inside, your name just fades away. In years to come people assume you were a nobody. But that's not always the case. They say crime doesn't pay but I'm telling you that's bollocks. If you do it right, it pays beautiful.

'When I was growing up, I had a fantastic life, thanks to my dad. Me and my sister never wanted for anything. We went on the most beautiful holidays you can imagine all over the world. One year it was off to Egypt to visit the Pyramids, the next it was flying over a safari park in Kenya in a helicopter and after that it was watching the sun rise over the Sahara desert. None of it would have been possible without my dad doing what he did.'

With the likes of 'Flash' Harry Hayward and Charlie Kray being regular visitors to the family home and Freddie Sewell for an uncle it was, perhaps, inevitable that Tippett Jnr would ultimately be drawn into a life of crime himself, though it happened far sooner than anyone expected.

When his son was around twelve Tippett Snr took over the running of a small spieler in Lewisham, south London. It wasn't exactly a high-class venture – just three rooms above a kebab shop – but his reputation was enough to ensure that all the local faces made it their regular haunt, coming together several nights each week to play poker, kaluki and bet on horses.

'I was only twelve or thirteen and used to make the teas on a Saturday. The place was electric; it was really buzzy, full of characters, and pretty soon I got to know them all. The place was like a magnet for all the gangs, and young thieves off the manor would come in and out all day with racks of clothes, trays of diamond rings, you name it, all for a fraction of the real price.

'I remember being so excited every time I walked up the stairs to the place. Just the smell of the cigar smoke – everyone in there seemed to have one between their teeth all day long – would set my heart racing.

'The amount of money going round the place was incredible, especially in the days after some of the lads had a good result. I remember one robber who was losing badly at poker and was down to his last two grand, which was sitting in front of him, all in fifties. Rather than see it go to the bloke he was playing he just picked it up off the table and slung it into the gas fire. A couple of the younger guys ran to try and get it out but the bloke pulled out a .45 and shouted out: "Any cunt goes near that lot and I'll put a fucking bullet in his head."

'Every now and then you'd hear about someone from the club getting killed or stabbed or badly injured but none of it ever put me off. I was hooked on the life and I absolutely loved it. I began going sick at school just so I could get up to the spieler and be round everyone. At first my mum tried to get me out of it but after a while she just gave up. I think she knew in her heart I was going to go into the life. After all, I was born into it.'

The young Tippett joined the ranks of Britain's armed robbers just at the end of a thirty-year stretch when it had been the crime of choice of the criminal élite. Armed robbery had taken over from the previous favourite – safe-blowing – which had grown to epidemic proportions in the aftermath of the Second World War as disgruntled servicemen turned their skills with explosives into a way of making ends meet. Rapid improvements in safe design meant that by the late 1950s the job took too long and too much explosive was needed to make it viable.

Back then Britain was a wholly cash society and every factory or office would take in huge deliveries of it every Thursday to pay the staff their weekly wage. Despite the vast sums involved, armoured vans were a rarity and most of the deliveries were made by couriers, carrying the cash in simple briefcases.

In those early days robbing the couriers was all too easy and small gangs could come away with big money, using nothing more sophisticated that a couple of coshes. By the end of the decade twenty couriers were being injured in raids each week and something had to be done.

The introduction of armoured vehicles pushed the gangs in the direction of banks, the design of which had not changed for years. There was no CCTV, no security screening and wooden boxes full of notes sat on open view on the counter. (Many banks considered it essential to display large sums to impress customers.) But carrying out raids in enclosed spaces with large groups of people meant that coshes were no longer an option. Sawn-off shotguns became the weapon of choice.

The 1960s saw the first of the so-called 'project' crimes in which larger, more sophisticated gangs operating under a rigid leadership would tackle high-value jobs that required intricate planning. In 1962 one such gang raided the BOAC building at Heathrow airport. Wearing fake moustaches, bowler hats and pin-striped suits in order to blend in with the crowds, they carried special umbrellas in which the central spine had been replaced by a heavy iron bar.

The heist, organised by a certain Bruce Reynolds, had been expected to net half a million pounds but in the event the gang only got £62,000. (Although they managed to get clean away, Reynolds went on to organise the Great Train Robbery the following year; it proved to be his downfall – he and the rest of the gang responsible were eventually caught.)

By the 1970s improvements in bank security had forced the gangs back out on to the streets, where they began to target the cash-in-transit vans. One team found success by using chainsaws to cut through the side armour and pull out the bags of cash inside, while smaller outfits would often make do with 'working the pavement' – snatching one or two bags as the guard transferred them from van to bank. The most skilled practitioners would refer to themselves as 'pavement artists'.

In Britain, and London in particular, gangland was thriving and many gangs were enjoying a high level of success with armed robbery, but compared to the rest of the world the UK's gangs were still operating in the Dark Ages. In Europe and America organised crime was evolving into something far more serious and sinister, thanks to the increasing availability of drugs and the vast profits to be made, but in Britain crime was all about cash.

All of that changed with a single job: Brinks Mat.

It was just after 6.40 a.m. on 26 November 1983 that six armed men burst into the Heathrow depot of the security company Brinks Mat. The robbers disabled the sophisticated security system, tied up the guards, doused them with petrol and threatened to set them alight unless they revealed the combinations to the final locks.

ARMED ROBBERY

In the following days, police and security experts remarked on how well organised and professional the raid had been. The truth was different. That bit of work had been punted around south London only for a few weeks. Mickey McAvoy, a young hardman, and an old blagger called Brian Robinson had put the word out that they were looking for a couple of sensible lads to help them with an inside job. They had heard there would be £3 million in cash in the vault and the plan was to split it five ways. It was only when they got there that they found the gold. They hadn't expected it. They were so disorganised that they didn't even have a big enough vehicle to deal with it. They had to go and get a van. They were supposed to be in and out within minutes, but the job took nearly two hours.

Until the Brinks Mat job, London's villains had simply spent the cash they stole or hidden it in secret stashes, but the need to convert gold into ingots changed the face of British organised crime – and law enforcement – for ever as the gangs suddenly acquired skills in smuggling, money-laundering and a host of related activities.

But the crime also dealt a shattering blow to the already shaky notion of honour among thieves.

Tracking down those at the heart of the raid presented few problems for detectives: the fact that the robbers knew their way around the security system pointed to an inside job. When detectives discovered that one of the guards, Anthony Black, had arrived late for work, missing the robbery, they pulled him in for questioning and he soon cracked. Robinson, who had been living with Black's sister, and McAvoy were quickly arrested. What also helped was that, where a modern villain will be careful to avoid doing anything that might draw attention to them, the two main players had done little to disguise their new-found wealth. Within weeks of the robbery both men had left the council houses they were living in and had bought enormous homes in Kent for cash. McAvoy had two Rottweiler guard dogs called Brinks and Mat.

Mickey McAvoy was sentenced to twenty-five years and quickly tried to strike a deal to give back his share of the money in exchange for a cut in his sentence. But by then the money had vanished.

McAvoy, along with other members of the gang, made the mistake of believing his friends would look after his share of the gold so it would be waiting for him when he got out. Those friends included, among others, George Francis and Brian Perry.

Since 2000 there have been at least five murders linked to the Brinks Mat case. Many are convinced that a number of scores are being settled, while the whereabouts of the money – only eleven of the 26,000 gold bars have so far been recovered – remains a mystery.

When Jimmy Tippett's mobile phone rings once more a glance at my watch reveals that we've been talking for more than two hours. This time it's good news – his father has been released without charge and plans a night out on the town to celebrate. Jimmy sits back in his chair and runs a palm over the shadowy stubble sprouting from his chin. 'It's a strange thing, being part of a London gang. It's not like being in the Triads or the Cosa Nostra. There's no initiation ceremony or anything like that, nothing formal, but that doesn't mean there aren't codes of conduct, accepted ways of doing things. And the most important rules are, no matter what happens, you don't fuck people over and you don't grass.

'The people I was working with, they were my friends and their dads were friends of my dad. We had all grown up the same way so the whole gang was a hundred per cent trustworthy. You always knew that, whatever happened, no one was ever going to turn grass because their whole family would be against them.'

They targeted mostly Securicor vans, pavement work. Tippett Jnr was the youngest so he learnt from the rest of them. They had a combination of experience and inside information, which meant they knew which vans to go after and when to get the team together.

'On the day of a job the tension was just incredible, almost too much. I was actually physically sick a few times. When you're waiting for it to start, it's nerve-racking stuff. A second is like a minute and every minute is like an hour. You become totally paranoid, convinced that everyone and his wife is looking at you. Then the signal comes and, bang, it's off. We'd always work it the same way – two of us would approach the guard from behind and one of them would hold a gun to the back of his thigh. That way he knows that if he tries anything and you let one off, his main artery is fucked and he's going to bleed to death.

'Most of the time the guards would do whatever you said but a few times they resisted and you let a few shots off into the air. The bang and the flame would normally be enough to bring them into line, but every now and then we had to use a bit of violence.

'When it's done you end up with one or two of those security boxes that they used to carry the cash in and then the hard part is getting the money out. One time I was so excited when we got back that I opened it up right away. And, of course, it exploded and the purple dye went everywhere. Every note in the box was covered with it. And my mate was laughing his head off, saying, "Ah, Jimmy, you fucked it up, you fucked it up big-time."

'I was pretty worried but we just ended up using it all in ticket machines on the Underground. You'd buy a single ticket, put the note in and get the change back. Even with the dye it still worked fine and we ended up in the south London press – they did a big story about the fact the money that had been nicked had ended up in the machines at Brixton.'

But Tippett Jnr has moved on from armed robbery. 'Now it's all changed, especially so far as the big jobs are concerned. It's all about CCTV, Big Brother watching you all the time, the helicopters are up in so many minutes and you can't fucking move. I used to think that if things got really bad, I might have to go back to it but now I'm not so sure. Half the cop cars on the street are those armed-response units. The minute you start waving guns around, you're asking for big trouble.'

By the late 1980s the police had started to shoot back and the risks of being caught and doing time paled alongside the ever-growing risk of ending up brown-bread. In July 1987 Michael Flynn and Nicholas Payne were shot dead by police during an attempted robbery of a wages van at an abattoir in Shooters Hill, south London. A few months later it was the turn of Tony Ash, shot dead during a wages snatch at the Bejam supermarket in nearby Woolwich. Another member of the gang, Ronnie Easterbrook, fired six shots at police from his old Webley revolver hitting one officer in the leg. He was reloading when a police marksman shot him in the shoulder. (Later Easterbrook famously tried to escape on the way to court by blowing a hole in the police van carrying him there using a lump of Semtex he had hidden in a piece of foil from a Kraft cheese triangle. The charge exploded inwards rather than out and Easterbrook lost a finger.) In 1990 Kenny Baker was shot dead by police near Reigate in Surrey, during an attempted raid on a Securicor van with the notorious brothers Dennis and Mahmood Arif.

Each fatal shooting brought with it fresh controversy, mostly on the issue of whether the criminals had been given an adequate chance to surrender and whether there was a general policy of shoot-to-kill. Either way the incidents, along with the introduction of greatly increased prison penalties for carrying firearms, persuaded many villains to look again at the way they operated. Little wonder, then, that some of the biggest and most successful robberies of recent years have been carried out by gangs who decided it was far better to leave their guns at home.

It was 6.18 a.m. on 11 February 2002 and British Airways flight 124 from Bahrain had just touched down two minutes ahead of schedule. The 187 passengers were keen to disembark and there was an audible sigh throughout the plane as the captain announced that their journey to the terminal would take a little longer than usual. Not only had they been assigned to one of the airport's 'remote' bays, meaning they would have to board a coach to get to the terminal, but they had to wait for some high-value cargo to be unloaded before they could get off.

Soon after the plane had pulled into bay four and the engines had been switched off a British Airways van, driven by a single security guard, rolled into view. A flap opened at the back of the plane and eight heavy-duty crates rolled down a conveyor-belt so the guard could load them into the back of his van. The crates contained a mix of currencies, chiefly American dollars and some Middle Eastern cash, and were due to be transported to another part of the airport for a connecting flight to New York. In all there was around £3 million in untraceable, used bills.

The guard then disappeared into the back of his vehicle to check the boxes against his manifest. At that moment, two Asian men wearing BA uniforms pulled up in a Renault van decked out in the company's grey, red and blue livery. The new arrivals explained that there had been a mix-up with the work rota and the crates should be placed in their van instead. When the first guard hesitated and suggested calling his supervisor for confirmation, the men pounced. They leapt from their vehicle and pushed him to the ground, tying his wrists and ankles with plastic ties.

The robbers hauled out the cash, dumped it in the back of their van and drove away. Within minutes the guard had freed himself enough to get to his radio and hit the panic button. Across the airport complex, alarms sounded and all exits were sealed but it was too late: the robbers had sailed unchallenged though the checkpoint and vanished into the streets of west London.

The hunt for the van didn't last long. It was found two miles away in Feltham, consumed by a ball of flame. The money and the gang had long gone. In the space of little more than fifteen minutes two unarmed men had somehow managed to pull off one of Britain's biggest ever cash robberies and got clean away.

The whole operation screamed 'inside job': details of the movement of currencies are known to just a handful of people. Not only that, the van involved had been taken from the maintenance shed. Despite this, thorough monitoring and interviews with all those who had access to the appropriate information failed to deliver a single clue as to who was responsible.

And then, a little more than four weeks later, it happened again.

In the early hours of 19 March, twenty-two-year-old security guard Sundeep Sidhu had been sent out in his van to meet South African Airways flight 234, newly arrived from Johannesburg. As a supervisor watched from a separate vehicle – part of a routine staff inspection – Sidhu loaded two silver cash boxes containing almost £3 million in mixed currencies into his van and set off to complete the transfer.

Sidhu's van moved off as normal but after only a few seconds lurched suddenly to one side, then the other, and began accelerating hard towards the nearest exit. There was no answer from Sidhu's radio, and by the time the supervisor had sounded the alert, the precious cargo was outside the airport perimeter.

Fifteen minutes later a sobbing Sidhu called the police – 'I've just been robbed at knifepoint.' He explained that as he'd started driving off, two men appeared in the back of his van, threatened him with a knife and ordered him to continue through security checkpoints off the airport. He followed instructions to take the robbers to a getaway car in a deserted country lane two miles from Heathrow. He had called the police as soon as they had left.

Sidhu said his attackers were Asian and in their mid-twenties – identical to the two men involved in the earlier robbery. The Flying Squad – the Metropolitan Police specialist armed-robbery division – were convinced they were dealing with the same team. 'The descriptions of the suspects in both robberies are very similar and so was the method they used,' said a spokesman later that same morning. 'You would think they would be satisfied with what they got last time.'

Apart from the obvious greed of those involved, the other thing that struck the investigating officers was that, if anything, this robbery was even more audacious and daring than the first. The South African Airways flight had arrived just minutes after a separate flight from Cape Town carrying several prominent dignitaries. The two planes had taxied close to one another and at least fourteen armed guards were on the Tarmac to protect the VIPs. This meant the two robbers had had to sneak past to get on to the van. They had also had to guess which of the two vehicles the money would be placed in.

Sidhu had worked as a part-time security guard at Heathrow for more than three years when the ordeal happened. Like all of ADI's guards he had been positively vetted as posing no criminal or terrorist threat. But as the day went on, police began to suspect that, far from being abducted, he had driven the van willingly and been a key part of an elaborate robbery plot.

Although supposedly traumatised by his experience, on the night of the robbery in March, Sidhu was seen with his brother Harjit, twenty-five, talking animatedly on a park bench near their home in Uxbridge, Middlesex. The brothers were then seen meeting up with a small group of friends including Anil Parmar, Manish Bhadresa and Harbhajan Padda, and continuing what appeared to be an exciting conversation.

It aroused suspicions enough for a major surveillance operation to be launched. But while police could film Sidhu and his friends talking, they were not able to get close enough to find out what they were saying or plant bugs. They hoped one of the gang would lead them to the place where they had hidden the money, but after weeks of close monitoring there was nothing. With more than twenty hours of silent video under their belts, the police employed the services of Oxford graduate Jessica Rees, profoundly deaf since being struck with meningitis at the age of four. The mother of two can lip-read with an unprecedented level of skill and accuracy. She can tell what is being said even when the subject is facing away from her, speaking with an accent and wearing a heavy beard.

The tapes turned out to be an absolute goldmine. One showed Harjit sitting with Padda in a car park at the end of a cul-de-sac in Hounslow. After watching it through once, Rees replayed it, this time translating the silent words. 'No one's suspected . . . the police have not sussed anything,' said Harjit. 'They've got no evidence. If the police think it's me I'll just say, "So, then, where's the money?" They won't have a thing on us.'

Another tape showed Harjit and Parmar meeting outside a Southall pub to discuss the various ways they could change the dollars they had stolen into sterling without arousing suspicion. Yet another, filmed at a local branch of McDonald's, showed them talking about dividing up the haul: 'Everybody gets £250,000. We've got it stashed, it's all over the place.'

Rees even managed to work out what the gang members were saying while they spoke on mobile phones, and it was this that led police to a lock-up garage owned by Padda in Twickenham where they found two holdalls containing £2 million in US dollars, sterling and euros.

Rees's evidence was so damning that, once confronted, Sidhu and the others immediately pleaded guilty to all charges, but there was no evidence to suggest they had anything to do with or knew anything about the first robbery.

For now, at least, the gang responsible for that robbery remain at large. No one seems to know anything and those responsible have more reason than ever to keep their mouths shut.

There are two observations that can be made about the Heathrow robberies. The first is that high-value armed robbery is no longer the exclusive preserve of white, working-class gangsters, a sign of just how much the business has changed in recent years. With many of the larger, better organised gangs now putting their efforts into other areas, the void has been filled by a wide range of newcomers.

The second is that, having pulled off such a slick operation, the only way the gang responsible will now be caught is if someone within their ranks or on the fringes of their organisation spills the beans.

Once a rarity, today's underworld is awash with informants, snitches and grasses. Many top criminals maintain their premium positions and their liberty only because they continually supply police with information about the activities of others.

The old codes of conduct are increasingly being pushed aside and replaced by an every-man-for-himself attitude. Another theory behind the murder of George Francis was that he had not only helped himself to the Brinks Mat gold but pointed police in the direction of some of his enemies.

Despite their increasing numbers, those who grass are still

considered the lowest of the low and risk spending the rest of their lives looking out for the bullet with their own name on it. This is particularly true for those who decide to grass to evade a stiff prison sentence for their own crimes. But every gang is different and there are many who believe that, because of the situation they found themselves in or the people they were working with, they simply had no choice but to give evidence against their former colleagues.

CHAPTER TWO

By the time I get to meet him, Steve Roberts has all but ceased to exist.

It has taken weeks of coded phone calls and secret messages to bring the two of us together, and during that time the price on his head has risen dramatically. There are now literally dozens of gangland figures after his blood, and such is the level of hatred that if word gets out I've seen him, I too could become a target.

Until a few months earlier Roberts was a key member of Britain's most notorious gang of armed robbers. Led by the violent and unpredictable Sean Bradish, often accompanied by his younger brother Vincent, the gang was responsible for more than a hundred raids, which netted millions of pounds in cash.

While many armed robbers spend their lives looking for 'El Dorado' – the one big job that will set them up for life – some of the best of today's blaggers focus on smaller, softer targets, varying their methods of operation just enough to prevent the police picking up the scent.

Legendary heists like the Great Train Robbery or the Brinks Mat raid may have amassed millions, but in every case the main players were behind bars or on the run within a matter of weeks. By contrast, the Bradish gang remained fully active yet at liberty for the best part of a decade, and although their individual hauls were smaller, they made more than enough to fill their lives with fast cars, exotic holidays and weekend-long parties fuelled with vast quantities of drink and drugs.

But within a few days of our meeting Roberts will be no more. All his old bank and building-society accounts will be shut down, his National Insurance number will be withdrawn, his passport destroyed and his birth certificate deleted. Every possible path that someone might use to try to track him down will be blocked: it will be as though he had never been born.

The reason is simple: Roberts grassed on Sean Bradish. 'I know I pissed a lot of people off with the way I was behaving and that a lot of them would be only too happy to see me out of the way, would pay money to see me dead,' Roberts says bitterly, 'but what Sean did was completely out of order. Once I heard that he was trying to have me killed, I knew I had no choice. I had to betray him.'

Having broken the ultimate criminal code and agreed to give evidence against the other members of his gang, Roberts is set to become a member of the Protected Witness Programme. But just before this transformation takes place he agrees to give me a chilling insight into the life and times of a modern-day pavement artist.

'How did it all start? I honestly don't know. The first part of my childhood was fine, really happy. I had a good upbringing and my family are good, honest people. I've got a bunch of brothers and sisters but I'm the only one of them who has ever been in trouble with the law.'

The problems started when he became a teenager.

'I was sent to a Roman Catholic school, which was fine apart from the fact that there was a Church of England school right next door and there was always trouble between the two of them. Someone seemed to get attacked every day and that someone always seemed to be me. It got so bad that I got permission to go to school late and leave early, just to avoid the other kids, but I couldn't handle it so I decided to leave. I started hanging around with a bad crowd instead.

'I was hanging out in Harlesden, which is where I grew up, and everywhere I went I was surrounded by drugs and guns and criminals. There was no escape from it. Of the people I grew up with, some of them have died from overdoses, some of them have been murdered and the others are going to spend the rest of their lives in prison. I got into stuff like stealing cars, burglary and street robbery, and the older I got, the bolder I became, the less I cared.'

Then things became a lot more serious. 'Two of my best friends were these two massive black guys, Roy and Chris. One day they came round to see me and said they had a proposition. They'd been getting quite heavily involved in the local drugs scene, selling crack and cocaine around the Stonebridge estate, and they'd found out about a dealer over in west London who had a big stash of drugs and money in his flat and decided to rob him. The reason they needed me was because the guy had been robbed before and didn't trust black guys. White guys were another matter and if I posed as a potential buyer, Roy and Chris figured he'd be willing to open up the door and they'd have a chance to rush him with the guns and take everything off him.

'It worked like a dream, so we started doing it more and more. Pretty soon we became quite sophisticated. I managed to get hold of a police badge and walkie-talkie and started posing as a copper. I would knock on the dealer's door, show them the badge, explain there had been an accident, and ask if I could use their phone because my radio wasn't working.

'As soon as they opened up, a bunch of us would rush in, tie them up and put guns to their heads. Sometimes they refused and it would all get pretty violent, really nasty, but most of the time, once they saw the size of the guys I was working with – Chris was six foot seven and weighed nineteen stone, Roy was almost as big – they usually gave it all up.

'It was a good living. One time we came away with forty-six thousand pounds in cash, another time we got a kilo of cocaine and more than four grand in cash. The best thing about it was that, no matter what we did, no matter how much violence we used, how many guns we carried or how much we took, the people could never go to the police. It was the perfect crime.'

As the 1990s progressed, incidents of 'taxing', as the robbery of drug-dealers became known, reached epidemic proportions and became increasingly violent. In May 1993 a notorious thirty-four-year-old Yardie, Christopher 'Tuffy' Bourne, bit off more than he could chew. He and his posse travelled to a crack-house based in a council flat at 54 Vassel Road, Brixton, south London, to carry out their second robbery of the premises in two months.

The first raid had generated a healthy haul – two kilos of cocaine and crack, £10,000 in cash and a number of thick gold chains from around the necks of the occupants. Four weeks later, hearing that the crack den had fully restocked, Tuffy decided to return.

But this time it was a set-up and he was met by a volley of hot lead. Trapped between the wall and the reinforced steel door, he was totally outgunned. Three bullets lodged in his chest, two more passed right through him and a further ten were recovered from the wall behind him. Immensely strong, Tuffy managed to stagger out of the flat and collapse on the street, only to be discovered bleeding to death by his ten-year-old son, who happened to be passing.

In the underworld the message was received loud and clear: the dealers were no longer soft targets and were prepared to defend themselves or retaliate. It meant that the only safe way to rob a dealer was to kill him. In October that same year, three men robbed and executed Ghanaian drug-dealer William Danso, chasing him around his south London home and firing more than seventeen shots. As the killers left they came across PC Patrick Dunne, a popular community beat bobby who made his rounds by bicycle. PC Dunne, who had been called to a nearby domestic incident, walked towards Danso's home to investigate the noise of gunshots. When he was ten metres away, he was shot in the chest by a single round from a 9mm automatic. He died instantly and his killers allegedly laughed as they fled the scene.

Other deaths followed as the trend gathered momentum. For those involved in the 'taxing' business the choice was either get out and move on or stick around and risk ending up on a murder rap. Luckily for Roberts, new opportunities were just around the corner.

'I used to drink in a pub called the Coach and Horses just off the Stonebridge estate. At the time there were at least eighteen well-known armed robbers who would meet there to drink, chat and celebrate whenever they had a good pay-day. Sean, Vincent and a few of their mates were regulars and, although I didn't know them, I was instantly attracted by their lifestyle.

'I was doing pretty well, making most of my living from stealing cars and robbing dealers, but the money the two of them were making was just incredible. They also knew how to make the most of it. They drove around in flashy cars, were always going off on holidays to the Caribbean or staying in posh hotels in and around London just to enjoy a bit of luxury. Everyone in the pub knew how they made their money – armed robbery – and the more I got to know them, the more I knew I wanted to be involved.'

At the time the Bradish brothers were working for a man called James Doyle, known in underworld circles as the Ayatollah because of his ruthless leadership style. A clever and cunning career criminal, Doyle had worked out that if he only ever attacked relatively small targets where the haul was never particularly high, changing tactics and using different members of his team to carry out the actual robbery, the police would assume the raids were the work of random amateurs rather one single gang.

He began by focusing his attention on bookmakers' offices and then, just as the Flying Squad began to suspect the string of attacks might be linked, moved on to building societies, then banks. The Doyle gang's biggest ever haul was a relatively modest £36,000, but with one or two successful raids being carried out on an almost weekly basis, there was always more than enough money to go round.

Doyle perfected his technique, and it was through him that the Bradish brothers learnt the skills that served them so well in later life. A typical robbery would begin with two members of the gang going on the morning of the robbery to steal two cars for the getaway. Doyle would select the target but rarely go inside himself. Instead, positioned in a nearby phone-box or at another vantage-point, he would supervise the action.

The actual raid would be carried out by two gunmen, backed up by a driver outside. They would arm themselves with weapons from an arsenal of sixteen guns and thousands of rounds of ammunition that Doyle kept, somewhat ironically, in bank safety-deposit boxes. Wearing masks or crash helmets, the two men would burst in. One would clear the tills while the other kept guard and a watch on the time to make sure the raid was completed before the automatic alarm system kicked in.

Doyle ruled the gang with an iron fist, punishing anyone who let him down with extremes of physical violence. When he heard that one of the gang had taken more than his fair share of the pot, he beat the man unconscious with the nearest weapon to hand – a frozen chicken.

'I met Doyle a few times and he was an absolute lunatic. The man spent as much time working on his wardrobe as he did planning the robberies. It all came on top for him when he was caught red-handed in 1995 and sent down to await trial. While he was on remand he convinced the prison to let him go to Moorfields Hospital in London about this long-standing problem he had with his eye. He'd been a few times before and knew the place well. After his appointment he asked to go to the toilet, and once he was inside, some bloke runs in with a shotgun, forces the coppers escorting him to get on the floor, then unlocks the handcuffs. He got away for a while but ended up getting caught in Ireland and sent down for twenty-four years at the Old Bailey.

'By a stroke of sheer luck, Sean and Vincent were having a day off when Doyle was picked up so they were still out and about when the rest of the gang got put behind bars. They had a little break, then decided to carry on, forming their own little firm. They had their own guns and all that but were having trouble finding someone reliable to steal cars for them. That's where I came in.

'I got a couple of cars for Sean and then he asked if I wanted to come along on the robbery. I agreed like a shot. We picked up a couple of shotguns, some surgical gloves, and disguised ourselves with bandanas, sunglasses and caps. We set off and ended up parked around the back of the Thomas Cook in Edgware. Sean went in first and I followed close behind. He then shouted at the cashier, "Open the fucking door!" She turned round and her face was a picture. Then she says, "Oh, God, not you again" – he'd already robbed the place about a dozen times before but he hadn't told me. He said, "Yeah, me again, so open the fucking door." And she did. Sean went through to where the cashiers were sitting, grabbed a few bundles and then we legged it. The whole thing took less than twenty seconds and we came out with twenty-four grand. It was incredible.'

After losing his cherry, Roberts quickly became a regular member of the team and soon found himself living the life he had previously only been able to admire from afar. The Bradish brothers had a well-established routine to celebrate the end of each robbery, and Roberts joined in eagerly. 'Most times we would do the robbery on a Friday morning early, at about nine a.m. Then we would book into a flash hotel and count the money, and have a glass or two of champagne.

'After that we'd go to the nearest shop and buy a whole new outfit. Everything we had worn during the robbery would be thrown away so there would be no forensic evidence. We always bought designer clothes – everything had a label. But once we'd done a robbery, it would just be trash. You'd go out and buy a brand new pair of smart Nike trainers for a hundred pounds and the next day you'd bin them. It was madness, absolute madness.

'Then it would be off to the pub for a bit of dinner and a few more drinks. By eight p.m. we'd start taking the cocaine and then go out. We'd hit the town, the clubs and pubs, pick up a few girls and enjoy ourselves. Sometimes they were prostitutes – quite often, in Sean's case, because he wasn't the best-looking man in the world – but often other girls would latch on. We'd be tossing bundles of money around like confetti, and once they smelled it, they'd be on you like leeches. We wouldn't stop until Monday morning, and would easily spend three thousand pounds on drink and drugs and women over the weekend.

'Sean wasn't into drugs that much, but he liked to experiment every now and again. Vincent and I were always bang on it. Towards the end I'd be drinking vast amounts, take up to twenty ecstasy tablets and an ounce of cocaine. We had some great times. I remember once when Vincent was at a club and he got so out of his nut he got off with this bird who turned out to be a transvestite. He came back screaming and then spent the next two hours marching up and down yelling, "I'm gonna kill it, I'm gonna fucking kill it." We just laughed our heads off.'

The extravagant lifestyle soon attracted police attention but, having spent years being followed by the police while working for Doyle, the Bradish brothers were more than ready.

'It became a bit of a game, finding the police and winding them up. We knew what some of the bikes and cars they used for surveillance looked like – we spotted them so many times in so many places – so it was never that difficult. If there was a team plotted up watching us, we'd call 999, describe the car and tell them the men inside were acting suspiciously. The police would always turn up and by the time they realised they'd fucked up the surveillance operation, we'd be long gone.

'We all had nice cars – BMW 7 series, Porsches, Mercs – and we'd for ever be finding tracking devices on them. We'd pull them off and stick them to buses or trains, just to send the police on a wild-goose chase. They were never going to catch us in the act because we always used stolen cars for the raids and I'd leave it until the last minute to nick them.

'Every time we did a job, we used anti-surveillance techniques. All the usual stuff – twice round a roundabout, indicate one way and turn the other, pull over and let traffic go past. Before we hit the target, from the moment we left the house and ever afterwards, we'd be constantly watching everything around us just to be sure they weren't on to us.

'We never got over-confident, though. We knew we had to keep up or, rather, stay one step ahead of what the police were doing if we wanted to be able to carry on living the life. In the end, just to be even safer, we started doing the robberies on motorbikes. We would be flying around so quick and dodging in and out of traffic that they could never follow us.

'We started working more randomly. Sean would often just turn up at my house in the morning and ask if I fancied going out on a job. Then we'd just drive about looking for somewhere to rob. One time the two of us were riding about on his motorbike and happened to pass a Securicor van making a delivery. We rushed back, picked up a shotgun and got back just in time to see it leave. Then we followed it until the next delivery and took one of the bags off the guard at gunpoint.

'I loved it. Before each raid the adrenaline would get going and sometimes it would be so overwhelming that as soon as it was over I would throw up.'

But there were problems. Although they became good friends, Roberts began to worry about Sean Bradish's increasing violence: 'Before we went into a bank, Sean would wait to make sure there were a few customers around. That way he had someone to threaten if the staff were a bit slack about letting him in to get at the cash. There were a few times when he came close to pulling the trigger and I started to feel it was only a matter of time before he killed someone.'

Sean's violent nature was soon spiralling out of control. 'One particular night we were in a pub and a man rumoured to be a rapist came in. A few of us took him outside, gave him a few punches and kicks, and left it at that. But Sean wasn't satisfied. He took a half-pint glass, smashed it, then rammed it into the man's face about thirty times. I had never seen so much blood. We tried to stop him but he turned on us. He'd become an absolute animal.

'A few nights after that he tried to shoot two police officers with a gun that I had bought and given to him. He'd just done a job with this bloke, Andy, and a couple of uniformed coppers happened to be passing by. They gave chase and Sean got out this 9mm automatic, held it up a few inches from the head of one of the coppers and pulled the trigger. Nothing happened. It jammed.

'If Sean had just gone to the getaway car right away then he and Andy would have been fine, but because of Sean pissing about, Andy ended up getting caught while Sean got away free. I went to visit Andy in the nick and he was so pissed off. He said if only Sean had done what he was supposed to do, it would never have gone wrong. But Sean's only concern was the gun. He was really pissed off at me that it didn't work. He had really wanted to kill the copper. Andy ended up getting twenty-one years.

'Sean was going crazy, it was like he was addicted. There were times when he'd get a gun and go out on his own, riding a mountain bike, looking for somewhere to rob, looking for trouble. I couldn't help thinking that he was just itching to kill someone and I didn't want any part of that.

'One time soon after the incident with the gun I was watching *Britain's Most Wanted* and a bit of CCTV footage came up of a recent robbery in some building society. The men in the film were wearing masks but I could tell straight away that it was Sean and Vincent, I could just tell. They grabbed the money, and Sean let a shot off at a guard as he was lying on the floor. It was totally unnecessary, there was no need for it at all.'

Tensions within the gang grew but it was only after a bungled attempt to raid Barclays Bank in Greenford, west London that Roberts realised the time had come to go straight: 'We had just got inside when I saw two men in suits jump out of a car and go to the boot. They were CID, who just happened to be in the area for a shoplifter, but my first thought was that they were Flying Squad and they were going to the back of the car to get their guns out. I screamed at Sean and we legged it out of there and round the corner to the alleyway where our motorbike was parked. I didn't want them to see the registration of the bike.

'He threw me the shotgun and as they came around the corner I told them to get their hands up and get against the wall. Then Sean came up on the bike, I hopped on the back and we sped away.

'Afterwards our nerves were shattered. We parked the bike, booked into a Holiday Inn in Croydon and went out on a major drink-and-drugs bender. Although we had only been in the bank a few seconds, we still managed to get four thousand pounds. We didn't have time to empty the tills but one customer had just been given an envelope and we took that. But I knew it had to stop. I knew that if Sean had been holding the shotgun instead of me, he would have let one go.'

During the escape, however, Roberts had lost his hat. It was later found, and he was identified from DNA in a hair found inside. Roberts was now firmly in the sights of the Flying Squad, who launched Operation Odie in a bid to put him and the rest of the gang out of business. But although the squad had masses of evidence, they decided to wait and catch the gang red-handed to ensure they had little chance of escaping conviction.

In the meantime, all too aware of just how close the police were getting, Roberts decided to retire and leave the Bradish brothers to their own devices. 'I had lost a lot of friends, either murdered or ending up in prison for the rest of their lives. I could see myself going the same way. I was also fed up with being followed by the police all the time, day and night, so I went back to being a bricklayer.

'Once I gave up on the robberies, it wasn't like I decided to go straight or anything. I thought I'd try my hand at buying and selling drugs, but that turned out to be the worst idea in the world because I would just end up taking all the drugs myself or sharing them with friends. One weekend, just before my birthday, I bought five hundred ecstasy tablets. I thought I'd have a few but mostly sell them and make a bit of extra money. But I ended up having a bit of a party and a bunch of friends came over to the house and we started taking them all. We just stayed inside, ordered takeaway food and necked the tablets the whole time. We were at it for days and days. There was so much rubbish in the house that in the end we brought the wheelie-bin from outside into the living room and just chucked stuff in that. It took a week to recover but the next weekend we did it all over again. I never made a penny out of those tablets.

'I was getting myself into a right state. When you're living that kind of life, spending so much time off your face, the paranoia builds up and the violence gets to you. It's in the air and, no matter how hard you try, sooner or later it gets into your blood.

'I'd bought some cocaine off this team of white guys, big nasty bastards who were friends of Sean. It was only a couple of thousand pounds' worth and the deal went smoothly, but a couple of weeks later they started hassling me, saying I hadn't paid them enough and that they wanted more. I couldn't fucking believe the cheek of it so I decided to go after them, teach them a lesson.

'I was a total wreck by then. I'd gone from using twenty-five pounds' worth of cocaine a night to more than a thousand pounds' worth every single day. All in all, I must have put the equivalent of a three-bedroom detached house up my nose in the space of a year. I was totally wired.'

Sitting with Roberts, who for the most part is softly spoken and, despite the rigours of gang life, retains his youthful, boyish looks, it is hard to imagine that he is capable of great violence. It isn't long before the illusion is shattered. 'I caught up with them one night and went crazy. I chopped a couple of them up with a machete, shot one of them in the eye and chopped them over their heads and legs.

'I knew that after that I was in an awful lot of trouble. The drugs were too much, they were killing me. It was hard to give it up but it was a choice of live a normal life or die.'

With Roberts gone, Bradish struggled to find a suitable replacement for a raid and, a few weeks later, begged his old blagging partner to rejoin him. Roberts refused and Bradish took on a couple of last-minute replacements. During the raid he was caught red-handed by the Flying Squad. True to form, Bradish was carrying a loaded sawn-off shotgun and had a dozen spare cartridges in his pocket.

'The only reason Sean got caught was because he had gone out on a job with two guys who had never been involved in a robbery before. They were total amateurs, didn't have a clue what they were doing. They did way too much planning. The car they stole for the getaway had been taken a week earlier and had just been sitting around. The police knew what it was going to be used for so they kept an eye on it. When the police pounced, the getaway driver was actually asleep. He was sitting outside the bank in the car waiting, which is the wrong way to do it – you're supposed to be driving around, otherwise you just draw attention to yourself. Sean should never have been working with them. They didn't have a clue what they were doing and that was his downfall. But he didn't see it like that, he didn't see it like that at all.'

Instead, as he languished in his prison cell awaiting trial and watching the evidence mounting up against him, Sean became increasingly convinced that Roberts had somehow tipped off the police. His response was a predictable one: using his contacts on the outside, he made plans to have Roberts killed.

In the meantime the same Flying Squad team that arrested Bradish had tired of waiting for Roberts to commit another robbery and decided to arrest him at home, using the DNA evidence they had recovered from the raid. At first Roberts was resigned to the idea of a fifteen-year stretch and kept his mouth shut, but then he found out about what Bradish had been planning and began to see things differently. And that was when he decided to become a grass.

'People talk about honour among thieves, but there isn't any these days. Sean had no hesitation in taking a contract out on me. If I had done the "right" thing and kept my mouth shut, he'd have got someone to put a bullet in my head. No amount of explanation would have convinced him that I wasn't responsible for him getting nicked so, as far as I'm concerned, he left me with no choice.

'It meant I had to face Sean in court. At first I was really shaky and felt sick: I just didn't want to do it. But after an hour in the box I started to focus. I knew I had to get the conviction. It wasn't a nice thing to do but, fuck me, it had to be done.

'It was hard. I was very close to Sean, very close. As mad as he was, I always knew where I stood with him, and at the end of the day, I thought he was a nice guy. I didn't feel that way about Vince, he was very sly and slimy. Right from the start I never trusted him. Each and every time I have done a robbery with Vince he has either fucked up or not been there to back you up. Sean was solid. If you went to do a robbery with him, he was there one hundred per cent. Vince only ever cared about himself.'

During the trial a former girlfriend of Roberts took the stand and accused him of lying. She said that he was only betraying the Bradish brothers because she had had an affair with one of them and that he was being driven insane by jealousy. 'The jury saw right through her lies. I think she'd been got at. It shows just how much power these people have. That was why I had no choice but to go down this path.

'But at the end of the day it's also a new start. It's a chance to get away from the lifestyle, the people I was hanging out with and all the things that were killing me. I'm fitter and healthier than I've ever been. I'm drug-free for the first time since the age of thirteen. If this hadn't happened, I'd be dead now. I have no doubt that being arrested by the Flying Squad saved my life.'

At the end of the trial, Sean Bradish was given four life sentences for his part in the robberies while Vincent received a sentence of twenty-two years. As he was led away Sean seemed resigned to his fate. He shrugged his shoulders, looked up at his friends in the public gallery and shouted, 'Have a Guinness on me.'

In return for his co-operation Roberts was sentenced to just eight years and will serve his time in a special part of the prison system known as the 'Bloggs' unit. Designed as a 'prison within a prison' and used to hold those who are giving evidence or assistance to the police in cases of serious crime, all inmates in the unit are known to staff simply as 'Bloggs' followed by a number. Their true identity and reasons for being in the unit are known only to senior management.

The Bloggs prisoners are kept separate from all other inmates and have to cook their own meals – as every Bloggs has a price on their head, the risk of them being poisoned is simply too high.

Once released from the unit Roberts will be given a brand new identity and provided with a modest home somewhere in the United Kingdom. That's when his real problems will begin. Having lived a life with tens of thousands of pounds at his disposal, he will have to get used to living on a weekly wage. Many of the Bloggses find they simply can't handle it.

GANGS

Henry Hill, the real-life inspiration for the Ray Liotta character in the film *Goodfellas* who joined the federal witness protection programme, summed up the difficulties: 'The hardest thing was leaving the life. Even at the end, with all the threats I was getting, I still loved the life. Now I have to wait around like everyone else. I'm an average nobody. I get to live the rest of my life like a schnook.'

It was only a few years before Hill returned to his old ways, getting himself arrested for a drugs conspiracy. He was not the only leopard who found it impossible to change his spots – at least one in three Bloggses go on to commit crimes under their new identities.

The Bradish brothers may be behind bars and set to remain there for the foreseeable future, but men who worked on the fringes of their gang continue to operate, sticking to the tried and tested pattern of targeting small, soft targets.

Yet despite the clear advantages of working in this way, there will always be blaggers who continue to dream of pulling off the one big job, regardless of the odds.

CHAPTER THREE

Mark Bryant stubbed out the remains of his third cigarette and poured the dregs of his coffee on to the grass. It was just after seven a.m. on 7 July 2000 and Bryant, along with two hundred of his colleagues from the giant supermarket warehouse at the Beddow Way industrial estate in the market town of Aylesford, Kent, had come to the end of morning break. On days when the weather was fine the staff would go outside and stand by the perimeter fence, even though the bleak, prison-like landscape of the estate generally offered little in the way of stimulation. But as Bryant filed back into the main building, all hell broke loose.

An armoured payroll truck driving down the road alongside the perimeter fence skidded to a halt as an eighteen-wheeler juggernaut jack-knifed directly in front of it, the two vehicles coming to a halt just a few feet apart. A split second later a pale blue Cargo van left a trail of burning rubber as it slid into position behind the payroll truck, cutting off the only escape route.

The raiders poured out of the vehicles. They wore overalls, body armour, full-face Balaclavas, rock-climbing helmets and heavy boots. Some wielded shotguns while others had pistols tucked into their waistbands. Gasoline-driven chainsaws were produced from the back of the van and two of the robbers ducked under the payroll truck and began cutting the hydraulic cables.

One of the van's security guards snatched his radio, ready to signal that the vehicle and its precious cargo of £8 million in untraceable bills were under attack. He stopped in his tracks when his partner pointed at the man now standing in front of their vehicle and shouting at them. He was holding up three army green magnetic limpet mines. Making sure the guards could see clearly, he armed the first by pressing a small button, causing a tiny red light to begin flashing. He then began fixing the devices to the bonnet. His words were unclear but the guards had no difficulty understanding the meaning: touch that radio and you're dead.

Traffic was building up behind the van blocking the road as commuters tried to get to work. When one furious motorist left his car to find out what was going on there was no hesitation: the nearest member of the gang levelled his heavy silver handgun, aiming just above the man's head, and fired two shots in quick succession. Once again the message not to interfere was received loud and clear.

Bryant and the other warehouse workers heard a muffled cry, 'Two minutes,' then watched as one of the men who had been cutting cables emerged from under the truck and attacked the hinges of the tailgate. The other ran across to a third juggernaut parked on the opposite kerb. He tore away a red plastic traffic cone from the rear, revealing a fearsome metal spike, hopped into the cab and reversed at high speed.

Through their side mirrors, the terrified guards in the payroll truck realised what was about to happen and braced themselves for the impact. The spike smashed into the centre of the rear doors, throwing the truck forward ten feet and making a small hole in the thick metal skin. Another muffled cry, 'Again,' and the spiked juggernaut drew back. The second impact was even harder, throwing the guards up against the windscreen like a pair of rag dolls. Two of the raiders inspected the hole: it was getting bigger; the cash was almost within reach. A series of hand signals were given and the spike was lined up for a third time.

By now Bryant and several other eyewitnesses had flooded the police emergency line with calls about a robbery in progress. Before the van could be rammed again, one of the gang who had been monitoring police frequencies on a scanner screamed the order to abort.

An unarmed traffic-patrol vehicle, staffed by officers Claire Jones and Steven Elliott, had been despatched to the scene, but as soon as the pair turned the corner into the estate, they realised the robbers were expecting them. Jones and Elliott found themselves staring down the barrels of several shotguns. There was nothing they could do. Elliott slammed his Range Rover into reverse and pulled back to safety while Jones called in armed back-up.

But the gang had already started their getaway. They piled into the back of the blue Cargo van and tore off towards the main town. In less than a minute they had reached a sharp turn in the narrow road close to a historic bridge over the river Medway, only barely slowing down. Shocked pedestrians watched as the van appeared to lose control, skidded off the road, through a fence and over a grass verge.

By the time the police caught up, the van had been abandoned and the gang had vanished. It would be an hour before a man walking his dog along the river would call in to complain about a group of young tearaways in a speedboat racing down the river at 40 m.p.h., and the mystery of just how the robbers had got away was solved.

Although they had failed to get any money, the raiders had displayed such military precision and expert planning that suspicion initially fell on soldiers from a nearby army barracks, until the bomb-disposal experts discovered that the limpet mines were nothing more than tinned meat pies that had been painted green, then fitted with magnets and flashing lights.

Detective Superintendent Andy Dolden, the tall, bespectacled head of the Kent County Constabulary Serious Crimes Unit, arrived at Beddow Way a little after eight a.m. Within thirty seconds, he knew exactly who was behind the raid.

Since April his unit had been running a covert surveillance operation against Lee Wenham, a thirty-three-year-old mechanic and scrap-metal merchant suspected of involvement in large-scale auto theft. Wenham was part of an extensive family of wealthy gypsies, and earlier in the year had paid £220,000 in cash for Tong Farm, a sprawling complex that included an apple orchard and several large warehouses. Wenham had quickly made the farm the base of his operations and had been seen driving a variety of stolen vehicles in and out of the premises. He had long been rumoured to be a main supplier of getaway vehicles for armed robberies and now, for the first time, police had hard evidence of his involvement.

The surveillance operation against Lee Wenham had so far yielded little that could be translated into anything but the most minor charges, but as soon as Dolden arrived at the scene, he knew he had hit paydirt. 'I immediately recognised the getaway van from the surveillance we'd been doing at the farm,' he says. 'Part of me wanted to go there right away and arrest everyone but I had to hold back. I had no idea if the whole gang was going to be there, and by the time I'd managed to get a firearms team together, any evidence would have been destroyed. The only charges we'd be able to make stick would be petty auto theft and that just wasn't worthwhile. Instead I decided to do nothing. Wenham didn't know we were watching him or the farm and that gave us the upper hand. The robbery had clearly taken a lot of planning and money, and the gang weren't going to walk away empty-handed. It was a dead cert that they would strike again.'

In fact the gang had struck once before.

Back in February an armoured Securicor van carrying £10 million in cash had been ambushed after leaving a depot in Nine Elms, south London. In an identical series of events, eighteen-wheel juggernauts had been used to block it at the front and rear, and two members of the gang had cut the hydraulics using miniature chainsaws.

The raid had been hastily abandoned after the unexpected and frankly farcical intervention of a frustrated motorist, whose car had been boxed in by the truck carrying the ramming spike. Blissfully unaware that there was a robbery in progress, the man had snatched the keys from the ignition of the truck and stormed off in search of the driver to give him a piece of his mind.

When the time came to ram the armoured truck, the keys were nowhere to be found. Eyewitnesses saw the raiders frantically searching one another's pockets and scrabbling about in the gutter in desperation before deciding to abort.

Seconds later, each of the blocking vehicles exploded in a ball of flame. The raiders then ran to the back of a nearby abandoned power station on the banks of the river Thames where they climbed into a waiting speedboat and made good their escape.

The February raid had come under the jurisdiction of London's Metropolitan Police so Dolden did not learn of it until hours after the Aylesford raid had taken place. Although it could easily have been a copycat crime, it took only a few cursory checks to confirm that the same gang had been responsible. All the blocking vehicles at the Aylesford raid had been fitted with incendiary bombs like those used at Nine Elms, but the gang had fled the scene so quickly they did not have time to detonate them. More tellingly, every vehicle at Aylesford had a spare set of keys taped to the top of the driver's sun-visor. Any lingering doubts quickly faded when detectives examined the vehicle containing the Aylesford ramming spike. Etched into one of the supporting girders were the words: 'PERSISTENT ARENT (*sic*) WE'.

Forensic tests on the getaway van at Aylesford confirmed what Detective Dolden already knew. Saliva on a pair of rubber gloves found on the dashboard belonged to Lee Wenham. A bucket in the back of the other van bore the fingerprints of another member of the gang: Terrence Millman, a fifty-eight-year-old career criminal known to have been involved in dozens of high-value armed robberies dating back to the early 1980s. Millman had spent almost half his adult life behind bars. But robbery was the only thing he knew.

Within a few days of the Aylesford raid, Millman and Wenham were placed under twenty-four hour surveillance and Dolden set about trying to work out where the gang might strike next. 'We knew what they were after: high-value loads in armoured trucks with close proximity to rivers for an easy getaway so that's what we started looking for,' says Dolden. 'We came up with three possibilities – the two places they had already tried, or a third Securicor depot in Dartford on the edge of Kent. This seemed by far the most likely target.'

With too few firearms teams in the Kent force to cover all three targets and one falling partly outside its jurisdiction, Dolden called Detective Superintendent John Shatford, head of the Flying Squad. The pair knew each other well, having joined forces on a kidnapping case earlier in the year, and Shatford had also been in charge of the Nine Elms robbery investigation.

Teams of detectives from the two forces met every few days to discuss the surveillance operation. Wenham and Millman had both been observed driving in and out of Tong Farm in various stolen vehicles, including a bright yellow bulldozer, and all the signs pointed to another raid being planned.

But just as contingency plans for dealing with the three most likely targets were being finalised, the officers received a report that Lee Wenham had made a visit to the Millennium Dome.

Built at a cost of £758 million, and launched with the slogan 'One amazing day, one year only', the Millennium Dome had been billed as a grand celebratory exhibition and amusement park that would appeal to everyone. Housed in the world's biggest tent and built on a former brownfield site on the banks of the river Thames, it had quickly become an expensive and embarrassing joke. The number of visitors had been fewer than half the predicted figure, the exhibits had been almost universally panned for being dull and insipid, the chief executive had been unceremoniously fired and the Government had been forced to step in on three occasions to inject vast sums of money to prevent the exhibition closing. Even a spectacular speedboat chase sequence using the Dome as a backdrop at the beginning of the James Bond film *The World Is Not Enough* had failed to spark any interest in the real thing. In short, the Dome was a big waste of time.

The surveillance report about Wenham ran to dozens of pages that were full of the most mundane detail, but what made the note about his visit to the Dome stand out was that Wenham had also visited the exhibition the week before. And that was really, really odd, because the whole point about the Dome was that no one was going there. So why on earth had Lee Wenham gone twice?

None of the officers on the team had been to the Dome, but Detective Chief Inspector Lee Catlin of Kent Constabulary vaguely recalled some details of the launch and rushed off to his computer to check the Dome's Internet site. He returned a few minutes later and spread several freshly printed pages on the table. Dolden scanned the information and whistled softly. 'I'd say that counts as a high-value load,' he whispered.

'Right on the river too,' added Shatford. 'I've gotta tell you, guys, I think this is what they're after.'

The global diamond corporation, De Beers, had decided that the Dome was the ideal venue to display their premier collection. The centrepiece was the 203-carat Millennium Star, the largest internally and externally flawless pear-shaped diamond in the world. It was being displayed with eleven rare blue diamonds. Essentially priceless, the collection had been insured for $350 million.

To steal the diamonds would be to pull off the biggest robbery in the world ever. It would also require a minor miracle. De Beers had spent more than £2 million on security and the specially built vault housing the diamonds was considered impregnable. There were sophisticated pressure pads, time locks, cameras and optical sensors throughout the structure. The walls, ceiling and floor were of reinforced concrete and steel four feet thick. The display cabinets themselves were built of bomb- and bulletproof glass designed to withstand sixty tonnes of pressure without so much as a scratch. According to the manufacturers it would take at least thirty minutes of sustained attack with heavy, industrial machinery even so much as to scratch the glass. The vault was deemed so safe that no guards were posted inside – it simply wasn't necessary.

Then there was the Dome itself. Security had been designed in the light of warnings from the FBI that it might be targeted by dooms-day cults or terrorists on New Year's Eve. Banks and banks of monitors fed live pictures from 170 CCTV cameras directly to a central control room where dozens of staff could react to the slightest problem in a matter of minutes.

The idea of Lee Wenham going up against such overwhelming odds didn't add up either. Previous intelligence tests had shown that Lee Wenham had an IQ of just seventy and a reading age of seven. The general consensus was that he was pretty dumb, but surely even he wasn't stupid enough to attempt to break into the Dome. And why would a gang that had only ever attacked vehicles suddenly turn their attention to a vault?

It made no sense until Shatford finished the last of a flurry of phone calls and called the rest of the team together to make an announcement. 'You're not going to believe this,' he said. 'The diamonds are being moved, the exhibition is going to Japan. They're going to load them into an armoured truck and drive them to the airport.'

'When?' asked Dolden.

'September the first. Two weeks from today.'

The Flying Squad began life in 1919 as the Mobile Patrol Experiment, a rapid-response unit dedicated to armed robbery. The nickname was a reference to the fact that they were the first detectives to be issued with cars and the only ones allowed to pursue criminals into any police division.

During the 1970s their exploits had been immortalised by a television drama, *The Sweeney* (from the Cockney rhyming slang Sweeney Todd = Flying Squad), which portrayed its officers as hard-drinking men prone to violence in both their personal and professional lives. It was uncomfortably close to the truth – in a few cases. Many Flying Squad officers were specially selected because they had grown up in an area of London known as the Bermondsey Triangle, where the vast majority of top armed robbers seem to hail from. For years it was not uncommon for Sweeney detectives to find themselves arresting people with whom they had been at school.

Such close links with the criminal community inevitably bred widespread corruption and, more than once, huge numbers of officers were fired or jailed. By the time Shatford took over in mid-1999, the squad's reputation was in tatters and there was even talk of it being disbanded. A new corruption scandal had surfaced and several senior officers had been imprisoned after allegations that, rather than catching villains, they had been planning and carrying out robberies. Shatford knew only too well that in saving the diamonds he would also be saving the reputation of the Flying Squad.

In the early hours of 1 September, a Brinks Mat armoured truck left the Dome *en route* to Heathrow airport. It was empty, the diamonds having been smuggled out secretly as a precaution the day before. Two firearms teams followed close behind and four others had been posted along the route, but it was soon clear there would be no raid. At the time that the truck pulled out of the Dome complex, Lee Wenham was still in bed, Terry Millman was at home with his family, and all of the suspect stolen vehicles were in the warehouse at Tong Farm.

But a chance sighting was about to change everything.

Just after nine thirty a.m. Detective Sean Allan, one of several Flying Squad officers posted at the Dome as a back-up, made a frantic call to Shatford's cellphone. 'Guv, Ray Betson has just come in. And he's got Bill Cockram with him.'

Forty-year-old Raymond Betson was just about the most cunning and sophisticated armed robber Britain had ever produced, having amassed a personal fortune well in excess of £10 million in a series of daring raids. Despite topping the Flying Squad's most-wanted list for five years, detectives had not been able to produce a single scrap of evidence against him.

Betson had never worked, never paid tax and had no social-security number, yet in 1997 he had moved from his grim east London apartment into a £500,000 mansion with his lover and their child, paying for the property in cash. Every item of his clothing, right down to his underwear, bore a designer label, and a brand new Mercedes and a top-specification Range Rover sat in the driveway of his home.

William Cockram, forty-nine, was Betson's right-hand man and lived in equal opulence with his wife and two children. The pair had grown up in the same street in south London and become partners in crime at an early age. Although both men had previous convictions, they were for minor offences. Between them, they had spent barely a year in jail.

They both owned properties around the world, and what money they could not hide or launder they spent on a champagne lifestyle. To celebrate the new millennium, Betson and Cockram had taken their wives to New York on Concorde and watched the fireworks from a skippered yacht on the harbour. Each ticket for the event, which included a black-tie ball and accommodation in penthouse suites at the Four Seasons, cost £30,000.

Meticulous and aware of every new advance in forensic science, Betson had avoided capture by becoming a master of police tactics. He invested in the latest scanning devices and practised techniques designed to frustrate attempts to keep him under surveillance as a matter of course. Even on the shortest, most innocent of car journeys, he would double back on himself, run red lights or drive around roundabouts several times. Previous attempts to tail him or place bugs in his home had all ended in disaster.

Betson had made sure no one was following him on his way to the Dome, but once he arrived he relaxed. With dozens of tourists milling around he never noticed the slim blonde female detective with the video camera filming him from a discreet distance. Assuming they were safe, the pair did little to hide their intentions. When Cockram went into the diamond vault, he spent several minutes examining the cabinets, feeling for joins and seals, even getting down on his knees to look for weak spots underneath. He then filmed the vault with his own video camera. The pair left the Dome, walked around it and along the banks of the Thames, pointing out the location of nearby jetties and other features. It was obvious that they were working with Wenham and Millman.

Later that same afternoon, they met Aldo Ciarrocci, a former boyfriend of Cockram's eldest daughter, at a shopping centre further down the river. As they used his video camera to play back footage of the vault, Cockram was heard to say, 'I thought it was pie in the sky but after being round there I can't believe it. Security is so light. I kept thinking it can't be true. But it is. I'm telling you, boys, this is a gift.'

David James, executive chairman of the Millennium Dome, had been in the job just two days when Shatford and Dolden came to see him on 7 September to outline the plot to steal the diamonds, which had now returned from Japan and were back on display in the Dome's vault. The previous day the sixty-three-year-old former industry troubleshooter had managed to secure an additional £47 million in government funding to keep the Dome open, despite a growing public demand for it to be shut. Despite the extra money, the whole project was hanging by a thread. The last thing he wanted was any bad publicity.

'I listened to what they had to say and I was absolutely horrified,' says James. 'The plan was to keep the Dome running as normal and then let the robbers – who would almost certainly be heavily armed – into the diamond vault, give them a few minutes to start attacking the display case and mount an ambush. I had a vision of a massive shoot-out between the police and the gang with members of the public caught in the middle going down like ninepins. I told them straight: there was no way I was going to let it happen.'

But Shatford, who had now taken overall control of the operation on behalf of the two police forces, was adamant that striking before they reached the vault would be even more dangerous as the robbers might scatter and take hostages.

All argument ended when Shatford announced a new plan: he would scare the robbers off from the Dome and they would move on to a new target. The police would have no idea where so would be able to do nothing about it. If someone got hurt and it emerged that an earlier opportunity to arrest the gang had been blocked that would be the worst publicity of all. James reluctantly agreed to let the raid go ahead.

All through September, the gang made preparations for the

robbery, unaware that the police were watching their every move. Wenham began adapting the bulldozer, removing sections to make it lighter and enable it to carry four men rather than one; he also joined Betson, Cockram and others to test a speedboat and a nearby harbour. When it proved too slow, Millman was sent out to buy another, getting the receipt made out in the name 'Mr T. Diamond'. Millman also bought an industrial nailgun, a device capable of firing nails with the force of a bullet, hard enough to penetrate solid steel.

At the same time analysts working for the Flying Squad identified more than sixty days between mid-September and the end of the year (when the Dome would close for good) when tidal conditions were right for the raid to take place. On each such day, up to 150 armed police officers would move into the Dome in the early hours of the morning. Some would be positioned behind a false wall in the back of one of the exhibits; others would disguise themselves as cleaners, hiding their guns in black rubbish bags as they mingled among the visitors.

By the end of October there had been around twenty such full-scale alerts but no robbery. As the logistics of having so many firearms teams at the Dome on so many mornings began to affect policing in other parts of London, Shatford came under increasing pressure to drop the operation on the grounds that it looked as if the robbery would never happen. In a series of heated arguments he pleaded for more time and won a temporary reprieve.

At Tong Farm, tensions within the gang were also reaching boiling-point. James, a friend of Betson who had been brought in to drive the getaway boat, had stormed out and refused to take part in the raid. He had become increasingly uncomfortable working alongside the ageing Terry Millman, who was rapidly becoming a major liability.

In early October, Millman had been stopped by police while driving one of the stolen vans they intended to use in the diamond raid. A breath test showed he was way over the alcohol limit and he was due to appear in court at the end of November. Rather than cleaning up his act, Millman got drunk again and crashed yet another of the gang's stolen vans. He ran away from the scene of the accident before he could be caught.

No one could understand it: Millman had always been a consummate professional and such reckless behaviour was out of character. What he had failed to tell the rest of the gang was that, earlier in the year, he had been diagnosed with terminal stomach cancer. He had taken part in the raids at Nine Elms and Aylesford in a bid to get enough cash to secure his family's future. With both robberies having ended in failure, he desperately needed the raid on the Dome to work out. As his depression grew, so did his drinking problem. But to the other members of the gang, it just seemed that Millman was losing his edge. Originally a key member of the team, he was relegated to a more junior position.

But with James gone the gang was still left with the problem of what to do about the getaway boat. Without it the raid could not go ahead. 'Don't worry,' Cockram told his colleagues. 'I know someone who knows about boats. I'll sort it out.'

All his life Kevin Meredith had struggled to make ends meet. The thirty-five-year-old softly spoken father of three had set up a charter-boat business from his home town of Brighton on the south coast of England but barely made enough to get by. The previous year Cockram had booked Meredith to take him and a few friends on a fishing trip and the pair had become friendly. In the weeks that followed, Cockram had taken two more trips and Meredith found himself telling his passenger all about his financial problems. His mooring fees were due and he was unable to pay: he might have to consider selling his business.

'How much do you owe?' Cockram asked.

'About fourteen hundred pounds.'

'Is that all? I can lend you that, no problem. Don't worry about paying it back, just give it to me when you can.'

Meredith had accepted the money gratefully and did not hear from his benefactor again until 3 November when Cockram called and suggested they meet. As they sat in a bar on the edge of Brighton marina, Cockram asked for his money.

'I don't have it,' said Meredith. 'You know I don't have it.'

'In that case,' replied Cockram, 'could you do me a favour and drive a speedboat for ten to fifteen minutes? I'll wipe the debt off if you do.'

Meredith swallowed hard. He knew little about Cockram, but the few conversations they had shared, his easy access to money and the company he chose to keep screamed that this man made his living outside the law. 'I'm not sure,' Meredith mumbled. 'I don't think I can.'

The smile faded from Cockram's face. 'Why not?'

'Speedboats are a whole different game from the boats I take out. I've never driven one.'

'There'll be time to practise. You can learn. It can't be that different.'

'I don't know, Bill, I think I'm going to have to say no.'

Cockram leant forward and hissed, 'I think you need to think about this more. Not just for yourself. Remember your wife and kids.'

The next morning Meredith told his wife he was travelling to London to help a friend with some building work and set off for the capital.

John Shatford awoke on the morning of Monday 6 November with the unshakeable belief that something big was about to happen. He would have put money on it. At eight thirty a.m. he sat in the control room of the Dome and watched a monitor as live pictures were fed to him of Millman's white van towing a speedboat towards the north bank of the river Thames. Twenty minutes later the bulldozer, which had been moved into a warehouse a few minutes' drive from the Dome, emerged and started trundling towards the site. Shatford began pacing back and forth in anticipation. 'I knew it was coming. It was all happening and they were on their way to us.'

50

But as quickly as it had started, so it ended. The bulldozer stopped, turned round and headed back to the yard. Millman towed the boat back towards Tong Farm. Shatford didn't want to believe the police operation had been blown, but it was a possibility. By now at least four hundred officers knew about the ambush. If the gang had someone on the inside, they would know all about it. With Betson's track record, it was even possible the gang were just toying with the Flying Squad.

In fact, the decision to abort at the last minute had been made by none other than Kevin Meredith. As he and Millman struggled to get the speedboat into the water, Meredith realised the tide was simply too low to allow the boat to be launched. With no river getaway possible, Betson decided there was nothing to do but wait until the following day.

The morning of the seventh found Shatford in a more sombre mood. He remained calm as, once again, the bulldozer emerged from its hiding-place and Millman's van towed the speedboat towards the river. This time the boat was launched and, within minutes, Meredith was carrying out practice manoeuvres before opening up the throttle and heading east towards the Dome. Following the instructions he had been given, he steered into a small creek, tied up and waited.

Just before nine a.m., Millman's van pulled up on a small road by the banks of the Thames a mile and half downstream of the Dome. He slipped on a hard hat and fluorescent jacket, then took out several traffic cones and placed them around a large pothole in the road. The rest of the gang would also dress like construction workers. It was the perfect disguise.

The only thing Shatford knew for sure was that, at some point, the robbers would have to go into the vault. How they would get there was anyone's guess. The favourite theory had been that they would simply come in through the main turnstiles and retrieve weapons they had hidden among the exhibits, but extensive searches had failed to find anything. The bulldozer, the police thought, was probably there to block the road, nothing more.

In the event, Betson's chosen method of entry surprised everyone.

Betson had driven the bulldozer right up to the perimeter fence of the Dome with Ciarrocci, Cockram and another of their associates, Robert Adams, hiding in the back under a blanket. He pulled to the side of the road and flicked on his radio: 'Five minutes.' He and the others then pulled on full-face gas masks.

Meredith received the message, fired up the speedboat's engines and headed across the Thames to the Millennium Pier, which sat adjacent to the Dome building.

Betson gunned the engine of the ten-tonne bulldozer and slipped it into gear. It shot forward and crunched through the outer fence, snapping two concrete bollards and a lamp-post as if they were made of matchwood.

Shatford was horrified. It looked like they were going to drive the bulldozer straight into the Dome. Around a hundred visitors, including a party of schoolchildren, were milling around inside. Shatford ordered his men to move as many people discreetly away from the vault as possible. 'We tried to thin out the crowd as much as we could but there had to be people there otherwise the gang would have suspected something was wrong and aborted the job. We had to let them get into the vault.'

The bulldozer continued picking up speed as it crashed through a set of locked gates and entered the main grounds of the Dome. Betson made a sharp right turn and headed towards a Perspex shutter that formed part of the outer wall of the Dome itself. It shattered into a thousand pieces as he tore through it at 35 m.p.h. A handful of visitors and two undercover police officers dived out of the way, narrowly avoiding being crushed, as Betson pulled up right outside the vault.

Cockram and Adams leapt from the bulldozer and ran towards the diamonds, while Ciarrocci jumped down and threw the first of four smoke grenades, filling the arena with a thick blue haze.

Inside the vault, Cockram reached the tall glass cylinder that held the Millennium Star and pulled the nailgun from the canvas bag slung around his shoulder. He fired six times, making a small star-shaped pattern, then stepped aside to let Adams hit the area with a sledgehammer. After two hefty blows, there was a fist-sized hole in the glass directly in front of the Milennium Star. Using £750 worth of tools, the gang had breached the £2 million security systems in just twenty-seven seconds.

'I couldn't believe how easily the glass went,' Adams would say later. 'I only hit it twice. I was twelve inches from pay-day. I almost had it in my hand. It would have been a blinding Christmas.'

Watching the scene unfold on the monitors in control room, Shatford barked the order: 'Strike, strike, strike.' The 'cleaners' pulled guns from rubbish bags; dozens of armed officers in black combat gear emerged from all around and raced towards Ciarrocci and Betson. Utterly overwhelmed, outnumbered and outgunned, they surrendered without a shot being fired.

Inside the vault Adams and Cockram were oblivious to what was going on until a stun grenade landed at their feet. Trapped inside the vault they knew there was no escape and threw themselves to the floor.

Outside the Dome, armed officers in police speedboats descended on Meredith while others arrested Millman. A team led by Dolden moved in on Tong Farm and arrested Lee Wenham. In the days that followed, the number of visitors to the Dome soared dramatically as people flocked to the scene of the crime. After eleven months, the boast of 'one amazing day' had finally come true.

As the gang had been caught red-handed, prosecutors expected them to offer little in the way of defence when the case came to court. However, it soon emerged that Betson and his men had planned what to say in the event of being captured almost as carefully as they had planned the robbery itself.

Under English law there is a subtle distinction between the act of robbery and the act of stealing: the former includes the use or threat of violence and carries a maximum sentence of life imprisonment. A charge of stealing implies the perpetrators did not intend to cause any harm to anyone. The longest jail term available is seven years.

Betson, Cockram, Ciarrocci and Adams pleaded guilty to conspiracy to steal but not guilty to conspiracy to rob. The fact that none of the gang had been carrying guns during the raid – much to the surprise of the Flying Squad – worked heavily in their favour. Only Meredith denied both charges. Millman, who finally succumbed to his cancer, died six weeks before the trial began.

Once the prosecution had completed their case, Betson took the stand. Cocky and confident, he told the jury that, as borne out by his criminal record, he had never been involved in violent crime or armed robbery and instead made all his money from tobacco-smuggling. While he admitted trying to steal the diamonds, he knew there was no possibility of anyone getting hurt because the Dome was practically empty that morning.

'How could you possibly know that?' asked the lead prosecutor.

Betson cleared this throat and faced the jury. 'Because we had a man on the inside. A policeman called Michael Wearing, my brother-in-law.'

Betson explained that Officer Wearing had been one of a small team assigned to patrol the exterior of the Dome during the first half of 2000. While working there he had struck up a friendship with a man named Tony who worked security at the building. Between them, they had hatched the plan for the raid and taken the proposal to Betson.

Wearing was hastily brought before the court. He had served with the Metropolitan Police for more than twenty years and had an unblemished record. He had married the sister of Betson's wife in 1991 and become godfather to Betson's son. But if Betson had hoped family loyalty might save him, he was very much mistaken. Wearing's most painful moment in the witness box came when he admitted that back in 1998, two years before the attack on the Dome, he had made a confidential report to his senior officers suggesting that his brother-in-law had been responsible for several robberies. Betson swore under his breath as the revelation emerged.

The arguments raged on with the defence claiming this was just a clever ploy on Wearing's part to cover himself. Cockram and

Ciarrocci took their turns in the witness box and supported Betson's account. Not only had the mysterious Tony suggested the raid, he had also funded it. Cockram and the others were on 'wages' of £100,000 to do the job. 'I thought the diamonds were only worth a couple of million,' he said. 'I was shocked when it turned out they were worth a lot more.'

Only Robert Adams refused to go into the witness box, anxious that his previous criminal history should not come to light. During the early 1980s he had been jailed for six years for attempting to kill his wife.

The allegations against Wearing soon collapsed. The officer had never made any secret of his relationship with Betson to his superiors on the force, and the Flying Squad had been aware of the connection all along. The idea that Wearing had provided any help or assistance for any element of the robbery was dismissed as utterly false.

In the end it was the weakest link, Kevin Meredith, who condemned them. As experienced, hardened criminals, every other member of the gang had said nothing during arrest and interview. Meredith, however, had started talking within minutes of being handcuffed on the boat and only stopped when he was joined by an attorney and advised that he might be better saying nothing.

But it was too late. The court heard Meredith on tape saying he had been threatened by Cockram and had only agreed to take part in the raid because he was in fear of his life. Most crucially Cockram had told him: 'Don't worry, we won't have shooters or anything. But we'll have ammonia, and if anyone comes up to us, that will put them straight down on the floor.'

It was enough to convince the jury that the gang would have had no hesitation in using violence and, apart from Meredith, they were all convicted of the more serious offence. Betson and Cockram received eighteen years, Ciarrocci and Adams got fifteen each while Meredith came away with five.

Their arrest and capture might have been a complete surprise but on their way to prison, the gang were finally let in on the biggest secret of all. As soon as De Beers heard there was a threat to the diamonds they had replaced them with crystal fakes. Even if the raid had gone according to plan, they would not have got their hands on the real gems.

Like so many of the hugely ambitious 'project' crimes that had gone before, the great Dome robbery ended in failure and stiff prison sentences. Little wonder that for the latest generation of would-be blaggers growing up in the traditional breeding-grounds of the Bermondsey Triangle, armed robbery has lost its appeal.

Those who manage to avoid being shot by the police or grassed up by the people they thought were their friends still face the prospect of at least fifteen years in prison, even if they were unarmed. And, under the three-strikes-and-you're-out system, a third conviction means an automatic life sentence.

Under a new clampdown even little-league robbers acting out of desperation face stiff sentences. Take the case of nineteen-year-old Teresa Hall from West Bromwich, who had been a model student before falling in with a bad crowd. Within the space of a few months she had fallen in love with an older man with a heroin addiction. When she could no longer subsidise his habit she helped him raid their local Total petrol garage, the boyfriend brandishing a handgun while Teresa filled a bag from the till. The pair escaped with just £311. A week later a second raid at a One Stop shop went wrong when the owners were alerted by a panic alarm. Hall sprayed CS gas at them. Arrested and charged, she said in mitigation that she had only gone along with the raids to help her boyfriend. Despite this she was jailed for nine years.

'It's just not worth it,' says Jimmy Tippett Jnr. 'When you do a robbery and stick a gun under the nose of some bank clerk, half the fucking world goes out looking for you. There's the bank, the insurance company, the cops, *Crimewatch*, *Most Wanted* – the lot of them. But if you fly over to Amsterdam and bring back an ounce of charlie in your underpants, it's almost as if no one gives a fuck.

ARMED ROBBERY

These days, if you're talking about crime, you're basically talking about drugs. It's all about money, isn't it?, and until someone finds a quicker or better way of making money than through drugs, that's the one people are gonna be sticking with.'

COCAINE

CHAPTER FOUR

At first it seemed like little more than the tragic suicide of a successful racehorse owner who, in a moment of madness, had simply gone too far.

When the body of forty-nine-year-old Eugene Carter was found hanging from the rafters of his plush Kent home in February 2001, most of his friends in the equestrian world believed it was because he couldn't live with the shame of a brutal road-rage attack the previous year. Although he had not yet been charged or even arrested, the police were closing in fast and Carter knew only too well that he risked losing everything he had worked so hard for.

'His behaviour was becoming increasingly unpredictable,' said a former colleague. 'He was withdrawing into himself more and more, shutting off from the outside world. I wasn't that surprised when I heard – it was obvious that he was under an incredible amount of stress.'

The trouble had started when Carter, who owned at least a dozen prime racehorses, went inexplicably berserk after finding a bicycle parked in an alleyway off Chislehurst high street that he wanted to drive down. Visibly shaking with fury he climbed out of his sleek black Mercedes, picked up the bike and, swearing to himself over and over again, threw it over a nearby wall.

The cyclist, a thirty-one-year-old Iranian, came out of a nearby barber's, saw what had happened to his bike and confronted Carter. It turned out to be a terrible mistake. Carter launched into a vicious attack, kicking and punching the man to the ground, then repeatedly smashing him in the head with a house brick, all the while spitting out a stream of racist gibes. Leaving his victim bloody and unconscious in the gutter, Carter then walked back calmly to his car and drove away.

The incident had been seen by dozens of eyewitnesses and, though none was able to recall the registration number of the vehicle that had been involved, they had all seen enough of the attacker's face to help put together an identikit picture.

'People came to us and described a man who looked identical to Carter,' says one police source connected to the inquiry. 'The name came up time and again. We were closing in on him and he knew that. I guess that's why he did what he did.'

Eugene Carter was far more than a petty thug and fan of the sport of kings; he was just about the biggest drugs baron that London has ever seen. A true underworld pioneer, Carter was singlehandedly responsible for creating the vast and lucrative market for cocaine that exists to this day. Only now can the real story of his life be told.

At the start of the 1980s, few people in the world of British law enforcement were concerned about cocaine. Average Customs seizures for each year of the preceding decade were a mere seventeen kilos while the haul for the whole of 1984 had been just thirty-five.

Cocaine abuse had looked like becoming a problem during the first World War and the early 1920s but never really took hold. It was expensive, had a reputation as a 'champagne drug' and was far more strongly associated with American culture. Back then if the British wanted to snort something that would keep them up all night, they generally preferred amphetamine.

Heroin, on the other hand, was widely seen as the scourge of society: in 1984 a massive 312 kilos had been seized. Government statistics estimated that there were more than fifty thousand addicts in the country, a figure that was rising fast, and newspapers and magazines were filled with stories about the developing 'heroin crisis'.

But as 1985 drew to a close the picture slowly changed. Cocaine seizures suddenly doubled and Interpol agents described the British market as 'an unpicked plum', warning that the detailed profiles used to spot potential cannabis and heroin smugglers were failing to catch those bringing in the white stuff. That same year, soon after Scotland Yard's Drugs Squad made their biggest ever single seizure – a whole six kilos – the *Sunday Times* dubbed cocaine 'the new threat' and detailed how the saturation of the American market was set to lead to a huge surge in European seizures. A few days later the *Financial Times* noted nervously that the wealth and power of the world's cocaine barons was becoming 'unassailable'.

Within months David Mellor, then Home Office minister, toured Bolivia and Peru to distribute cocaine-fighting aid aimed at helping to prevent the drugs reaching the UK. It was too little, far too late. Shortly after Mellor's return, Assistant Commissioner John Dellow of the Metropolitan Police warned that there was growing evidence to suggest that 'violent and evil' criminals from South America were hard at work trying to set up a drug-distribution centre in Britain.

Soon afterwards Richard Lawrence, then chief investigation officer of HM Customs and Excise, was describing cocaine as 'the greatest concern for the future' because of signs that the South American organisations were trying to create an infrastructure in the UK to sell and market their product.

In fact, that infrastructure had existed for some time. With its common language and large Colombian population, Spain was the natural port of entry for Colombian cocaine. The traffickers received a boost when changes to Spanish law decriminalised the possession of cocaine unless the amount involved greatly exceeded an individual's personal needs. Though not changing the legal status of large-scale smuggling, the new liberal attitude meant the local police were often diverted to other duties, giving the drugs barons virtual free rein.

The cartel operatives arrived in Spain to find hundreds of leading British gangsters *in situ*: following the collapse of the extradition treaty, they had set up home on the now infamous Costa del Crime to settle back and enjoy a hassle-free life. But few of them had retired completely. After some initial reluctance to get involved in drug-trafficking, a few of these old-timers began to dabble in the cannabis trade, facilitating the movement of tonnes of resin from Morocco to the UK. The vast profits and relatively low risks (especially compared to armed robbery) soon attracted interest, and by the time the South American cartels arrived, the British were well placed to assist them. By the end of the decade high-profile seizures of multi-kilo loads were becoming a regular occurrence, yet masses of cocaine was still getting through, the price was falling and demand was growing fast.

But cocaine would never have taken off in the UK unless it had been carefully marketed to create a growing demand. Not only had that already been done, but it had virtually all been the work of one man.

Eugene Carter got his first introduction to the criminal life courtesy of his uncle. Johnny Carter was a legendary face who, during the 1950s, had run racetrack gangs for the likes of Jack Spot and later hit the headlines after a dramatic knife fight with none other than Mad Frankie Fraser. Growing up on the fringes of the underworld, Eugene first made his living from his family business – scrap metal. A traditional rag-and-bone man, he rode up and down the streets of south London in a horse-drawn cart collecting rubbish.

He spent a lot of time with his cousins, the Walker brothers, who in the early 1980s were ranked alongside the top armed robbers in the capital, and would wile away hours drinking at Charlie's wine bar in Lewisham, a popular haunt for many south London faces. It was there that Carter became friendly with the likes of Jimmy Tippett Jnr and Brian Reader, later convicted of handling gold from the Brinks Mat robbery.

Although he never became an armed robber himself – friends say he lacked the courage – it was the aftermath of the Brinks Mat job that first set Carter on the path that would ultimately lead to his untimely death.

With most of those responsible for stealing or handling the gold bullion behind bars within a year, south London was suddenly awash with friends and relations of the gang who found themselves looking after vast sums of money. Some simply buried the cash, others invested in property. Carter was the first to see the potential of the fast-growing cocaine market and invested in that instead.

His system was so simple and so foolproof that not one shipment was ever intercepted. Carter had become friendly with some of the staff in the Colombian embassy and, using their diplomatic privileges, they brought in hundreds of kilos of super high-quality cocaine with them on every trip. (This method of smuggling is still widely used, though rarely uncovered. In October 2003 a diplomatic bag containing £1 million worth of cocaine was intercepted on its way to the Sierra Leone high commission in London. The drugs were found by United Nations officers – acting on a tip-off – who gained special permission directly from Sierra Leone's president to open the bags before they left Africa *en route* for Gatwick.)

'Carter always had money,' says Jimmy Tippett, 'but within the space of a few months he went from having a bit of money to having absolutely fucking millions. I was just a kid but I'll never forget some of what I saw during those days. I was doing little favours for him, driving his car and delivering bits and pieces. I remember one time he was at the races and he took two hundred grand with him and blew every single penny. Not only that but by the time he left he owed the bookmakers an extra sixty thousand that he'd got on credit. The man had millions and millions and he didn't give a fuck. I'd never seen people do that sort of money, not ever and not since.

'Eugene wasn't the only one who got rich. The Brinks Mat robbery turned all of south London around. It saw a lot of people moving out of their council houses into big eight- or nine-bedroom mansions in Kent or Essex. And it saw a lot of people moving into coke as well. In those days the only people the Colombians would deal with were the old faces – that's why you had people like Eddie Richardson and some of the Great Train Robbers like Jimmy

Hussey and Tommy Wisbey getting done for drugs in the early nineties. Nowadays that's all changed and they'll deal with anyone. But back then they were only really dealing with Eugene and he was cleaning up.

'Nowadays no one could afford to be that flash – the police would be on them like a shot, and now with all this asset-recovery stuff, you'd never get away with it. Back then it was different. The police might have had an idea that he was up to something but his system was so tight and he kept himself so far removed from the actual street sales, he was virtually untouchable.'

Carter's excessive lifestyle soon earned him a nickname – Eugene Cartier. His party trick was to take off his Cartier watch and smash it on the floor in the middle of a nightclub to the astonishment of those around him. His favourite piece was a diamond-studded square Rolex that had cost him £170,000 and had originally been commissioned for the Sultan of Brunei. He also regularly wore a baguette diamond ring worth £250,000. These and a few other bits and pieces meant Carter could boast that he never left the house with less than half a million pounds' worth of jewellery on him.

'He drove around in a Rolls-Royce Corniche convertible, which he'd bought brand new, paying ninety grand in cash for it,' says Tippett. 'I drove it once – he was at the races and wanted some extra money to put down some bets so he gave me the keys and asked me to go and fetch him thirty grand. When I got back he put the lot on one horse. It came in fifth or something but he didn't bat an eyelid, he just laughed.

'Eugene had so much money that he just didn't know what to do with it all. He'd go out clubbing for the night and think nothing of spending ten thousand on bottles of Cristal champagne.

'He was rich and surrounded himself with people who were willing to do anything for him, but the truth is that nobody liked him. The reason is that he was a horrible, horrible cunt. He was the sort of person who would open up a gram of charlie in the VIP section of our favourite club and wait until a little crowd gathered around him. He would have a snort, give maybe one other person a snort and look up at all the people waiting for their turn. Then he would pretend to sneeze, blow the whole lot over the floor and say, "Whoops, sorry."

'Then he'd pull out another gram and do exactly the same thing again. He used to do stuff on purpose, always psychological, playing with people's minds. I once saw him throw three grand on the floor of a club, then sit back and watch people fighting to get the money. He had a real inferiority complex because he was a real ugly bastard, all cropped ginger hair and a big nose. He used to set fire to fifty-pound notes in front of birds to try and impress them. The only way he ever got laid was through the money and being flash so that's the way he behaved.

'The police soon got wind of what he was up to and spent a couple of years keeping him under non-stop surveillance but it was a waste of time. They saw him have a few meetings and even hand over the odd bit of cash here and there but there was nothing to link him to drugs at all. Rather than swoop and get him for something small, they wanted to wait and take him for something that would put him away for a long, long time, but that just wasn't going to happen. He was too careful for that. Or, at least, he was at the start.

'Doing coke was a very different experience back then. For one thing the quality was excellent. You would have a little toot and you would know all about it. I guess the Colombians wanted people to get a taste for it to help develop the market so the stuff coming over was virtually pure. Nowadays even before it gets here it has been cut to shit. The Colombians got to the point where they started thinking, Why bother getting money for just one kilo when we can cut it two or three times and still make loads of money? Plenty of people out there are having a good time and they're more than happy with the money they're paying, but they don't know what they're missing.

'Because it was so good, people couldn't get enough of it and they were always coming back for more. That meant the money just kept rolling in, much faster than Eugene could ever spend it. No matter what he did, there was always more just around the corner.

'He bought this massive house in Chislehurst, paid a million pounds for it, and would have wild parties there with loads of champagne and coke and caviar almost every weekend.

'But Eugene was using more coke than anyone. But for the fact that he wasn't paying for it, he would have been his own best customer. After a few years the pressure really started to get to him. He was getting more and more paranoid and more and more out of control. Coke's the last thing in the world you need if you're feeling like that, but Eugene just couldn't leave it alone. He'd give up for a week or so and try to sort himself out, but then he'd be right back on it, worse than before.

'Anyone else would have had to stop: they would have run out of money or be so busy stealing and selling their body that they wouldn't have time to do any drugs. But Eugene was so rich there were no limits to what he could do. Before long he was spending six or seven grand a night on coke. It was incredible.

'The parties continued but Eugene wasn't enjoying any of it any more. He'd lock himself in his room for six or seven hours at a time and talk about the fact that people were after him. A few times I saw him on a really bad day and it was sad to see him like that.

'Around that time he started paying money to hitmen to go and shoot people. He was convinced someone was trying to take his monopoly away from him. He just couldn't see that the thing with the embassy was so sweet that there was no way anyone could challenge him.

'The paranoia took over and he got into a big beef with a rival gang who were controlling the coke trade in north London. Eugene was in charge south of the river but convinced himself that the other gang wanted it all to themselves. Then that thing with the cyclist happened and the stress was just too much.

'There was a theory that the rival gang had been responsible, that they'd gone to his house with guns and made him hang himself. Whichever way it was, his death was the end of an era and those that had become rich as part of his drugs empire soon found themselves in need of another supplier. But not everyone minded when Eugene died. A lot of people owed him a lot of money for coke so they ended up having a right touch. One geezer I know owed him for thirty kilos so he couldn't have been happier.'

For the first five years of its life, cocaine wasn't cocaine at all. The active ingredient of the humble coca leaf was first identified in Germany in 1855 by chemist Friedrich Gaedecke who named it erythroxyline. Four years later a second chemist, Albert Niemann, managed to isolate the product and renamed it cocaine.

Hailed as a wonder drug and fabulous health tonic, cocaine was sold openly over the counter, even in Harrods, and became a popular ingredient in many wines and medicines. There were toothache cures, coca cigarettes that were guaranteed to lift depression, chocolate cocaine tablets that mixed the best of both worlds.

Robert Louis Stephenson wrote his classic *The Strange Case of Dr Jekyll and Mr Hyde* during a week-long cocaine-binge, while polar adventurer Ernest Shackleton explored Antarctica propelled by tablets of Forced March, which, taken hourly, promised to 'allay hunger and prolong the power of endurance'. The 1880s also saw the launch of Coca-Bola chewing gum – 'a powerful tonic to the muscular and nervous system, enabling the chewer to perform additional labour and relieving fatigue and exhaustion'.

The cocaine-infused wine, Vin Mariani, received glowing endorsements from royalty, prime ministers and even the Pope. Coca-Cola was introduced in 1886 as a valuable brain-tonic and cure for all nervous afflictions, and promoted as a temperance drink 'offering the virtues of coca without the vices of alcohol'. The new beverage was invigorating and popular and little wonder: until 1903, a typical serving contained around sixty milligrams of cocaine. All traces of the drug have long since been removed.

Totally unaware of its dangers, many doctors began prescribing cocaine as an antidote to morphine addiction and soon found themselves with patients dependent on both. People have been underestimating its power ever since.

It wasn't until 28 July 1916 that the possession of cocaine without a prescription became a criminal offence, and not until 1920, the year the Dangerous Drugs Act was passed, that the use of cocaine went underground. It resurfaced in the America of the 1970s, popularised by hard-living rock bands and movie stars alike, but found few takers outside this élite market. In 1972 just one in eleven Americans between the age of eighteen and twenty-five had tried cocaine. Within a decade that figure had risen to one in four, and the first evidence of equally startling growth began to appear on the other side of the Atlantic.

Today hundreds of thousands of occasional users take the drug and suffer no ill-effects, though for some it is all too easy to fall into the trap of addiction, which is what happened to Steve Roberts and Eugene Carter.

In the golden days of organised crime, drink and drugs were shunned by the men who considered themselves part of a noble profession. Going out to celebrate a job done well was one thing, but drinking before an armed robbery or other 'job' was heavily frowned on. One of the big differences with today's villains is that many of them, like Tippett, Roberts and the Bradish brothers, will happily spend most of their time in a drug-fuelled haze. And, as Tippett knows from bitter personal experience, that can cause problems in itself.

'Charlie changes people in lots of ways, but the paranoia it brings is the worst thing of all. I remember one night I'd been out drinking with my mates Lee and Frank, both of whom were sons of villains, and a guy called James Lawlor, who was a bit of a blagger. We were all in the Crown in Southwark Park Road, snorting lines of coke and drinking. When it got to closing time none of us were ready to call it a night so we went back to Lee's flat just up the road to carry on.

'We were all having a great laugh and a few more of Frankie's mates joined us. Between us we must have got through at least two ounces of coke and by four a.m. we were completely wasted and the paranoia was starting to set in.

'I was sitting next to James and he suddenly pulled one of those old-fashioned cut-throat razors out of his pocket. He was playing around with it, flicking it back and forth. I hadn't seen one like that for donkey's years so I asked if I could have a look. He swung the blade over and tried to cut me with it. I managed to move out of the way just in time but he still caught my neck.

'Then it just turned. We all started fighting each other and it was all for no reason. It was one big fucking tear-up. We were all charlied up and E'd up, and it just got too much. James turned into a complete fucking psycho, he was out of control, trying to cut everyone. Punches and kicks and bits of furniture were flying around all over the place. Me and Lee managed to get James to the door and kicked him out but we were convinced he was going to come back and get us. We barricaded the door and sat there with a little 410 shotgun waiting for it. Every little noise we heard was like pure hell. It was the longest night of my life.'

Three weeks later Tippett read a story in the paper that made him realise he'd had a lucky escape. Lawlor and his friend Brian Stead had been out on a pub crawl when they ended up at a place called the Gin Palace club in the Old Kent Road. There they happened across Ray Brooker, a devoted family man but even more devoted social drinker. Brooker had been due to go to his daughter's nativity play but chose to spend his time drinking with Lawlor and Stead instead.

They travelled back to Stead's flat and carried on drinking and taking vast quantities of cocaine. When Lawlor left the room to go to the toilet, Brooker remarked drunkenly, 'I'm going to do him one of these days.' As soon as Lawlor returned, Stead told him what had been said. Lawlor then grabbed a .38 pistol and shot Brooker in the mouth. Both men then stabbed him repeatedly.

Once Brooker was dead Lawlor called his brother, Jason, who came to the flat and helped the pair to cut up the body in the bath.

'But then as they were driving the body to the dump James

reaches into one of the bags, pulls out Brooker's arm and starts using it to make hand signals. Then some girls go past and he uses the arm to wave at them. He was an absolute psychopath. It turned out he'd been working as a hitman for a couple of the south London gangs and had killed at least three people. At the same time he'd been involved in loads of different armed robberies. The police had been waiting for him to do another – I think they were hoping he'd try to shoot his way out and they'd get the chance to kill him on the job. Now he's doing life instead.'

It used to be the case that only a few well-known criminals, mostly in London, had direct contacts with the Colombians. Now it's spread across the whole country.

Curtis 'Cocky' Warren, a Merseyside drug baron, who is now serving time in the Netherlands, was one of the first, and dozens have followed in his footsteps.

In Manchester throughout 2002 Donovan Hardy ran a massive cocaine empire from behind the façade of a mobile-phone shop. Hardy would send his cash to Colombia – either directly, via Panama, or by paying money into his bank account on the Cayman Islands – and pick up the drugs in the Netherlands. He employed several couriers, who would bring back small batches of cocaine, usually around two kilos at a time, from a stash of up to a hundred kilos that he kept in the false ceiling of a flat in Rotterdam.

In Scotland in the early part of 2003 a four-man gang led by James Mair paid £1 million direct to a Colombian cartel for a half-tonne consignment of cocaine and a further £50,000 for dozens of bales of raw rubber, which would be used to conceal the drugs on their journey from Panama.

But even for those who fail to link up directly with the South Americans, there are still vast sums to be made from the cocaine business. This has prompted police in London to change tactics and go after the mid-level dealers, who had been virtually left alone for many years while detectives focused on large-scale importers and street sellers.

COCAINE

According to intelligence sources, these entrepreneurs are vital to the supply chain. Some are hardened criminals, involved in gang and drug activity, but others are seemingly respectable business people running food outlets, property and import/export companies that act as fronts for illegal activities.

It took only three weeks for me to track one down.

CHAPTER FIVE

I hear Rick long before I see him. His gravelly Yorkshire tones cut through the hubbub of the pub in Norton, just outside Doncaster, where I've spent the last forty-five minutes waiting for him to arrive.

He bustles through the swing doors, laughing like a drain as the teenage girls on each of his burly arms giggle and make wide-eyed kissy faces at him. Rick is a stocky six-footer and, notwithstanding the beginnings of a neat round beer-gut protruding over the top of his black jeans, looks supremely fit and formidable. His dark hair has been cropped to disguise the early stages of male-pattern baldness and he wears a perfectly tailored smart-but-casual dark grey jacket over a black T-shirt. Confidence oozes out of every pore: the first impression is that of a high-class spiv, the sort of man you'd find selling brand new Jaguars and Bentleys rather than second-hand Fiestas.

Rick heads straight for the bar so Billy, who has set up the meeting on my behalf, nips over to let him know I am there. Eventually, having installed the two girls at a corner table and picked up a bottle of premium beer, Rick wanders over. He eyes me cautiously and makes no attempt to apologise for being so late. I know better than to mention it: he is, after all, one of the biggest coke dealers in the North-east and he's taking time out to speak to me purely as a favour to his friend Billy.

The air of confidence crumbles alarmingly when I pull out my MiniDisc recorder and place it on Rick's side of the table. By the time Billy and I have reassured him that there's nothing to worry about he has drained his first bottle and returned to the bar for another, stopping off to talk to the girls once more on his way back.

Finally Rick returns to the table and sits himself down, seemingly eager to get the whole thing out of the way as quickly as possible. 'Okay,' he says, with a half-sigh. 'Tell me what you want to know.'

My first question is the most obvious one: of all the town and cities in the North-east, why does Rick base himself in Doncaster? Rick smiles, settles back in his chair and sips his beer while nodding slowly. 'I know what you mean,' he says. 'It's not so long ago that, as far as drugs were concerned, all roads led to London, end of story. Everything was controlled from there and passed through there, regardless of where the stuff finally ended up.

'Don't get me wrong, London's still important, it's kind of like the main hub, always will be, but Liverpool, Birmingham, Bristol – they're all moving up the ladder. These days a lot of the big shipments miss out London all together and go straight to the regions 'cos that's where the demand is.

'So why Doncaster? Well, it's a big city and it's central, especially to Yorkshire. A lot of people come together here. There are always a lot of faces in Doncaster and a lot of activity. There has to be. The reality of the drugs trade is that the big players are a lot more spread out than a lot of people would think. Otherwise it just wouldn't work.'

Born in Leeds, Rick moved to Grimsby at an early age and, after working as a doorman and gaining a reputation for being useful with his fists, found himself drifting into a world of crime. 'It were never a deliberate choice, like, it just sort of happened. You start out doing little favours for people, and before you know it, you're at it yourself.'

After dipping into protection and debt collection, Rick turned to large-scale bootlegging, one of the first in his area to do so. He made a small fortune almost overnight but ended up in prison for eighteen months after being caught during a random Customs sweep. It was soon after his release that he was invited to join the criminal equivalent of the Premier League. And, surprisingly, it was all courtesy of the Kray twins.

* * *

In March 1969 Ronald and Reginald Kray were convicted of the murders of Jack 'The Hat' McVitie and George Cornell, and the detectives responsible for putting them away felt confident that their gang – the Firm – had also been brought down.

Not so. Despite remaining firmly behind bars for the next thirty-odd years, the Kray twins were able to use the extraordinary power of their name not only to keep the Firm going but to amass around £5 million as their share of the proceeds of their new criminal enterprise. Some of their income came from books and film deals as well as payments from newspapers and magazines for exclusive interviews. Other money came as the result of legitimate 'sponsorship' arrangements through which dozens of businesses – at least ten of them debt-collection agencies – set up deals in which the twins received a cut of the profits in return for allowing them to use the Kray name.

But the bulk of their income came from the criminals who wanted to advance up the career ladder and knew that being a part of the Firm was the way to do it. A typical deal would involve an up-and-coming gangster writing to the twins and asking whether, in return for a retainer of, say, £800 per month, they would endorse him. If they agreed, the twins needed do nothing more. The up-and-coming gangster would be able to say he was part of the Firm and join the list of those allowed to meet the twins in person.

During such occasions the newcomers would find themselves rubbing shoulders with regular visitors who were noted members of the old guard, men like Joey Pyle, Freddie Foreman and Tony Lambrianou, who had long since retired from a life of crime. While the old-timers swapped war stories, the newcomers would be introduced to one another. The system worked like a dream: without ever leaving their cells, the Krays helped put together dozens of drug deals, robberies and other scams. Throughout their prison career the twins never masterminded any direct criminal activity but their knowledge, criminal contacts, and the sheer power of their name made them pivotal figures in the underworld.

According to Ronnie's widow, Kate Kray: 'If somebody needed something or wanted something it would cost them money from the moment they walked into Broadmoor or prison to see one of the twins. They never organised crimes but they were there to make introductions and advise for money.

'Ron was the kingpin. Villains from Scotland, Wales and all over . . . they didn't know each other but they all knew Ron. So if you had some villains from Liverpool coming down to London to do a bit of business they would pay Ron to make the introductions. He never wanted to know the details of the villainy – the only thing he was interested in was how much his cut was going to be.'

In time-honoured tradition, Ronnie and Reggie referred to this money as their 'pension' and it soon amounted to far more than the twins could ever spend themselves. Some of it was diverted to charity, some sent to keep their wives, friends and 'colleagues' who had fallen on hard times out of the gutter. There was more than enough to go round: almost all the payments were made in cash and Kate Kray alone was picking up at least six £800 'pensions' each month. She once collected a single package that turned out to contain £85,000.

Membership of the Firm (which continues to flourish, despite the death of its founders) means instant access to a trusted network of top criminals with international connections. And in an underworld where 'grassing' is fast reaching epidemic proportions, the Firm stands out as an organisation that lives by the rules of organised crime as they stood in London in the mid-1960s. Parents, particularly mothers, are to be treated with the utmost respect, women and children are to be kept out of the line of fire, and the police are to be treated with utter contempt.

These are values that Rick holds dear. 'When I'm grafting, I only ever work with people who I've known for a long time or people who have been put on to me through the Firm. Dealing with proper people who I know I can trust, it might mean I end up waiting a little bit longer for the deal to come through but at least when it does, I know it's a hundred per cent safe.

'You need to be part of a trusted network. The downside of being somewhere small is that everyone knows who the main players are and you soon get to know one another. You have different levels. If you take the drug scene you've got your street dealers, the guys who deal to them and then the ones who import. Up to a certain level, everyone sticks together but when you get above that, when you get to where I am, no one will deal with anyone else because no one trusts anyone else. At some time or another everyone in this town has worked with everyone else and at some point they've all fallen out with one another.

'If you deal with sensible people you are not going to get fucked over. At least, that's the theory.' I ask Rick to elaborate. 'I have always been part of the old school and gone with the old-school rules. You don't fuck with people and that means you can come back again and again and again. You get a good name for yourself and you get some respect. Your name starts to be given out to other people. But if you decide to rip someone off for twenty grand, you're only ever going to do it once.'

I ask Rick to take me through the main commodities that he deals with and the relative merits of each. 'A few years ago everybody was coming out of the drugs game and going into cigs and spirits. The money was good, and if you did get caught, the sentences were nothing. But now they've really clamped down on the bootlegging, pushing the sentences so that they're on a par with cannabis, so people are drifting back into the drugs game again.

'As far as cannabis is concerned, there's no money in the resin any more unless you're involved at a very, very high level, hundreds of kilos at a time. It's that cheap over here now that it's just not worth it. A few years ago you could bring it in for six or seven hundred a kilo and get two grand for it all day long. Now you're lucky if you can get eight hundred for it. There's still good money to be made in the quality herbal stuff, like skunk, but it's a lot bulkier so it's harder to smuggle.

'Heroin? I can't comment on that because I've never touched it and I never would. I don't like the idea of going around creating junkies. Es are going for a pound apiece. You used to be able to make good money but not so much now. You have to put a shitload of cash up front and you're taking a big risk for not that much gain.

'The cigs business, it's gone a bit silly now, it's way too competitive. You have to pay up front and there's no money to be made unless you're bringing back containerloads. But once you start doing that the risk goes up tenfold. When I got into it, there were only a few people involved and you could make a good crack out of it. But not any more. Everybody's selling cigs, you go to every corner shop or every car-boot sale and they're all over the place.

'Charlie is where the money's at. The game has changed a lot since the old days but it's still the main earner. I once heard someone say that drug-dealing was a thousand times more addictive than drug-taking and they were dead right.'

Rick drains the last of his bottle and I offer to buy him another, fighting my way through to the crowded bar and waiting what seems like an eternity to get served. When I finally return Rick can't remember the point he was about to make so I ask him what he considers to be the key attributes of a successful smuggler.

'You have to be a bit of a gambler. The fact is there's no way in the world that Customs can stop every single container that enters the country – if they did the whole world would grind to a halt. They've got their sources, they've got their intelligence, but most of all they've got their profiles. If they have a plane coming in from Bogotá and another coming in from Milan, well, then, it's obvious where the risks are. So my job is to play their game in reverse, to work out what they're looking for and do everything I can to make sure my shipments don't get flagged up.

'When you get involved in the big shipments, I'm talking tonnes, then you're in for a lot of sleepless nights. You put your money down and you're waiting six months before you even know it's got into the country. And even then you're a long way from being home and dry. If Customs are on to you, they ain't gonna pounce right away. They'll wait until you've got it back to your warehouse or wherever. Touch wood, I've never been bubbled up – and, more than anything else, that's the way you get caught these days.

'I've spent time out in Spain, working with people there. There's a lot of Brits in the area, especially around Puerto Banus on the Costa del Sol because there's the huge marina there. A lot of the smugglers are using the big yachts to pick the stuff up because they know they're less likely to get stopped than if they do it with some scruffy fishing-boat. You can bring the stuff right up into the heart of the town, and from there it's easy. No Customs, no borders, nothing.

'But there's a lot of police activity in Spain now so more and more people are doing it through Portugal or flying it direct to the former eastern bloc where you can still bribe Customs and police and whatnot to get it through. Instead of hooking up with the expats, a lot of the gangs are doing their own trafficking now. Once the supply is sorted out, they don't need to get anyone else involved. That means there's even less chance of getting grassed up, you can control it, put a real lid on things.

'Once it's in Europe it's just a question of hiding in the HGVs and getting it through the tunnel or sea ports or sometimes just sticking it in the post. But even at my level, more and more people are looking to buy straight from South America. Some of those people who work on the cruise ships, cabin crew and such, are doing very nicely because of that.

'A lot of the stuff I deal with comes in via Ireland. There's a lot going on over there because the Irish navy consists of something like two rubber dinghies and one of those inflatable bananas. There's so much coastline, they just can't patrol it all. It's absolutely wide open.'

When I start to ask Rick about the usual quantities he deals with, one reason for his initial nervousness soon becomes clear. A few days earlier one of his former colleagues was arrested in connection with a £15 million consignment of cocaine, heroin, amphetamine and cannabis that was smuggled through the Channel Tunnel from Holland. The route and methods have both been utilised by Rick in the past.

'His firm is based up in Bolton and basically doing in the North-west what I'm doing in the North-east. They'd done the run ten or eleven times before with no problems. They just got unlucky this time around. They were always careful. The drugs were hidden in containers of chemicals so there was no smell to leak out. The lorry drivers would be given pay-as-you-go phones just as they left and those same phones would be thrown into the sea while they were on the ferry coming back so there was no way they could ever be traced.

'He had a legitimate business in Amsterdam that wasn't making any money but gave him plenty of excuses to go back and forth. The people were earning good money, though. The lorry drivers were getting paid ten thousand a time, and that's on top of what they were earning anyway. That's why I think they were just unlucky. He hadn't pissed anybody off, he was working with everyone who might have been an enemy.

'As well as bringing in his own stuff, he would offer other people a service bringing their drugs to the UK, charging upwards of eight hundred pounds per kilo, which is a good way to make money. You never want to be too greedy but every time a truck comes through without being stopped, your first thought is always, Fuck, I should have put a bigger load on it. It's the same with a container. Each one can carry up to five hundred kilos of coke but you never fill them up all the way just in case. But once they get through, you're kicking yourself that you didn't brim the fucker.

'They say it was fifteen million pounds but that's bollocks. That's final street price and when you're an importer you never see that. At this level what you're looking to do is either double or quadruple your money as soon as you get it in the country. If you want to take it all the way and make millions, you can, but you have to get out there yourself and sell ten-pound bags of the stuff. It's just not worth the risk.

'If you get caught with a million pounds' worth of coke, what they basically mean is that they've nabbed someone who has just lost two hundred grand. I'm not saying people aren't making money out of it, of course they are. Just that it's not quite the same as what you read in the papers. Not unless you're bang at it day and night. And then it gets difficult because you end up with more money than you know what to do with and the only thing to do is invest it back into more shipments. I know people who've made fortunes only to lose it all when some big shipment goes tits up.

'Once you get the stuff, you pass it on to your dealers. A lot of firms put it out on bail – you know, give it to people on credit. You hand over the drugs and they've got, say, two weeks to come back to you with the money. I try not to work that way because it causes all kinds of problems.

'The rule is, whatever happens, the buyer still owes the money. They can walk out of the gaff, get hit by a car, drop the lot down the nearest drain or get picked up by the police, but they still owe the money. As soon as you take drugs on tick, as soon as you take it on bail, you're liable. There's nothing the police love more than catching someone with a few grands' worth of gear on bail 'cos they know the pressure the man's gonna be under.'

Rick runs a club he uses to launder some of his profits and also to provide a 'secure' environment for his dealers to trade in. A number of wholesale importers and distributors also own or have some involvement with pubs and clubs and use them as outlets for similar purposes.

'The people at the lowest level of the pyramid, the guys who are selling grams and wraps, they're the most visible. They're the most replaceable and they're also the ones who are most likely to get caught. It's not for me. I'll leave that to the street gangs. I'd rather take the money and run.

'You need to stay one step ahead. You work on the principle that you're being followed or watched or listened to twenty-four/seven. You don't take your eye off the ball. Whether you're going out grafting or whether you're going down Morrison's for a pint of milk, you behave in exactly the same way. When you start doing things different, that's when you stand out.

'But as far as I'm concerned, the whole thing with police and Customs is like natural selection. There are a lot of good people in this game but there are a lot of idiots as well. Occasionally they get lucky but for the most part the people they're pulling in are the weakest and worst that there are. It works out well for us. It keeps the courts busy, keeps the public happy and means there's more money left in the pot for us.'

I switch off the tape and it is almost as if Rick sighs with relief. He tells me he feels far more comfortable knowing that his words are not being recorded and quickly begins to open up even more.

Rick confesses that the part he finds hardest at the moment is not bringing the drugs into the country but getting the money out to pay for them. He has plenty of 'friendly' *bureaux de change* that he and his fellow gang members use to change small-denomination notes into European currency, but actually getting the cash out to Spain or Amsterdam or Ireland to pay for whatever is coming in is becoming increasingly problematic.

Getting the money out used to be something that Rick did with the help of a flamboyant restaurateur and club owner by the name of Peter Beaumont-Gowling, known to his underworld contacts as David Simpson. The fifty-two-year-old playboy-entrepreneur was the driving force behind the Joe Rigatoni restaurant chain in Newcastle and he also owned a string of bistros in the Darlington area. Having worked in restaurants in Paris and Denmark, as well as the Four Seasons in New York, his reputation in the highly competitive industry was second to none.

Beaumont-Gowling enjoyed the fruits of his success to the fullest degree. He owned houses across Britain and also in Spain, had several prestige cars, including a Bentley and a stretch limousine, and kept a luxury yacht moored on the Costa del Sol. His work in the entertainment industry naturally brought him into close contact with the gangland élite, which in turn attracted the attention of the police, but although they kept a close watch on him there was never any evidence of wrongdoing.

One night, having tracked their target to a hotel in Chelsea and bugged his room, detectives listened in as Beaumont-Gowling ordered and received visits from thirteen prostitutes, one after the other, and drank so many bottles of Dom Pérignon that the hotel bar actually ran out. The following morning Beaumont-Gowling was arrested just as he was about to board a flight to Heathrow to Dublin. He was carrying two suitcases, which, when examined, were found to contain a total of £576,000.

'Peter was one of those guys, not really a gangster, but someone who fancied the lifestyle, liked the image that went along with it. He made all the original approaches. It was he that wanted to know if there was anything he could do,' says Rick. 'It worked well for a while, but then he got careless. And when it all came on top, he just couldn't handle it.'

Gowling crumbled under questioning. He admitted being paid £35,000 a time to take cash-filled cases to Ireland and said he had already completed around ten such trips, either from Heathrow or Newcastle, by the time he was caught. He also confessed that the south London-based drugs-smuggling syndicate he was working for was making at least £500,000 per week, but stopped short of naming any members of the gang.

Jailed for eleven years, Beaumont-Gowling was ordered to hand-over £310,000 from his bank account, £50,000 in shares, and £12,000 pre-paid on a credit card, crippling him financially. The money he was carrying was also confiscated.

The day he left prison, Beaumont-Gowling told his local paper, the *Newcastle Evening Chronicle*, that he craved more success: 'Irrespective of how I felt in relation to my sentence and an excessive fine, I have conducted myself very gracefully throughout. I believe my debts to society have been paid in full. I'm determined to leave the past behind and I am looking forward to continuing my life in a productive and sensible manner.'

It wasn't to be. Just before midnight on Valentine's Day 2001, Beaumont-Gowling's girlfriend arrived at his flat in the trendy Jesmond area of Newcastle and found him slumped in a corner of the living room. He had been shot repeatedly at point-blank range in the head, chest and back.

With no signs of a struggle and no evidence that someone had forced their way into the flat, police concluded that Beaumont-Gowling had almost certainly known his killer and had willingly opened the door to him. He died less than a month after his release from prison.

Rick won't reveal anything about why he was murdered but says that an anonymous letter, sent to police more than a year after the shooting, hit pretty close to the mark. Photocopied and written in thick black ink it read, 'It seems that someone is going to have to explain why Beaumont-Gowling had to go. He thought he could walk straight back into the business. He was special once and made us lots of money, but he couldn't keep his head down. He had to be seen with the birds and play the big spender. It was all bad publicity. When he went down it was bad news for both producers and investors. We had to fill the void. Confidence had to be restored. Sacrifices were made. Whatever plans he made couldn't be allowed to happen. We couldn't take the chance. The decision in the end was easy and best done quickly. Who was going to miss him? Just his women. No loss, really.'

With Beaumont-Gowling gone, getting the money out has become more problematic than ever. 'That's the hardest thing right now. The police and Customs, although they make a lot of noise about street values, they know the truth about what we pay for the stuff. They know that if they hit the money on the way out, it's gonna hurt just as bad as if they get the drugs on the way back in so now they're getting two bites of the cherry. They're putting more and more resources into it: you've even got sniffer dogs going up and down fucking train platforms looking for people with money. Once you didn't have to worry about it, now it's become a big deal.'

Holding on to the cash is simply not an option. Attempting to spend it in the UK draws too much attention and state-of-the art forensics techniques mean that notes contaminated with certain batches of cocaine can be used as evidence to link those found with the money to the rest of the smuggling operation.

The way the gangs get round it is to use the same methods for getting the drugs in to smuggle the money abroad. It is strapped to the bodies of couriers, hidden in false compartments of suitcases, inside the spare wheels of cars and vans and sometimes even split into small bundles, stuffed into condoms and swallowed.

'But getting the money out is a problem in itself because it gets bulky real quick,' says Rick. 'You see all these films where people talk about having a million quid in a little briefcase, but that's bullshit, you'd never fit it in. The money from street sales comes to you in small, used notes and they add up pretty quickly. If you sell a kilo of coke at street level, you get back six kilos of banknotes.'

Rick drains the last of his bottle and gets ready to leave. 'This whole business is about identifying the problems and finding solutions. For me that's a big part of the buzz.' He pauses and grins. 'That and the money, of course. They can make it harder – which will only put the price up – but they're never gonna stop it 'cos it's just getting more and more popular. You go to the northern working-men's clubs, and all the lads, they're all at it in the toilets, having a line in between their pints of Newcastle Brown.

'People have a lot more disposable income these days so they can afford to indulge every now and then. I'm not putting people out on the streets, I'm not leading anyone astray. I'm just providing a service. It's just another form of entertainment.'

But while those operating at the higher end of the trade may justify their actions by claiming to be providing nothing more than adult recreation, the truth is that much of the momentum behind the cocaine market comes from the ever-increasing demand for its far more sinister, deadly and far less socially acceptable derivative: crack.

CRACK

CHAPTER SIX

Hidden behind deeply tinted windows, the Black and White café in the St Paul's district of Bristol has a tiny mock-marble counter where you can buy traditional Caribbean fare, like ackee, salt fish, curried goat and jerk chicken. But almost no one comes here for the food.

In a society where open dealing is no longer out of the ordinary, the Black and White café stands out from the crowd as one of the most blatant hard-drugs dens in Britain. By all accounts, the café has been raided more times than any other premises in the UK. One single weekend in the summer of 2003 saw three separate raids, which resulted in seventeen arrests and the recovery of thousands of pounds' worth of Class A drugs.

The drug deals around the café are now so frequent and so open that locals refer to it as the hypermarket. Open selling also goes on at the local pub and a nearby branch of the Tastee takeaway, but the Black and White is by far the most popular and best-known venue. The scene of countless shootings, stabbings and armed robberies, the café is at the epicentre of the increasingly violent gang activity surrounding the global trade in crack cocaine.

The first time I hear about the Black and White and its formidable reputation I'm nowhere near Bristol, I'm not even in Britain but more than 4500 miles away in the run-down streets of the Jamaican capital, Kingston. Even on the outer edges of the local drugs scene, the Black and White is widely talked about as the place to go to score, deal and meet the local dons.

For twenty-six-year-old Michael Andrews it was spending time at the Black and White that got him into dealing in the first place. When I met him he had been back in Jamaica for five weeks, having been deported for a number of drugs offences. In England he was feared and respected as a ruthless operator. A hugely successful crack-dealer, he had money, a nice car, fine clothes and plenty of women. In Jamaica he had nothing. In a quiet roadside bar in uptown Kingston, his tongue eased by a near-endless supply of Red Stripe and Swiss-style pork chops, Michael told me his story.

'My experience,' he said softly, 'is just an unlucky one. I have some family in England, in Bristol, and my dad used to live there so my gran said she'd pay for my ticket so I could have a holiday. That was how it all started, just a holiday.

'I got there and saw it was a very different kind of living. Life was nice and easy. When a man migrates, especially when he is from a certain section of Jamaica, the life he sees in England – it's like heaven. I know many people who didn't even know what a toilet was until they came to England. One man who visited me said on day one, "Bwoy, that toilet is nice, for when it flush it bring you back clean water with which to wash your hand."

'Right away I met a nice girl and we were having fun, but after two months she got pregnant. I thought to myself, Okay, you've got responsibility now – this was my first child – so I thought, Why not stay? I had a visa for three months and it was about to run out. I wasn't thinking of marrying, I wasn't thinking at all. I just thought that somehow everything would be okay.

'You've got to live, you can't expect your family to support you for ever so I went out and found work. I was doing a bit of plastering for a guy, mixing the muck for him, doing some skimming. I was learning quite a bit, but after a little while the recession hit and the building trade was doing nothing much.

'I didn't have a National Insurance number so I couldn't get any other kind of job. But I had to do something to survive. One portion of chicken and chips might cost less than two pounds but when you can't even buy that for yourself, you feel bad, especially when you've got a kid coming. The baby was only a few weeks away and I was suffering. The girl was on the social, but that money, you can't do nothing with it.

CRACK

'I was living in Bristol and I used to hang around in the Black and White café with a few guys I knew from Jamaica. Some of them used to sell stuff on the front line. They knew I had nothing and one of them said to me, "Come and sell some weed, it's easy."

'I'm gonna be honest with you. The first time I went on the line, I bought just an ounce of black hash. I didn't want to get too deep. But within the space of an hour that was sold out and I bought two more ounces and went back on the line. I'd just doubled my money in an hour. At the end of that first night I went home with about two ounces of black, an ounce of weed and three hundred pounds in my pocket.

'So I say to myself, "Yeah, a few hours and I get this! Come on, I'm going to do this full time." So I start waking up in the afternoon, going on the line, coming back at six in the morning, sleep until midday, then hit the streets again. After about a month, life started to get nice, real nice. I was making money, wearing pretty clothes and ting. The girl was all right and we were ready for the baby. Everything was sweet.

'Then a friend of mine, his name was Squitty, he used to deal coke on the same line as me, he approached me. And now a bit of greed got caught up in me. I said to myself, "Why not sell some cocaine?" The first time I bought a sixteenth of an ounce, the smallest portion, for a hundred and fifty quid. I got on the line at five p.m. and the first man that came up to me five minutes later bought four grams. In the space of ten minutes it was all sold out and I had made one fifty on my one fifty.

'I started dealing coke big-time. Then I started cooking crack and selling that too. And that was the best business of all. The cash comes in so fast you don't know what to do with it all. I was making big money – four, five thousand a week – but still, even then, I wasn't thinking. I had a flash car, flash clothes, flashy girls all over the place. I might have been living in Bristol but I would drive up to London or Birmingham or Manchester just to go clubbing. I was all over the place because I had money.

'And ting was cheap. A lot of people who smoked crack would go out and shoplift and steal and rob, then give you ting in exchange for the drugs. And they'd be desperate. I got a Rolex, a brand new Rolex, for less than a hundred quid's worth of crack, then I just sold it on for five hundred quid to a man that wanted one. Other times people would go out ram-raiding or hire girls to go out shopping with stolen credit cards and bring back televisions and hi-fis. You could get everything and anything and never pay full price.

'And then little by little I had people working from me. Some of them were friends that I knew from Jamaica who had heard what I was doing and wanted a piece of the action for themselves. Others were people that I met here and decided that it would be better to work with them than to go to war with them.

'But war was always a possibility. I got a gun, a Magnum 357 Python, and I didn't have to pay for it. I was driving with some friends one day and the gun was brandished. But as a rougher man than them, as someone more ragamuffin, I held on to it and said, "Hey, lend me dis." You see, they were my posse, my crew, and I was the leader. So there was a pecking order and because I was the Don, anything like that would be taken by me. Then I'd be out there on the line selling my drugs, and one of the guys from my crew would come up to me and say, "I'm skint, man, give me a bit of change," so then I'd give him fifty quid, twenty quid. Little money, little money, until he stopped asking and the gun was mine. Guns were always a priority for me, but at first it was for niceness, not to kill or such. We would be at a dance and a nice Jamaican sound like Stone Love would come up and we would take out our guns and salute and ting like that. But gun was for other ting too. Trouble was always just around the corner. I remember one time there was no coke in Bristol, none at all. I drove up to London. I had my piece on me. When I got there I went to see my friend Clive in Brixton. I said, "There's nothing in the country, man, I need some coke." So he sent me to a restaurant close to the Atlantic Road, a black restaurant. I went up to the counter and said I was looking for some stuff. The guy was a Jamaican, but you could see he had been in England a long time. He went around the back, and five minutes later he came back and told me to wait. I said okay, but then I saw a man come in and lean on the table to one side of me. I watch him and he watch me but still nothing.

'So I'm thinking, Maybe these guys think I'm playing with them so I reach in my pocket and pull out my money, big wad of cash, and slap it on the counter. "Don't worry, I'm serious," I say. "I need some stuff, there is none in Bristol." And right away I see the guy's eyes light up when he sees the money. He was thinking, Bristol's the country, so I'm a fool because London is the city and he's a Don.

'Fifteen minutes later, still nothing. I went up to the first guy and said, "What are you playing at?" Then a second man come in and lean on the table on the other side of me. Then I realised the man was calling down his friends, trying to get a team together. He had sent word. – "Come, there is money and a fool" – but they were scattered, they were taking time to get there.

'So then I just pop out my piece, point it at the man head and start talking raw: "You can't rob me, none of your friend can rob me, man will die if you wanna rob me. You're a pussy, I'm a cold-blooded Yard man." Then they started to realise who I was and they start to respect me. They were saying, "Cool, everything cris." I got my stuff. That's the closest I have been. I know in their hearts that they wanted to rob me but I would have killed them all if I had to. And once they knew who I was, it was no longer necessary.

'You see, I had a bad reputation because of the people I was dealing with. When I started to sell more and more I had to go to bigger and bigger people, people others were afraid to deal with. I got introduced to some of the real Dons, some white men, Irish, who were bringing untold amounts of coke into the country and selling it to everyone. One man took me to his home and on the table in the living room was just pure coke, a mountain of drugs. I was good business for them, and he said to me, "If there is anything you want, just ask. If a man messes with you just tell us and we will eliminate him."

'So people knew not to fuck with me. I was in the Black and White café one time when a lot of man was robbed. These people, black but British, came in with Balaclavas and shotguns and started taking people tings. I stood up and wait for my turn to be robbed but no man touch me. At first I wondered why but later I found that because of the man I was dealing with I had been branded. The robbers didn't want to get involved because they knew that somewhere down the line they'd get it back.'

Seemingly safe from other dealers, it was the police who finally brought the curtain down on Michael's world as he returned to a girlfriend's house one morning. 'I had a lot of women as well as my baby mother – I lived all over the place. I was at one of my women's yard and I had just come back from the laundry – I like to wash my own clothes. I threw them on the bed and told her that she should iron some. Then I heard a knock at the door.

'Now, a lot of cops in the area knew me but they didn't know exactly what I was up to, or I didn't think they did. So whenever they passed me by I would just say, "Look, it's the Bill," and laugh because of the television programme.

'The girl called out, "Who is it?" They called back, "It's the Bill." I thought, Gawd! I was thinking, What's this? I went to make my way out the back but when I look out the window I could see more policemen waiting for me. I knew I could never make it.

'The girl look at me, a bit confused, like, then she opened the door. These men come in and held on to me and said, "You're under arrest, suspected of being an illegal immigrant and of being involved in drug-trafficking."

'But these men were fools. They didn't bother to search the flat. I had an excess amount of cash, about five grand in fifties, twenties and tens under the pillow along with a large amount of drugs. But they never found them. My girl took the money and threw the drugs out once I had left. I was caught on the Tuesday and I was back on the plane to Jamaica on the Thursday.

'And now I am back and I have nothing. I never sent no money home, I never had no bank account. I had a excess amount of jewellery, nice gold chain and bracelet, diamonds, nice ting, but they took them all from me. The problem with us Jamaicans is that we grow up with nothing, and when we get something, we don't know how long it will last so we use it THEN! Straight! So now the only way I can get the life I want to live is to go back. Back to England. Back to Bristol. So that's what I'm going to do.'

Michael had promised to get in touch as soon as he returned to the UK and said that he'd happily introduce me to some of the main players in and around St Paul's. The weeks, months and years went by, and I heard nothing. Eventually I decided that the time had come for me to check out the Black and White café for myself.

I arrived in Bristol a week after the police had placed armed foot patrols on the streets for the first time to prevent a potential bloodbath between the city's indigenous drugs gangs and a new influx of Jamaican dealers who were fighting for control of the hugely lucrative crack trade.

The move marked the height of hostilities between the two factions. During the 1990s the city's drugs trade was entirely in the hands of a local gang known as the Aggi crew (the name was taken from the surnames of the founding members) but in 1998 six of them were jailed after being caught with more than £1 million worth of crack cocaine.

The vacuum that followed was filled by the Yardies – men like Michael Andrews – who not only picked up from where the Aggis had left off but also brought new levels of sophistication to the local drugs scene.

Instead of holding wraps of crack in their mouths, the street dealers operating in the area around the café placed the drugs in old Coke cans or milk cartons, which would then be left in the gutter. After handing over their money, customers would be directed to the nearest can. Suddenly there was no way to arrest the dealers – none had any drugs on them. Dealing on and around Grosvenor Road became so open that it quickly reached epidemic proportions.

There were knock-on effects too. To prevent their merchandise being swept away, the dealers started intimidating the council's utility workers. In at least one case a street-sweeper had a gun jammed up against his head. Refuse collections halted altogether in many areas, as did road repairs (dealers were also hiding drugs in the cracks in the pavement). The dealers then turned their attention to the workers attempting to install CCTV systems until they, too, gave up. Within weeks Stapleton Road, another notorious strip, had become known as the 'street of fear' with dealers, prostitutes and muggers operating with virtual impunity. In a seven-month period, 915 crimes were recorded along a 150-metre stretch.

To boost their numbers the Jamaicans also set up an immigration scam. By the time police discovered that a college set up in St Paul's was bogus, more than three hundred Jamaican 'students' had been granted long-term visas and entered the country. One year later, forty-five of those 'students' had been charged with drugs offences, eleven with weapons charges, one with rape and another with attempted murder. A further 121 were being detained on immigration offences while 148 remained on the run. Some of those still being sought are known to have committed several murders back in Kingston.

The Jamaicans also set up two money-laundering operations, one based in a greengrocer's and the other in a local takeaway restaurant. Between them the two premises helped transfer more than £7.5 million to Kingston, the result of an estimated 75,000 crack deals. Some of the money was being used to buy property, the rest to fund new drugs consignments to the UK.

Despite numerous police initiatives the drugs keep on coming and there is no solution in sight. 'We have made more than eight hundred arrests in the past eighteen months but on the streets the problem remains as bad as ever,' Detective Chief Inspector Neil Smart tells me. 'We've been very successful in the number of dealers arrested but because there's such a demand for drugs, if we go in and arrest six, ten, twelve dealers, there will be others. Each arrest takes my team off the street for several hours. Most of the time, the dealers are being replaced within minutes.'

One single event took the situation in Bristol from bad to worse. Three weeks before my arrival several key members of the Aggi crew were released from prison on probation and emerged eager to take back their turf. Within five days of their release, their faces hidden by Balaclavas as they brandished the guns they had stashed before going inside, they made a tour of local bars including the Black Swan, the Malcolm X Centre and Lebeqs and announced that they were back and taking over. They offered the Jamaicans a deal: they could stay and work in St Paul's, but they'd have to pay a tax of at least a hundred pounds per person per day.

Then, as a final mark of disrespect, the Aggis stormed into the Black and White café and robbed every person at gunpoint. As they handed over their money and possessions, the Jamaicans, a loose alliance of several gangs including the Hype Cru, the Mountain View Posse and the Back to Back gang, told the Aggi crew that they would not be paying them a single penny and that the only way to resolve the argument would be with guns.

And so it was. The next night one of the Hype Cru was shot through the back of the knee, then one of the Aggis was shot in the shoulder in a revenge attack. Then the Aggis began attacking the Hype Cru's street dealers, kidnapping some, pistol-whipping others and always stealing whatever drugs and cash happened to be lying around.

A few days later, in an attempt to draw the Jamaicans out into the open for a gun battle, they made their way to the roof of the council flats opposite the Black and White café and began firing giant fireworks towards the front door in an attempt to start a blaze that would have forced the occupants to evacuate. It failed and the Aggis retreated, but everyone at the Black and White café knows it is only a matter of time before they try again.

The air is thick with the cloying smell of cannabis and the wooden floor is vibrating with the sounds of hardcore reggae. A dozen people are milling about close to the pinball and video poker machines at the back of the place, while the main room is dominated by two snooker tables, both of which are in constant use. According to my sources the players, often as not, are the main dealers: packets of crack are taped to the base of each table, allowing easy access but frustrating police efforts to link the drugs to particular individuals.

For a split second everyone stops and stares at me – a new and unfamiliar face entering a tight-knit and often paranoid community. I march confidently up to the nearest snooker player and tell him I'm looking for Steve, the owner. The man I've asked has short dreadlocks poking out of his head at all angles, a roll-up hangs from the corner of his mouth and the whites of his eyes have that soft yellow glaze that mark him out as a long-time pot-head. He looks me up and down, leans on the end of his cue, then jerks his thumb towards the kitchen area where a few members of staff are milling about. Satisfied that I'm not a rival dealer or an undercover cop, everyone ignores me and goes back to their business.

I reach the kitchen counter and learn that Steve is not around but might turn up a little later. I flick through the menu, order some goat curry and spend a little time playing the video machine. Trying my hardest to blend into the background, I'm hoping to see a little action take place.

It takes a while before I realise it is going on right before my eyes. Subtle handshakes, pats on the back and other gestures are all part and parcel of the routine of exchanging drugs and money. It's all done so carefully and so skilfully that it's easy to see why the owners have such a hard time stamping it out. Within half an hour I see half a dozen deals, though I have no idea if crack, heroin or cannabis is being sold. I also notice that a couple of the dealers appear to be wearing bullet-proof jackets. No one here is taking any chances. Particularly the police.

That same afternoon they launched a series of raids on the homes of the Aggi crew who, as a result of breaching the conditions of their parole, face being returned to prison. It's a short-term measure at best. In some cases, it will be only a matter of months before the gang members are released again.

Out of change and full of surprisingly good curry, I head back on to the streets. Walking along I avoid making eye-contact with the people standing at every corner. These are the lookouts. Every now and then they move, whistle or give off some kind of signal. Around thirty seconds later a police patrol car will drive past. No one seems too worried – even if the police see something it takes them way too long to respond. Normally they would get on their radios and have back-up in place in seconds but the local gangs have obtained so many scanners that the officers are forced to communicate on their mobile phones instead, a process that takes considerably longer.

As night falls a party starts up in a house at the end of an alleyway just off Drummond Road. Three men in black T-shirts, with thick gold chains hanging from their necks like glittery nooses, eye me suspiciously as I walk past. Music pumps out through the walls so loudly that I can feel the paving slabs under my feet vibrating in time with the beat.

As I walk down Pemberton Street into Brunswick Square a girl climbs out of a nearly new silver saloon car and stands on the side of the road as if she is waiting for a bus. I've stumbled into the heart of the red-light district – a bright yellow sign warns that cars passing through the area are likely to have their licence numbers recorded – and as I walk past she catches my eye. I keep walking.

Nowhere in Bristol is the power of the crack trade more apparent than in the vice world. Police estimate that the city's two hundred prostitutes each spend an average of £1100 per week on the drug, creating a thriving market worth more than £11 million.

I pass more ladies of the night, some of whom proposition me, some of whom do not. I'm almost at the end of the square when a youngish-looking girl steps out from the shadows in front of me. 'You after a bit of business, love?'

She's pretty but looks pale and unwashed. She is wearing an oversized coat, a black crop top that exposes her midriff, and a faded denim skirt covers the tops of her bare, battered legs.

'Maybe. How much?' I ask.

'It's twenty-five for a blow-job but you have to wear a condom. A fuck is forty with and sixty without.'

'I'll give you sixty, but to be honest, I'm more interested in talking than fucking.'

'You what?'

I explain that I'm a novelist and that in my latest book one of the characters spends time in a red-light district and that I've come down to the square to carry out some research. My little lie is a calculated move: experience has taught me that if people think something is destined to be turned into fiction, rather than kept as fact, they are far more likely to open up.

The girl agrees – she tells me her name is Leanne – on condition that we take no longer than ten minutes, the average time she spends with her clients. That way she won't lose any business.

We walk to my car and drive close to her usual place of work – the wall of an old graveyard next to a meeting-house. Once there, Leanne decides she needs a change of scenery so I offer to buy her a cup of coffee in a nearby café. After dumping five sugars in her cup and stirring well, she takes a huge gulp and begins to tell me about life on the streets of St Paul's.

'A couple of years back when I started on the game, all the girls were on brown [heroin], nothing else. Then the dealers starting selling what they called 'party packs' – a bag of smack and two free rocks. We all got hooked but, surprise, surprise, once we did, the rocks started costing money. It's all so fucked up. Now the only time people take brown is to help them come down.'

Leanne is scruffy, she speaks quickly, fidgets a lot and at times her eyes seem unfocused, but despite this she is attractive and interesting. She is a long way from what I expected of a crack addict.

As we talk, I tell her that I find it difficult to understand how someone of such clear intelligence and personality could end up in a situation like this. 'I do what I do because the money is good, it pays for my drugs and I don't have to answer to anyone. I'm hooked on both. There are women out there who tell me they've managed to kick crack but they can't kick walking the streets because there's nothing else they can do which gives them anything like the same money and freedom.

'But right now, there's only one thing that separates you from me and that's the rock,' she says. 'It's a feeling you can't explain, that you can't live without. I love it but at the same time I hate it. Crack will run you ragged. With heroin, you can get up and do things, and when it's time to go to bed, you're ready to go to bed. But with crack you don't want anything else. It pisses me off. I've seen the good turn bad and the rich go poor, sometimes within weeks. There are strawberries and raspberries out there now and there never used to be. That's how bad it is.'

In the bizarre pecking order of prostitutes, Leanne explains, strawberries and raspberries, also known as chickenheads, are the lowest of the low (high-class, high-price call girls are at the top). Instead of being paid cash for sex, they receive only drugs, often just a single rock. 'They get so desperate that they can't even see it makes sense for them to get some money and buy their own stuff. You always swear you'll never sink that low, but I've done it a few times. All the girls have.'

One coffee turns into two, and then I buy Leanne a sandwich. We're getting on well, almost flirting with one another as we talk about her life and the way her work affects her relationships. It's almost like some kind of weird date, although we both know nothing sexual is going to happen between us. Or, at least, I don't think it will. It's a cliché, I know, but I can't help thinking she's getting off on the idea of someone wanting her for her mind rather than just her body.

She asks where I'm staying and without thinking I blurt out the name of my hotel. It's nearby and she suggests we go back to my room and continue our conversation somewhere quieter. For the first time I feel apprehensive. I manage to sneak her past the receptionist and we giggle as we clamber into the lift and make our way upstairs.

Once inside, Leanne's true motivation for seeking more privacy becomes abundantly clear. She removes her coat, perches on the edge of the bed, then reaches into her battered black bag and pulls out a plastic water bottle. The screw cap has been replaced with a mass of masking tape and silver foil and there is a short glass pipe, sealed with Blu-tack, poking out of the side. She reaches inside her bra, under her left breast, and pulls out a tiny clingfilm wrap containing five small pieces of magnolia-coloured rock.

She watches me watching as she loads one of the rocks on top of the foil and heats it with a flame from her lighter. The inside of the bottle fills with a pale smoke, which she then inhales through the pipe. 'Well, you said you wanted to see what it was all about,' she says, between puffs.

I pull up the chair and sit down facing her. I've read about taking the drug, but seeing someone do it right in front of me is something else. I'm horrified but at the same time I'm absolutely fascinated. I wait for some kind of transformation, but nothing seems to happen. Rather than becoming manic and running around the room like a crazy woman, Leanne actually seems to become quieter, lying back on the bed as her eyes glaze over. She lets out a low moan. 'Ah, yeah, fuuuuuuuuck,' she sighs.

Is it, I ask, really that good?

Leanne smiles big and wide. She rolls over and leans forward on the bed, resting her chin on her hands, a Cheshire-cat grin on her face. She pushes a stream of translucent smoke out of her pursed lips and the air around me is filled with a smell that's something like sweetened burning plastic. 'Oh, yeah,' she says softly. 'It's good. It's really good. You ought to try it.'

And with that she props herself up on her elbows, loads a fresh rock on top of the lid and passes me the pipe.

CHAPTER SEVEN

No one quite knows who invented crack. There are reports of it appearing in Amsterdam in 1978 but, probably because it was a little too harsh for mellow Dutch tastes, it soon faded away. Two years later it surfaced in the Bahamas and quickly took hold to the extent that, by the end of 1982, there had been a massive increase in the number of psychiatric admissions to hospital on the islands.

By 1983 the drug was filtering across the water to Miami, then up to New York and beyond, particularly Los Angeles where the black street gangs began pushing it like there was no tomorrow. The first ever newspaper report on crack appeared in the *Los Angeles Times* in 1984, and within a few weeks American law-enforcement officials were warning that within three years crack would have swept across the entire country like a firestorm, a prediction that turned out to be a ghastly underestimate. In August 1985, not one of the tens of thousands of telephone calls to America's national cocaine hotline concerned crack. By February 1986 every other call was from a user of the new drug.

Grim accounts of what the drug had done to America's inner-city ghettos surfaced. There were tales of teenage crack-head mothers selling their own babies to get the money for their next hit, of twelve-year-old dealers involved in shoot-outs with the police, and countless acts of violence committed by those under its influence. In 1988, 73 per cent of all children battered to death by their parents in the New York area were the offspring of crack-users, while around 40 per cent of all homicides in the city were said to be crack-related.

The speed at which crack spread surprised everyone, with the possible exception of the dealers. They knew only too well that by pricing the new product well within the reach of society's lowest common denominators there would be no end of takers. At a hundred dollars a gram, cocaine was still having trouble leaving its jet-set roots behind. At ten dollars a hit, crack wasn't just cheap, it was a miracle of modern marketing.

And marketing is exactly what was responsible for bringing crack to the masses. Regardless of who invented it, it is now widely accepted that the Colombian drug cartels were responsible for pushing the drug into the ghettos.

The best of the cartels, and in particular the Medellín cartel during the time it was being led by the infamous Pablo Escobar, treated the cocaine trade very much as a business. At the time 80 per cent of cocaine-users in the United States were white, middle-aged and affluent. There were some younger people, thirty-five and under, who had money to spend, but the main market revolved around the trend-setter industries of movies, television, music and sport.

Having experienced phenomenal growth, the market suddenly began to collapse and the street prices of cocaine fell, often dramatically. The rise of the 1980s gym culture and other health fads, as well as concerns about the addictive nature of cocaine, led many core users to cut back.

During a series of brainstorming sessions in the early 1980s designed to find solutions to the fading market elder cartel bosses recalled that during the 1950s and 1960s, when heroin was America's favourite drug of abuse, the black ghettos had formed one of the key markets. If they could find a way to sell cocaine to the blacks, they could open up a whole new world of profit.

The problem wasn't just that the blacks couldn't afford cocaine but also the hit the drug delivered wasn't intense enough to pull them out of the social deprivation they suffered in the same way that heroin did. The easiest way to make cocaine more appealing, and provide a more powerful high, would be to find a way to smoke it, but that presented all sorts of problems.

CRACK

Although you can smoke cocaine in its powder form – users have long mixed the drug with tobacco to create joints known as 'primos' – the process is hugely inefficient. At smoking temperatures, cocaine tends to burn rather than vaporise so the amount of smoke that gets to the lungs is extremely limited.

One solution was to create freebase, an elaborate chemical process during which the alkalide ether is used to 'free' the base cocaine from the hydrochloride powder form. But freebasing was incredibly dangerous – ether is highly flammable and dozens of people had burned to death in accidents. One famous incident involved the actor Richard Pryor, who set fire to himself while attempting to freebase on a plane.

Another was basuco, a brown paste produced as a by-product of the cocaine-manufacturing process deep in the jungle laboratories of South America. But basuco looked and smelt foul and the only people who used it regularly were the street kids of Colombia, who became zombies under its powerful effects.

Although it was the Medellín cartel that instigated the search for something as powerful as basuco but more palatable for American tastes, it was a chemist working for the rival Cali cartel that struck gold. Working on a hunch, he dissolved cocaine powder in ammonia, added water and bicarbonate of soda and heated it until the liquid boiled off. Crack cocaine had been born.

The effect of the drug alone was enough to guarantee its success. The instant euphoria that a rock of crack produces usually lasts forty or fifty seconds, a few minutes at the most, and a mere flash in the pan compared to the thirty-minute cocaine high or the three- to four-hour trip from a dose of heroin. But with crack, the high has no parallel. There isn't anything else like it. Around seven per cent of cocaine users go on to develop an addiction, and even then the process can take up to eighteen months. With crack, around 80 per cent of users go on to develop an addiction, usually within two weeks of their first smoke.

For those destined to get hooked, the first ten-dollar hit at first seems like a bargain but within minutes of their first puff, most users are begging for another hit. With each new intake the body's resistance rises so that more and more is needed to produce the same effect.

For its consumers the ultimate curse of crack is that, because the high is so short-lived, it's almost impossible to overdose. If you could afford it, you could smoke your way through $2000 worth of crack within a day and still come back for more. And even if you couldn't afford it, you'd still want to and you'd happily rob, steal or kill by way of trying. For dealers, crack is an equally intense experience. An ounce of cocaine will produce around fifty decent snorting lines but some 370 rocks of crack. For the dealer, selling the cheaper product will on average quadruple their profit margin.

The new drug swept across America within six months, but the journey across the Atlantic took a little longer.

In the autumn of 1986, Anthony 'Crumpet' Lemard choked to death on his vomit, face down in a police cell in west London. He had been arrested a few hours earlier after police were called to a block of flats a few miles away where they observed Lemard 'going berserk', brandishing a knife and 'acting crazy'.

When pathologists tested his blood and urine, they found the highest concentrations of cocaine ever seen in England. Experts were puzzled by how anyone could have taken such a huge amount. Then one official said Lemard might have been taking a new form of cocaine that enters the bloodstream more quickly and in far higher concentrations. Lemard had become Britain's first crack victim, though it would be years before the drug itself was seen.

Crack officially arrived in Britain in May 1988 when a few rocks were found in a council block in Handsworth, Birmingham. The following month small traces of the drug were found in a squat in Liverpool. In September of the same year a reinforced flat on the Milton Court estate in Deptford, south London, was raided and turned up the country's first crack factory. Dozens more cropped up to replace it and the estate soon became known as Crack City.

In November 1988 Paul Matheson, a fifteen-pounds-a-week van driver from Kingston, Jamaica, became the first man in the country to be convicted of selling, rather than simply possessing, crack cocaine. Touring the maze of walkways that made up the north Peckham estate in south London, an area once described as the most deprived housing development in Europe, Matheson and his minders would make at least a hundred deals a day. In less than six weeks he had sold more than £105,000 worth of crack until worried residents tipped off the police and he was arrested.

At his trial Matheson explained how, despite earning thousands of pounds for his bosses, he himself earned only a flat fee of £450 per week. The court also heard how, since his arrest, Matheson's family back in Jamaica had received numerous death threats. Not surprisingly, he refused to name his backers.

In February 1989, a monthly youth magazine asked me to investigate the rise of crack in the UK. Despite a few isolated cases I quickly discovered that there was far more hype than hard evidence. Most of the drug-users and drug agencies I contacted had heard of it, but had not yet seen it. A few hadn't even heard of it.

But two months later the tabloids were going crack-crazy, an event triggered when the head of the New York office of the Drug Enforcement Administration, Robert Stutman, came to Britain and delivered to startled police and Customs officials the following ominous warning: 'I personally guarantee you that two years from now you will have a serious crack problem – we are so saturated with cocaine in the United States, there ain't enough noses left to use the cocaine that's coming in.'

By the summer of 1989, around the time I started the research for my article, the north Peckham estate's dealers had gone to ground but I'd heard of crack being offered for sale in a couple of pubs close to Ladbroke Grove, west London, and, somewhat naïvely, I set off there one Thursday evening to see what I could find.

GANGS

It was dark when I arrived in the area and on my way to the first pub I bumped into a dreadlocked Rastafarian shouting and swearing at the barman who had just thrown him out. Rudy, as his name turned out to be, was steaming drunk. Well over six feet six inches tall and in his late thirties, he walked slowly with the aid of a stick – the result of a recent car accident. He was about to fall over when I caught him and listened patiently as he thanked me, then explained that he was desperate for another drink but the landlord had refused to serve him.

With no other leads to follow up, I offered to buy him a drink in the next pub in the hope that he might know something about the local drugs scene. It turned out to be an inspired move.

Rudy was celebrating that night because he'd just got out of prison for poncing – living off immoral earnings. Everywhere he went, local prostitutes would come out and hug him and silver BMWs with tinted windows would slow down and salute him with their horns. Rudy, I rapidly discovered, was an old-style ganja-trading Yardie, who commanded great respect around the Grove, even from the younger generation. And in his thoroughly inebriated state I was his new best friend.

We found another pub and I bought the drinks. We sat down in a quiet corner, chatting about nothing in particular. Periodically young hoods would pass by and stop to say hello. Almost all of them had some item of 'business' to discuss and eyed me suspiciously. 'Who's your friend?' they would ask.

'He's safe,' Rudy would reply.

And suddenly I was one of them. Any friend of Rudy's was a friend of theirs. About two months of undercover work had been accomplished in less than an hour.

Over the next week I spent every evening at the pub under some farcical pretext of having been offered a job, claiming that I was planning on moving to the area later that month and wanted to get to know my local. Thankfully no one ever thought to question this further.

I soon became friendly with Desmond, a forty-two-year-old

Jamaican fond of drinking brandy and port mixed together, who had lived in the capital for some fifteen years. As the evenings passed he began slowly to open up to me. He told me how he'd spent six years in prison for manslaughter in Jamaica after getting carried away with trying to persuade a floating voter which way to turn; how he ran a cocaine-distribution ring across the south-east of England packing the drug into tins of white Dulux paint and sending young couriers in overalls by bus, train and taxi to deliver to his small band of customers.

He explained how, despite a makeshift den having opened up above a newsagent's in Ladbroke Grove, crack hadn't taken off in a big way yet – the only people who seemed interested were the long-term heroin addicts who no longer got any buzz out of their addiction. 'But give it time,' he told me, 'give it time. Once you get a taste for it, you never gonna want to give it up.'

Even before Leanne made the offer and I took her makeshift crack pipe in my hand, I knew I wanted to try it.

I'd spent years researching the phenomenal growth of the crack market in the UK and spoken to dozens of dealers, users and recovering addicts about its effects, yet I still had trouble under-standing what it was about the drug that made it impossible to say no. I had listened time and time again to people talk about the 'intense high', the 'profound rush', the 'whole-body orgasm' and I had read every book, leaflet and newspaper article I could find on the topic but somehow still felt I was in the dark. Part of the problem, perhaps, is that while there have been many journalists and writers who have been addicted to heroin or who have taken cocaine and ecstasy or cannabis and written eloquently and ex-tensively about the highs, lows and in-betweens, the same doesn't appear to be true of crack.

Yet the effect of crack on society is fast becoming far more devastating than that of all the other drugs combined – such is the power of the drug that it has turned thousands of addicts into criminals as they desperately search for the cash for their next fix –

and the more I looked for the answers, the more it dawned on me that I was going to have to experience it first hand.

At this point I should say that in spite of (or perhaps as a consequence of) my line of work, my experience of drugs is extremely limited. I've never smoked tobacco (though everyone else in my family did) and have no desire to start. I puffed away at a couple of joints as a teenager but didn't like the feeling of being stoned so never pursued it. I've been offered cocaine more times than I can possibly remember but I've always passed simply because I never felt the need to say yes. As for ecstasy, magic mushrooms, heroin, LSD, uppers, downers, poppers, Special K, glue, I've been around dealers and users of them all but they've never appealed to me, even in the slightest.

My one radical moment came in the late 1980s at a massive outdoor rave in the shadow of Dungeness power station when, for no good reason, I decided to try speed. Unable to find a suitable surface from which to snort the powder, I opted to swallow it instead. The only effect I remember is that I couldn't get to sleep when I got home so I stayed up all night watching bad TV.

Long before I met Leanne I mentioned my intentions to a couple of close friends and immediately wished I had not. One in particular was utterly appalled and shocked at what she described as my 'wilful arrogance' in believing that somehow I wouldn't get hooked on a drug so powerful that it was notorious for being virtually instantly addictive.

Now, I have second thoughts, but after seeing Leanne in action, I am determined to go ahead. But as the pipe moves ever closer to my mouth, two separate sets of warnings echo around my head. The first came from a long-time crack addict who told me, 'If you've never touched drugs before, taking crack will do to your mind what lying in bed for a year and then running a marathon would do to your body. It's seriously heavy duty.'

The second is a dinner-party conversation with a friend, Humphrey, who works as a commissioning editor for a publishing company. He described at length the best proposal for a non-fiction book he ever received – a work by a man living on a notorious estate in north London who wanted to understand how so many lives had been devastated by crack. 'It started with lots of interviews and him spending time in crack-houses,' Humphrey told me, 'then, of course, he ends up taking crack himself. It was an incredible proposal but he's never going to finish the book. Once he tried it, he found he liked it and now he's an addict like the people he was writing about.'

I chase the thoughts out of my mind and focus on what's right in front of me. That's when I look at the glass pipe sticking out of the side of the bottle and see tiny specks of Leanne's saliva and lipstick clinging to it. I find myself wondering if she'd be offended if I wiped them away before putting the thing into my mouth.

I look over and see that she has her eyes closed so I reach across with my other hand and rub the end of the pipe between my finger and thumb. And at that moment a tiny, involuntary giggle bubbles up out of me. Here I am about to smoke crack – an act that could completely ruin my life or even kill me – and I'm worried about what? Catching a cold?

I pick the lighter off the bed and, copying Leanne's action, hold the flame just above the rock while placing the end of the pipe in my mouth.

And then I inhale.

And . . . oh, my God . . . it's . . . it's everything. It's absolutely everything. It's having great sex, it's finding out that you've won the lottery, it's getting promoted at work, it's finding a fifty-pound note lying in the street. It's being pissed at your favourite pub with all your best friends while the funniest comedian in the world does a show on stage. It's lying on a beach with the sun on your back, it's someone bringing you breakfast in bed, it's all the chocolate you've ever eaten in one single bite.

Smoking crack is all of these things, all at once.

I feel it in my stomach first, a warm buzzy glow that spreads through my body like a hot shiver. Then it hits my head and everything kind of explodes. I feel so alive. I feel incredibly alert, enormously powerful, like I could take on the world. My chest is pounding, hard, and there's a kind of rushing noise in my ears but it all feels great. It feels fucking amazing. I feel fucking amazing. I am fucking amazing! Fear, doubt, worry, concern – I don't know what any of them are any more. I could do absolutely anything and whatever I did I would do brilliantly. For the first time in my life, I understand the true meaning of euphoria. Who in their right mind wouldn't want to feel like this all the time?

But as I sit there, mouth open in shock and surprise, I sense the best of the feelings starting to drain away. So soon! I still feel amazing but not as amazing as I did ten seconds earlier and, oh, shit, it's fading fast. The lighter is still in my hand, a tiny fragment of rock remains on top of the foil. All I have to do to make it all right all over again is to take another puff . . . oh, God, I really want another puff . . . just one, just for a minute . . .

And now, at last, I understand just how dangerous this stuff truly is.

I'm lying on my bed in my hotel room. Leanne and her crack pipe are long gone and I have what promises to be a pounding headache building up at the front of my skull. I feel exhausted, like I've been running around for weeks.

I know I'll never touch crack again but that doesn't mean I don't want to. And the fact that I can't is starting to annoy the hell out of me. I take a deep breath, shut my eyes and massage my temples.

Outside, back on the streets of Bristol, the police may well have prevented a bloodbath by arresting all the members of the Aggi crew, but as a consequence they have left the crack trade entirely in the hands of the Jamaican gangs. It is part of a pattern that is emerging across the country.

Although London remains the centre of black-on-black violence, Yardies who now feel unable to compete there are moving out to new fields. Their usual trick, according to one Drugs Squad officer, is similar to that practised on Bristol's prostitutes. They arrive in a town and, through extreme force, take over the bulk of the heroin street dealing. They then begin to give away free crack with the smack until, having created a whole new addict base, they rake in the profits. In England and Wales, drug seizures rose in 2003 by 10 per cent, but the amount of crack cocaine seized during the same period more than doubled.

In early 2003 Jamaicans David Curling and Andrew Morrison were convicted at the High Court in Glasgow of setting up just this kind of drug-dealing operation in Edinburgh. Other Yardies have been arrested in Aberdeen, and police in Scotland say use of crack is rocketing. During the whole of 1999 there were four seizures of the cocaine derivative throughout Scotland. In the first six months of 2001, there were thirty-four, by 2003 seizures were showing an increase of 500 per cent with no sign of slowing. In Scotland in 1999, only two per cent of drug users said they used it. By 2002 this had increased to seven per cent.

In South Wales the M4 has become known as the 'crack highway' because of the vast quantities of the drug being driven along it. According to the Swansea Drug Project, crack is regularly seen on the streets of the city, with Jamaican gangsters said to be behind the bulk of the trade. They are also believed to be present in Newport and Cardiff.

In Bolton, Lancashire, police found forty-eight-year-old Jamaican-born Denis Reid selling crack on the streets. He had entered Britain through Gatwick two weeks earlier, officials had confiscated his passport and ordered him to return home. But instead of flying back to Jamaica he absconded and ended up in Bolton.

Even in Gloucestershire, often portrayed as a rural bolt-hole full of quaint cottages in chocolate-box villages, crack has made an appearance. Following an influx of Jamaican criminals and an explosion of gun crime, the local police force has been forced to introduce an armed-response team to the area for the first time.

GANGS

As the effects of my one and only crack pipe wear off completely, I find myself wondering how it could be that one tiny island so many miles away could have such a phenomenal impact on law and order here in the UK. There is only one way to find out.

CHAPTER EIGHT

I know I've been in Jamaica too long when I finally stop flinching at the sound of gunshots.

I've returned to the island for the first time in three years and, as soon as I land in the capital, Kingston, I realise I'm in the middle of a bloody civil war. It's the second week of October 2002, just five days to go before the polls open for the general election, and Jamaica is living up to its reputation as having one of the highest *per-capita* murder rates in the world.

So far forty-three people have been shot dead since the election was called nine days ago and the sound of gunfire echoes through the city at all too regular intervals. Flicking through the local paper as a taxi speeds me from the airport to my hotel I read that residents in the poverty-stricken downtown districts have taken to barricading their streets with abandoned cars, concrete posts and tree stumps in an attempt to prevent drive-by shootings.

Earlier in the week, motorcades led by both serving Prime Minister P. J. Patterson and opposition leader Edward Seaga were fired upon, and a candidate for the People's National Party, Jennifer Edwards, was shot at while campaigning in an area known as a stronghold for the rival Jamaica Labour Party. Edwards was then rushed by an angry crowd and slashed with a knife. She was forced to seek refuge in a safe-house until police could escort her from the area.

Elections in Jamaica are notorious for their violence, a legacy of the troubled 1970s when the two main political parties established their power bases in the ghettos of downtown Kingston, and reinforced the law with the use of hired gunmen. During the 1980 campaign, 844 people were killed in two weeks, most of them on election day. The battles occur because, particularly for the residents of the ghetto, voting a party to power isn't so much about the broader issues of lower taxes or trade deficit as the specific personal matters of whether your home gets connected to the local water and electricity supply.

Local MPs fight for seats by guaranteeing the desperately impoverished substantial financial aid for their communities in return for their support. For those living in the ghettos it is a short step to taking up guns to ensure everyone within a certain community votes a certain way or, better yet, that all those in a neighbouring community also fall in line.

Such tactics have been and are effective because Jamaican election results are often incredibly close. In 1967 the JLP won with 224,180 votes while the PNP polled 217,207. The results continued to be neck and neck until the 1990s, which saw three straight landslide victories for the PNP. Although there has never been another bloodbath like that witnessed in 1980, scores of deaths accompany every election.

A month or so before I arrived the two parties signed a pact in an attempt to halt the killings, both agreeing not to campaign in six key areas that always attract trouble. The areas that would be free of campaigning included the 'garrison communities' from where much of the violence emanates. Known by their unofficial names, which include Tel Aviv, Dunkirk and Southside in downtown Kingston, the garrisons are also home to the drugs barons that control the trade not only in Jamaica but in the UK and beyond. However, the aggressive advertising campaigns by the two parties, possibly thanks to a lack of libel laws, soon made a mockery of this. The JLP's snappy election slogan was: 'The PNP can go to Hell'.

Tensions within these areas always run high but anywhere that two rival communities meet is a potential tinderbox, regardless of whether there is an election or not.

Take, for example, the slaughter at 100 Lane on New Year's Day 2002. The whole of 100 Lane is considered a People's National Party stronghold. Park Lane, on the other hand, is a JLP stronghold, but the two are separated from each other by a narrow alley just a few yards long.

The attack was systematic and well planned. A gang of around fifty gunmen from Park Lane struck shortly after midnight. Dressed in trench coats, they first caused a blackout in 100 Lane by shooting out the local electrical transformer. Then, while one group set up roadblocks to prevent the police gaining access to the area behind and blocked access to the lane to keep them away, the other went from house to house killing in cold blood everyone they could find. No one was spared.

Andrea Simmonds, thirty-three, a barmaid, was executed by the sporadic spurt of bullets, her body forming a shield that apparently enabled her son, Sujay, eight, to survive. Eyewitnesses said her life might have been spared if it had not been for the angry order from a gunman who ordered one of his cronies to 'shoot the gal' after initially sparing her. As she pleaded for her life, dozens of bullets were pumped into her body.

The shooting went on for two hours, and when it was over, seven people were dead. The victims included two schoolgirls aged six and eleven, three women and two men. The toll would have been far higher but several of the houses had metal anti-burglar grids fitted to the doors and windows. Unable to get inside the gunmen simply sprayed their bullets through open windows.

The attack was said to be revenge for an incident a week or so earlier when a group of eight gunmen from 100 Lane, dressed in denim and military fatigues, murdered Glenroy Maize, thirty-two, a juice vendor of Park Lane, and wounded four others including a woman. That itself was in retaliation for a killing by the other side, all part of a bitter political feud that has been going on for years even though some of the residents have relatives in both neighbourhoods.

It was this same long-established political violence that gave birth to the Yardies. After each election gunmen loyal to the losing side would find themselves starved of funding and unable to purchase new weapons. The ruling political party would also have control of the police and order them to round up the other party's gunmen. In order to escape prosecution or, more likely, being shot dead by a police execution squad, they fled, first to the mountains and then beyond.

America and Britain were their first targets. From the late 1970s hundreds of Jamaican gangsters, the vast majority of them loyal to the JLP (who had lost the 1976 election), set up home in London, Miami and New York, almost always choosing the ganja trade as a way of making money. Between 1974 and 1978 the amount of herbal cannabis seized in the UK averaged around 2500 kilos per year. In 1979 the amount more than doubled to 6445. In 1980 it increased threefold to 18,419 kilos. The vast majority of this growth has been attributed to the work of one man.

In Jamaica Robert Blackwood, also known as Bowyark and Rankin Dread, had been the right-hand man of a certain Claude Massop, a notorious Don who ran the JLP garrison in the Rema district until he was shot dead by the police in the late 1970s. Blackwood's name had been linked to the murder of at least twenty-nine PNP rivals and a further four policemen, but bringing him to justice proved problematic. By the time one of the cop killings came to trial, three of the witnesses had been murdered and a fourth had 'lost his memory'. The charges were dropped.

After Massop's death Blackwood assumed control of the Rema district but after being involved in a shoot-out with two police officers he decided to 'go foreign', obtaining a false passport and fleeing to Britain under the name of Errol Codling in early 1978. Blackwood settled in London and, describing himself as a musician/record producer, first made his name legitimately, cutting a record, 'Hey Fatty Boom Boom', which reached the top ten in 1980. 'I was famous. I had the Mercedes. I had the flashy jewellery and clothes. I had it all. And there were always girls. Sometimes I had a different girl every night,' he would say later.

But Blackwood's heart wasn't in the music business and, after the glory of what turned out to be a one-hit wonder, he set about building a criminal empire. He opened a drinking club, ran a string of prostitutes, dabbled in counterfeit currency and funded a series of cannabis shipments to both Britain and America through a number of armed robberies. By the end of 1980 the ganja trade was worth an estimated $1.5 billion per year – more than the value of all Jamaica's legitimate exports combined – and the Yardies were awash with wealth.

At first, the vast majority of the illicit cash that gangsters like Blackwood made was channelled back to fight future election campaigns, and this is believed to be the main reason the 1980 election proved so violent. This time the JLP and, soon afterwards, PNP gunmen followed their counterparts abroad. Politics were forgotten and gunmen from the two parties fought it out over the best drug turf. Between 1980 and 1985 at least 1500 Jamaicans were murdered up and down America's east coast as gangs battled to control the ganja trade.

In Britain, the violence took longer to emerge and came not as a result of the existing trade in ganja but the growing trade in cocaine. The Colombian drug cartels had been expanding their operations in North America since the early 1970s and turned to the Jamaican gangs for help after experiencing problems in moving their product around.

In Britain, which, unlike America or Spain, had no sizeable Colombian community, the Yardies found themselves perfectly placed to form a strong link in the supply chain at street level. Men like Robert Blackwood soon switched to coke, and overnight drug-smuggling went from being a way of making a good living to a way of living like a god.

By early 1986 Blackwood was concentrating so heavily on cocaine that he had to buy his ganja from others. On one occasion he and four of his crew had made a deal with a Nigerian dealer named Innocent Egbulefu to buy £150 worth of cannabis. But Egbulefu wasn't so innocent. The batch of dope he sold Blackwood and the others was made up of herbs and tealeaves. On 1 March 1986 the five men he had ripped off paid a visit to his high-rise flat in north London. They smashed their way inside and, after explaining their grievance, threw him out of the window. It all happened so quickly that when Egbulefu hit the ground, eight floors and ninety feet below, he still had the remote-control unit for his television in his hand.

It was the first UK death attributed to Jamaican gangsters but it would not be the last.

On 23 May 1986 Jamaican Derek Walters was standing in the doorway of the Old Queen's Head pub in Stockwell, south London, when a man got out of a blue Mercedes, walked up to the thirty-one-year-old DJ and blasted him in the head with a shotgun at point-blank range. A few days later a doorman at Cynthia's night-club in nearby Brixton was shot through the head for trying to stop a gang of Jamaicans entering the club and shooting their real target – a rival coke-dealer. In early 1987 at a party in Acton, west London, 'Sammy Dread', wanted for at least three murders in Jamaica, blew the head off rival coke-dealer Alwyn 'Shankie' Alfred. As the gun went off the terrified crowd dived to the floor but those who were brave enough to look up as 'Sammy Dread' strutted out said that he was smiling.

In July of that same year, eighty-five representatives of US and Canadian law-enforcement agencies attended a conference in Miami to discuss ways of combating the Jamaican criminal gangs. Two detectives from Scotland Yard were sent along and reported back that the gangs now had several thousand members and associates, that politics, though still a factor, had taken a back seat, and that the gangs now had a single, well-defined business plan – to accumulate vast wealth through narcotics.

A specialist police initiative – Operation Lucy – was finally launched but it was already too little too late. Crack had arrived, the profits were higher than ever and, having been brought up in a society where violent death was commonplace, the Yardies had a willingness to show and use guns, both against one another and the police, that was completely unprecedented. The impact of Jamaican organised crime has been far greater than that of any other group in the UK. Since the first signs of Yardie activity surfaced here in the mid-1980s, they have carried out more than five hundred murders and five thousand gun attacks. If they are caught and sent back to Jamaica the problems begin all over again. Many of Jamaica's worst crimes are carried out by so called deportees – men who have been kicked out of Britain or the United States for drugs offences or violent crimes and are sent home. The deportees wait around only as long as it takes them to get hold of money and a false passport to return to Britain.

What becomes increasingly clear is that much of the violence and corruption in Jamaica is inextricably linked to what goes on in Britain, and vice versa. The top Yardies make frequent trips back and forth and there are dozens of cases in which hitmen have travelled straight from the island to the UK, carried out a murder then flown back on the next plane. At the same time, and despite their power and wealth in Britain, the Yardies still depend on the support of those in Jamaica – the place the vast majority ultimately yearn to return to.

'We know that the drugs barons are attempting to worm their way into the political process either at ground level or through other methods,' Superintendent James Forbes of the Jamaica Constabulary told me, the day after I arrived in Jamaica. 'You only need to look at the large number of drug couriers travelling between Jamaica and London to know there is a link. It is by no means far-fetched to say that certain people involved in the drugs trade in London and the rest of Britain are both financing and having a considerable influence on activities back here in Kingston. They are using money made from the drugs trade to disrupt elections and ensure their favoured candidates are brought to power.'

On my third morning I call the Jamaica Constabulary press office for details of a fatal multiple shooting in central Kingston. The officer who answers barely misses a beat when she asks if I could be more specific. 'We had quite a few of dem multiple ones last night, which d'ya mean?' We finally agree that the particular inquiry I am interested in is a triple murder in the western section of the city that has only just occurred. I rush to the scene hoping to find out more details.

I arrive to find a small crowd gathered around some wasteland and make my way to the front. The bodies of seventeen-year-old Garthan Powell, Errol Thompson, twenty-four, and his brother Ian, twenty-nine, are lying together, grotesquely twisted, in the mud of a sewage ditch. Each one has been shot in the head, execution-style, and the two brothers had been blindfolded and bound before being murdered. A bloodstained vehicle was found nearby and the trio are believed to have been kidnapped from their homes the previous evening. No gunshots were heard in the area, leading many to assume they were killed elsewhere before their bodies were dumped.

A group of burly firemen appear and help to lift the bodies away. Some of the crowd recoil in horror when something falls out from one of the bright blue ponchos they have used to cover the bodies as they load them on to stretchers. I listen in discreetly as a woman in the crowd tells a young man that she believes the trio were killed by PNP supporters over the theft of a gun.

There are, on average, up to a hundred murders per month in Jamaica, the vast majority in Kingston, a city with a population well short of six hundred thousand. Later that afternoon it is the turn of Glenroy Harris. The men who came to kill him left little to chance. When the police arrived at the scene they found twenty-eight assorted spent shell cases and two live rounds scattered around the labourer's body.

Eager to learn more about his death I persuaded a taxi driver to take me to the murder scene, Burke Road, in a ghetto in the west of Kingston. On the way we stopped at the local police station to get the latest information. When the desk sergeant learnt that I planned to visit Burke Road he was astonished that I didn't have an armed escort.

As we passed through the garrison known as Tel Aviv, my driver, George, pointed out the spot where he saw a man killed the year before. 'I heard this blam, blam, blam, and when I look round this man was lying on the ground surrounded by blood. He was trying to draw his gun but there was no strength left in his body. Some of these streets, outside election time you can walk down them but if you do that now . . .' George paused, took one hand off the steering-wheel and slowly drew a finger across his throat. 'I tell you, man, I am Jamaican, I was born in the ghetto and I love my country but me 'fraid these people. Me nah trust them. They shoot you dead and then apologise afterwards.'

Every side-street in Burke Road was blocked by a barricade. Most had graffiti declaring the street's allegiance to one or other political party. On the edge of Burke Road we stop to ask a woman selling sweets by the kerbside if she knew anything about the killing of Harris. 'I heard about it. I know the man, knew him well. The way I understand it, they kill him for the ganzi.' 'Ganzi' are the T-shirts in the colours of the two political parties. Harris, wearing his green JLP colours, was killed when he met a group of PNP supporters in orange.

When the woman learnt that I planned to walk down Burke Road and question the locals, she pleaded with me not to go. She then pleaded with my already nervous taxi driver not to take me. 'You see that street now, pure gunmen living down there. Nobody else.' I reached a compromise with my driver – he agreed to drive past the end of Burke Road so I could decide how safe it looked.

While the streets around were busy, Burke Road, two hundred metres of potholed Tarmac lined with ramshackle houses, was a ghost town. The silence was eerie. I decided to move on. Two hours later, a policeman was shot and killed at the junction of Burke Road and Spanish Town Road, just a few yards from where I had been, bringing to ten the number of murders on that one day.

The first thing visitors to the headquarters of the Narcotics Division of the Jamaican Constabulary notice is the lack of computers. Essential information such as fingerprint details and criminal records are still written by hand on index cards. The Jamaican Constabulary is woefully under-resourced. They are short of at least a thousand officers and recently suffered a 50 per cent cut in their petrol budget – paid directly by the Government to oil companies – leading to massive restrictions on the frequency of patrols.

From his sparsely furnished office Superintendent Gladstone Wright is the first to admit that he and his officers need help to tackle the increasingly sophisticated drug-smuggling centre that Jamaica has become.

'The smugglers are becoming more dynamic and the trade is growing all the time,' he said. 'In terms of what is happening in Britain, the trade has escalated sharply since 11 September. The couriers who would normally be travelling to America are unable to get their drugs through because security at the borders has become so tight. Cocaine is stockpiling in Jamaica and that is no good for the dealers – there is no viable market for the drug here. So it is all being diverted to Britain.'

One month twenty-three drug mules were caught on a single Air Jamaica flight into Heathrow. A week later a further nineteen were caught on a BA flight into Gatwick. Both aircraft were targeted for checks at random.

Before 11 September, 50 per cent of all drugs intercepted from airline passengers arriving in the United States were seized from flights from Jamaica, despite such flights making up less than three per cent of US air traffic. As Wright believes, much of this activity is now being directed towards Britain, and as much as 65 per cent of all the cocaine in the UK is smuggled through Jamaica. (Crack itself is rarely smuggled. It is far more profitable to smuggle cocaine, then convert it.)

'Becoming a drug mule is the most readily available form of employment in this country at the moment,' he said. 'It is a job that you do not need to be interviewed for or have any kind of qualifications, but you can earn more money than most Jamaicans see in a lifetime. The economy here is very bad at the moment and unemployment is extremely high. These people are easy prey for the dealers.'

The 'body packers' often prepare themselves for their smuggling trips by swallowing whole grapes. The money they are paid is directly related to the number of pellets they are able to swallow. On average a person's stomach can carry up to five hundred grams of cocaine – fifty to a hundred pellets, depending on the size – but many will try to increase their earnings by carrying a good deal more.

The pellets are often dipped in honey to ease their passage down the gullet. The mules will take tablets to induce constipation during the course of the trip. In earlier years the cocaine was stored in condoms but the fingers of surgical gloves, which are made of latex and are sturdier, are the current material of choice. The cocaine is compressed and formed into pellets using a machine, which supposedly ensures an airtight seal.

Despite this, dozens of couriers have had to be rushed to hospital after becoming ill while waiting to board planes at Kingston. At least ten die each year as a result of packages bursting inside them. In April 2002 a Jamaican woman, known only by the nickname 'Modern Girl' due to her taste in designer clothes, was found dead near the M45 in Northamptonshire. Aged around sixty, she had been in the UK for less than forty-eight hours before her body was found. A post-mortem showed she had swallowed ten packets of cocaine and that one had split, causing a fatal heart-attack.

Those who swallow pellets of cocaine receive the most publicity but the smugglers are also using a wide variety of other techniques; some are highly sophisticated. Cocaine has been found sewn into the seams of trousers, suspended in liquids, concealed in the soles of shoes and hidden in the handles of suitcases. One woman was arrested at Norman Manley airport with half a kilo of cocaine woven into her hair.

Police and Customs officials in Britain and Jamaica admit that a significant proportion of mules do get through. Once they have cleared Customs in Britain they travel to prearranged addresses where they are given laxatives to help them expel the packages.

But, according to Wright, his officers do not even attempt to catch all the drug-smugglers before they board flights to the UK. 'It is relatively easy to spot the novices. The people with cocaine strapped to their bodies look bulky or have an unusual gait, while those who have swallowed for the first time are often visibly nervous and panic-stricken. The problem is that we simply do not have the resources to deal with swallowers.

'When we identify them they have to be taken to hospital and placed under guard until the cocaine passes through their system to make sure they don't die. That can take around six days – in one case it was nearly fifty days – and we do not have the manpower to cope with that. We would never knowingly let someone board a plane whom we suspected of having swallowed cocaine, but I am certain that we could catch many more people if we had more resources to devote.'

The vast majority of drug mules are single, female and trapped in lives of poverty and desperation. A lack of state welfare means there is a daily struggle to feed, clothe and educate their children, and the fact that 22 per cent of women are unemployed means there is little money around.

There are cases of women who have become mules to pay for life-saving operations or medication for their relatives; others who simply hope to connect their houses to the local water and electricity supply. Some are forced into it at gunpoint. The families of those who are caught and imprisoned often find themselves the target of the gangs who want to know what has happened to their drugs. There have been incidents of families being executed by the drugs barons, who believe their shipments have been stolen by the mules.

The breeding-grounds for the mules are the shanty-towns on the edge of Kingston, where hundreds of single mothers struggle to raise families in dank, filthy one-room shacks made of little more than compressed cardboard. 'If you had to live the way these people live you might well be tempted to take drugs to Britain too,' says Olga Heaven, director of Hibiscus, a charity that aims to ease the plight of Jamaica's most poverty-stricken citizens. 'These are not professional couriers, they are women who have no other choices.

These are first-time offenders who don't drink, don't smoke, God-fearing women who have never done anything wrong in their lives.'

Despite a series of high-profile commercials on television and radio and related poster campaigns, the message doesn't appear to be getting across. 'The problem,' adds Heaven, 'is that the money they earn from just one trip is enough to change their lives for ever. A lot of them get caught but enough get through and come back with the money for those who are on the fence to decide it's worth the risk.'

The odds certainly seem to be in their favour. The entire Jamaican Narcotics Division is staffed by just 130 officers. By comparison, 150 detectives investigated the murder of TV presenter Jill Dando. Wright plans to expand the division to a staff of more than two hundred, but while having more officers will undoubtedly help, Wright acknowledges that the police themselves are part of the problem. Corrupt officers have been known to transport drugs in their own vehicles, to block off roads to allow planes to take off and land, and to turn a blind eye to shipments being smuggled out of the country in return for bribes.

In January 1999, 127 officers in the Portland Division were transferred after allegations that some had formed an alliance with members of a Colombian cocaine cartel. Eight months later the entire Special Anti-Crime Taskforce was disbanded after some of its officers were found to be selling drugs. More recently police officers have been caught selling gun licences to drug-dealers and helping smugglers to get hold of false passports for their couriers, enabling them to make repeated trips abroad without arousing suspicion.

Perhaps unsurprisingly when you look at the environment they have to work in – police officers and their families are regularly ambushed and murdered, often in the most barbaric way possible – Jamaica's police also have a reputation for going in hard and shooting first whenever there is the slightest notion of danger. In 2002 the police shot dead 133 suspects and sixteen officers died in shoot-outs. Although many complaints were made that police often shot at those who were unarmed, no officers were charged with murder. In July 2001, a joint police–army operation entered the JLP stronghold of Tivoli Gardens, west Kingston, reportedly to search for an arms cache. In the brutal three-day orgy of violence that followed, twenty-seven people were shot dead, including one policeman and one soldier. Pictures of dead bodies stacked three and four deep at the morgue shocked even the most gore-hardened Jamaicans.

But there are, of course, many honest and dedicated officers. A veteran of eighteen years, Sergeant Adele Halliman has spent the last six years specialising in narcotics and is now Jamaica's top mule-buster. Like Gene Hackman's character in *The French Connection*, she believes a sixth sense alerts her whenever a courier is around: 'I guess I have a gift. It's hard for me to explain exactly how it works but I just get a sense when someone is carrying contraband, and I am never wrong.' The day before I speak to her, Halliman arrested yet another British citizen, Michael Edwards, as he boarded a flight to London after a ten-day holiday in Jamaica. His luggage included a bottle of Sorrell, a local drink made from flower petals, which aroused her suspicions. 'There was something about the colour that wasn't right so I checked more closely. It turned out to be liquid cocaine.'

Halliman spends much of her time in the departure lounge of Norman Manley airport at the X-ray machines that scan every item of a passenger's luggage before they reach the check-in desk. 'It's a lottery. Some people will bring through five pieces of luggage hoping we won't have time to search them all. Others have just one piece because they believe they will look more innocent. We have even had people using their children in an attempt to distract us.'

Halliman feels frustrated because she says she hasn't got the resources to do a more effective job, but this frustration pales alongside that which comes from seeing how the Jamaican judicial system deals with those who are caught. Sentences are remarkably light, especially compared with Britain where even a first-time mule can expect to serve a minimum of six years.

CRACK

To see this for myself I make my way along to the dilapidated local courthouse at Half Way Tree where, although the air-conditioning failed years ago, protocol dictates that those addressing the magistrate must wear jackets and ties.

In the stifling heat of court number five one of Halliman's colleagues, Detective Constable Conrad Granston, repeatedly mops his brow as he explains why he had immediate suspicions about Diane Haddow. After opening her suitcase, he found thirty-three plastic bottles of medicated powder. 'I thought to myself this can't be right, nobody should need that much. She told me her daughter suffered from a severe skin complaint and that she had bought it to treat her, but it still didn't make sense.'

Granston cut open one bottle and found three pellets, each wrapped in black plastic. They contained cocaine and almost all the other bottles had similar contents. Haddow, a twenty-two-year-old from Tottenham in north London, was arrested at Norman Manley airport in Kingston as she prepared to board an Air Jamaica flight to London. In all, her suitcase contained around a kilo of high-quality cocaine.

At least seven other cases in the court on the morning I visited involved couriers arrested *en route* to London in the previous week. They included a woman who had swallowed ninety-nine pellets of cocaine, and a man who had attempted to smuggle cannabis in a false compartment in his suitcase.

Since I returned to London Jamaican Customs officers have also been posted to Heathrow airport to help interview suspected mules. Officers at both of Jamaica's international airports have also been given hand-held detectors that are able to pick up traces of cocaine in the body, on clothes or in suitcases. The introduction of the new equipment has led to an 80 per cent fall in the number of people trying to smuggle drugs into the UK by this method but officials admit that, in reality, the problem is as bad as ever. Instead of the drugs flying direct from Jamaica they are now being routed via non-traditional destinations including Belize, the Bahamas and St Maarten.

And as long as there are women desperate enough to risk everything on a flight to London, the problem will remain.

One Customs officer recounted the tale of Barbara, a thirty-nine-year-old mother of six who is now serving three years and nine months for carrying just 341 grams of cocaine. A street seller in Kingston, she was approached by a young woman who told her she could make much more money doing something else and led her to a little house just outside Kingston.

There, Barbara was shown piles of little parcels, containing 100 per cent pure cocaine. Each parcel was an inch or so long, made from the fingers of latex gloves and secured with tape. She was told to swallow a hundred and given six bottles of juice to wash them down, but managed to ingest just fifty-two.

She was paid the equivalent of £400 on the spot and told she would get another £1600 when she arrived in England. While on the plane she was told of a woman who had died with drugs in her stomach because one of the packages she swallowed had burst. It was the last straw. Stopped by Customs officers as she came off the plane, she immediately told them what she had done.

But she did not realise the high price she and her family would pay for her getting caught. Since she failed to meet the person she was supposed to deliver the drugs to in a café at Heathrow's terminal three, the gang who supplied them in Kingston assumed that she had stolen them. As punishment, they kidnapped Barbara's brother, stabbed him, then burned him alive.

As the price of cocaine continues to fall, so the use of crack continues to grow, often with alarming repercussions.

Crack is increasingly being used by the middle classes, people wealthy enough to fund substantial habits without resorting to crime. (This is ironic, considering crack was conceived and aimed at the working classes after the Colombian cocaine cartels found they had lost the middle-class market.) In the City of London, crack is increasingly being treated almost like a form of dare. Dozens of brokers and other financial workers take it every weekend, believing it to be the ultimate buzz and a natural release for the high-pressure lives they live. Experts worry that, although figures for crack use are showing a considerable increase, they mask the true picture as the wealthier, middle-class users who manage to avoid both the criminal-justice system and drug-treatment agencies are never counted.

As seen in Bristol, crack is also sweeping through the sex industry with devastating effect. Drugs workers in Hull say dozens of teenage prostitutes are now offering sex for as little as five pounds to feed their crack habit. In London's King's Cross, many women offer passing men unprotected sex for ten pounds – the price of a single rock in the capital.

One drugs liaison officer told me, 'When you mix crack and prostitution it becomes a twenty-four hour cycle. You go out and you work long enough to get a rock, then you go away and use it, and then you go out and do the same all over again. Eventually you need some sleep, so you take heroin in order to come down. Then you wake up and it starts again. Crack has become the new pimp and the girls are working harder than ever for it.'

Unlike heroin, with its trackmarks and pasty complexion, crack offers no obvious evidence of use or other signs that might put off the clients of a drug-using prostitute. Crack also reduces inhibitions and acts as a stimulant, allowing sex workers to operate for longer hours. The two industries increasingly operate hand in hand, with many prostitutes purchasing drugs on behalf of their clients and sharing them.

The first ever round of compulsory testing of offenders in Bradford in the summer of 2003 found that half of all those charged with theft, burglary and robbery had taken either heroin or crack cocaine. Half of those found to be using drugs have both heroin and crack in their bloodstream when they are arrested.

Increasing popularity is also affecting the way the drug is made and marketed. Crack cocaine has traditionally been produced in small quantities and sold on to street-level dealers and users, but more recently, gangs have produced crack in larger quantities to feed the growing market.

The drug is also becoming more common among clubbers. According to leading drug charity DrugScope, more young people are being pushed into experimenting with crack because there are so many fears over the effects of ecstasy use. 'There is growing evidence that clubbers are under the mistaken belief that cocaine is a safer option,' said a spokesman for the charity. 'Because they haven't seen scare stories about cocaine or crack, they believe that it is a better option than ecstasy.'

Experts say the shift in patterns of drug use has directly affected the type of crimes being committed at street level. Heroin addicts, previously identified as being responsible for the vast majority of property-related crime, traditionally fund their habits through activities such as burglary, breaking into parked cars, shoplifting and credit-card fraud. Crack, however, leaves heavy users edgy, paranoid and dangerously desperate. Because of this they are more likely to get involved in violent, opportunist crimes, such as mugging, mobile-phone theft and carjacking.

And there is no end in sight. With increasing numbers of crack addicts looking for an even greater buzz, drugs agencies across the UK report that, rather than simply smoking their rocks, the most hardcore addicts are now injecting them, which produces an even greater and far more addictive high.

Once described as the ultimate in 'disorganised organised crime', the Yardies and those who mirror their activities are becoming increasingly sophisticated. Money-laundering schemes have come in to replace wearing your wealth round your neck. Alliances are being formed with Turkish and Asian criminals to provide inroads into the heroin business (partly to increase profits but also so that heroin-users can ultimately be switched to the more profitable crack). The 'disorganised' tag is unlikely to last for ever, but the powerful association between Jamaica and brutal gun violence seems set to remain in place for the foreseeable future.

Although they continue to dominate the market for the time being, Jamaican criminals are ultimately set to be replaced by their

CRACK

British counterparts as the dominant force in the crack-cocaine business. Until this happens, however, Jamaicans will continue to be associated with drug-related gun crime, and any Jamaican with a criminal record will be referred to as having 'Yardie' connections.

It's a label the vast majority of law-abiding Jamaicans do not care for but admit, particularly while the murder rate on the island continues to be one of the highest in the world, that they can do little about.

Although Colombia has the cocaine trade, Italy has the Mafia and Turkey has the heroin barons, Jamaicans can take some comfort in that they do not occupy the number-one slot in the league of countries associated with organised crime. That dubious honour goes to none other than Nigeria.

FRAUD

CHAPTER NINE

Tao Savimbi's voice cracks with emotion as he recounts the day his father was brutally murdered right before his eyes. 'They killed him, shot him in the body and head sixteen times because of who he was, because of his position,' Tao tells me, in his thick African accent. 'I had to flee, I had to. My mother told me to run so I fled and sought asylum. If I had stayed . . .' there's a pause as Tao swallows hard '. . . if I had stayed, I would not be here to talk to you. I would be a dead man.'

I'm sitting in my office, both elbows on the desk, the phone pressed hard against my ear. I'm listening intently to Tao and trying oh-so-hard to stifle my giggles. Despite his best efforts to convince me otherwise, I know that his carefully constructed tale of woe is nothing but a sham. Normally I would dismiss the whole thing out of hand but this time I have decided to play along and see where it leads me.

It all started a month or so earlier when the following email popped into my mailbox with the subject line: 'Urgent Assistance Needed'.

Dear Sir

I am Mr Aroujo Tao Savimbi, son of the late rebel leader Jonas Savimbi of Angola who was killed by government troops on the 22nd of February 2002. I managed to get your contact details through the Internet myself largely due to time essence and I was desperately looking for a person to assist me in this confidential business.

Shortly before his death my late father was able to deposit a large sum of money with a security vault in Europe. The family is urgently in need of a very competent investor participant that we could entrust with the Certificate of Deposit and (PIN) Personal Identification Number Code to help us remove the fund from the security company since no names were used in securing the vault. The sum involved is that of Twenty-three Million and Six Hundred Thousand United States Dollars (US$23.6m) which my father had deposited in two trunk boxes with a Finance and Security Company in Amsterdam.

My family and I do not have any access to any of these deposits with banks in Angola and Europe so we really need your assistance in this transaction. Please if the proposal is acceptable to you, after getting the money out from the security company vault to your country, my family have agreed to offer to you 25% of the total sum for the kind assistance you rendered to us.

I have spoken with the security company that is operational Manager, he is ready and willing to release the two trunk boxes to whoever I issue a power of attorney in his/her names as the new beneficiary of the deposit.

I am, therefore, soliciting your assistance to travel to Europe to receive this money physically, set up bank accounts and transfer in bits into your home bank account before my government gets wind of the fund. My reason for doing this is because it will be difficult for the Angolan government to trace my father's money to an individual's account, especially when such an individual has no relationship with my family.

Moreover, the political climate in Angola at the moment is very sensitive and unstable. If you agree to proceed, I will send you a power of attorney and details of my contact at the security firm so that you will be able to proceed to Europe and gain access to and receive the funds on behalf of the family.

I plead with you to treat this issue confidential and urgent because it is delicate and it demands a great degree of secrecy. I would want you to reach me through my email address above *if you are interested to assist me. I sincerely will appreciate your response.*

Best regards and God Bless,

Tao Savimbi

Although it is true that a certain Jonas Savimbi, infamous head of the UNITA guerrilla movement, was killed in an ambush by Angolan government troops in early 2002, the email I received did not come from his son. Instead it was sent out by a gang of highly sophisticated Nigerian fraudsters, a small part of a world-wide network that is believed to earn more than £200 million each year from Britain alone.

Officially known as advance-fee fraud, it is most often referred to as the '419 scam' after the sub-section of the Nigerian penal code that criminalises the act of obtaining money by deception.

419 fraud started life in the mid-1980s when thousands of handwritten letters, supposedly written by doctors, lawyers or accountants but always in pidgin English, were sent asking for details of the recipient's bank account and a few sheets of their headed company notepaper to be sent back to the Nigerian capital, Lagos. The reason given was that a large sum of illicitly gained money needed to be transferred into a Western bank account. In return to playing host to several millions of dollars, the bank-account holder would be promised a substantial commission. The reality was that, having obtained all the details of a victim's bank, the fraudsters would use the headed notepaper to forge a letter requesting that the bank transfer the entire balance of the account to them. Now, thanks to the magic of email, the number of approaches has risen considerably in recent years. At first glance this scattergun approach may appear a waste of time, but if only one in every hundred thousand produces a response, the scam has paid for itself many times over.

The variations are endless but invariably there is something illicit about the funds: they have been smuggled out of the country illegally, are part of an accidental overspend that someone has managed to divert or they are assets being hidden from prying government eyes.

Apart from the supposed illegality of the enterprise, the other catch is that something always goes wrong before the money can be transferred. The only way round these bureaucratic hurdles is to stump up some cash – a relatively small amount compared to the vast wealth that is just around the corner. One hurdle leads to another and requests for money continue until the victim either gives up, goes bankrupt or both.

Although they almost always originate from Nigerian gangs, growing public awareness of 419 fraud means the emails now purport to come from elsewhere in Africa and the rest of the world. Requests for money often ride hard on the back of topical events: as with Savimbi, the death of any prominent African figure will lead to a rash of emails from sons, daughters and wives of the deceased, all claiming to have access to fortunes that were somehow squirrelled away. In recent years people have received emails from special-forces soldiers fighting in Afghanistan who have stumbled across piles of cash belonging to Al Qaeda and need help in getting it out of the country, from cousins of Iraqi chemical-warfare experts who fear their assets may be frozen, and from Kosovan charities desperate to find a new home for their enormous bank balances.

At first these new communications were still being sent out of Lagos but a crack-down by Nigerian authorities – who make up to fifty arrests each week – has forced the gangs to set themselves up further afield, greatly aided by the global nature of the Internet and the advent of high-tech communications. A telephone call to Nigeria can be easily and instantly transferred to anywhere else in the world with the caller being none the wiser.

One recent police operation in east London led to the arrest of a Nigerian who had succeeded in ripping off two businessmen, one in Alaska, the other in Australia (it is an unwritten rule of the scam that you don't fleece anyone in the country you are operating from). Both victims thought they were communicating with an official from the Central Bank of Nigeria in Lagos rather than a man sitting in a back bedroom in Leytonstone.

What particularly intrigues me about Tao's email is the Amsterdam connection: 419 victims are often invited out to Nigeria or other parts of Africa on the premise that they need to be there to oversee some paperwork before the final transaction can be completed. Regardless of the destination, such journeys are not to be recommended.

In July 2001 Joseph Raca, a sixty-eight-year-old former mayor of Northampton, travelled to South Africa to complete a business deal that had begun some weeks earlier with a letter offering him the financial opportunity of a lifetime.

Having made and received dozens of phone calls, all of which only served to convince Raca that the offer was genuine, the trip abroad was supposed to be a final formality: sign a few papers and earn millions of pounds in commission. Raca was met by a man and a woman at Johannesburg International airport and driven out to the suburb of East Rand where he was taken into a house to meet Mr Ford, the man he had been speaking with. For the first twenty minutes or so the conversation was jovial and friendly. Mr Ford explained that, although the money was ready and waiting, there were a few small problems. A cash payment of £7000 was needed before the final transfer could be made.

When Raca explained that he didn't have access to that kind of money, Ford suggested they travel to an ATM so Raca could withdraw as much as possible from his credit cards. When Raca refused, the atmosphere suddenly turned nasty.

'One of the men pulled a gun from the small of his back and placed it against the back of my head. One of the others started stripping off my clothes, frisking me and then taking all my possessions. They said they were going to shoot me and dump my body in the jungle. I really believed I was going to die and I was just trying to survive. I prayed and begged for my life to be spared. Ford took out a machete and tried to cut my ear off. Then they told me to wrap a towel around my knee to staunch the flow of blood as they were going to shoot me in the leg to show they meant business.

'I was very frightened. I'm not ashamed to say that I crawled and begged. They were using foul language and told me they would kill me if I didn't do everything they said.'

Raca was instructed to call his wife, Aurielia, in Northampton, and explain that unless she paid a ransom of £20,000 within twenty-four hours, he would be killed. But his captors had reckoned without the resourcefulness of the former Polish naval lieutenant, who first arrived in Britain fifty years earlier after jumping from his ship into the sea at Hull docks and claiming political asylum.

As his terrified wife listened to his plight, Raca broke into Polish and told her to call the police while he did his best to stall the gang. When he called back the next day, Aurielia informed her husband that the police were on their way. Having liaised with the South African authorities and traced the phone number, two Northampton detectives were flying to South Africa at that very moment to help with the rescue.

Raca's sudden confidence at the end of the call made the gang nervous. As police closed in on the house they fled, dumping Raca on the roadside. He had been held hostage for nearly fifty hours.

Raca was one of the lucky ones. When sixty-one-year-old Tory councillor and professional troubleshooter David Rollings left his home in Bristol to travel to Nigeria to retrieve some £2 million that had been fleeced from some of his business associates in a 419 scam, he was determined not to come back empty-handed. Rollings knew Nigeria well, having made dozens of business trips to Lagos over the years. Staff at his favourite hotel, the five-star Ikoyi in the heart of the city, greeted him warmly when he arrived on a breezy Saturday morning.

Rollings left early on Monday morning, hoping to confront the fraudster, but returned after just half an hour looking shaken. 'It was obvious that something was very wrong,' the Ikoyi's manageress, Fatima Mohammed said later. 'David was sweating profusely and appeared to be extremely upset.'

Refusing to be comforted by the staff, Rollings curtly demanded his key and returned to his room. Half an hour later, 'There was a terrific bang. Everyone in the hotel heard it and we all ran about knocking on all the doors trying to find out where it had come from. For a few minutes there was chaos, people everywhere, but then when we got to David's room there was no reply.'

Inside, Rollings was sprawled on the bed with a single bullet-hole in the back of his head. The room was neat and tidy – there had been no attempt to rob him. No gun was found in the room and his killer is now thought to have slipped away during the initial flurry of activity that followed the gunshot. They have never been caught.

A few weeks earlier an American finance consultant by the name of Gerald Scruggs had also visited Lagos, staying in the five-star Sheraton in the city's suburbs to oversee what he thought was a legitimate multi-million-dollar business opportunity that had fallen into his lap by way of a wealthy Nigerian lawyer.

Once Scruggs arrived, the lawyer, whom he had never met before, kept demanding more and more cash to 'sweeten' the final deal. After handing over thousands of dollars, Scruggs began to suspect that the glittering opportunity was made of fool's gold and refused to pay any more.

When they found him, just outside the hotel grounds, he had been necklaced – a car tyre had been strung about his neck, doused with petrol, then set alight. As with Rollings, his killers have never been caught.

In the past ten years at least seventeen people have been killed in Nigeria while attempting to recover lost monies. Anxious to avoid becoming the next victim I had little desire to travel to Lagos, but having planned a trip to Amsterdam anyway, I found myself intrigued by the idea of being able to meet face to face one of the 419 fraudsters targeting the UK.

Having read through Tao's original email a few times over the course of a week, I sit down at my computer and type a reply. I explain that I am the director of a small but profitable paper-handling company based in central London and that I'd be happy to help him in any way I can. It is less than twenty-four hours before I hear from him again.

Dear Tony,

I received your email. Thank you for your lovely kindness. I would like to take you back to the first message I sent to you and elaborate the kind of help I need from you.

First Step: As you must have read from my first message how my father was killed by Angolan Government troops because of his position. Due to this reason my mother advised me to relocate to the Netherlands where I am currently seeking asylum for safety reason and look for a trustworthy person who can handle the beneficiary to the said consignment and also arrange for a profitable investment.

Second Step: This fund was deposited in one of the private security companies here in the Netherlands by my late father, and as the next of kin, all the relevant documents have been passed to me. But due to the crises in my country and also my political status in Europe, I am not able to operate a bank account. For this reason I will submit the power of attorney and change of ownership to you in order for you to claim the consignment.

Third Step: You should know that we are taking you as our foreign business partner and also as a manager for all our further transactions.

Fourth Step: All the various accounts where the money will be deposited after claiming it from the security company will be opened by you in your name or your company name for security reasons.

Fifth Step: After I submit the documents to you and a copy to the security company you will be invited to come to the Netherlands branch office to sign the release of the consignment. Please send me your private telephone number in order to give you the other information.

Best Regards and God bless,

TAO SAVIMBI

This time I reply immediately, sending Tao my telephone number and telling him that, by a happy coincidence, I am planning to travel to Amsterdam on business in the next few weeks (though I neglect to mention that it is to research other chapters of this book). I tell him how excited I am about being able to help him with his difficulties and how much I look forward to meeting him. The next day Tao writes to me again:

> Dear Tony,
>
> Thank you for your co-operation concerning this transaction and I hope that you will be visiting the Netherlands very soon. Please try and send me your international passport number in order for me to meet with my advocate to write the power of attorney and change of the ownership to your name, since we are entrusting you as our overseas business partner.
>
> After submit the power of attorney and change of ownership you can open conversation with the security company as our overseas business partner nominate to become the rightful beneficiary to the said fund.
>
> Within the shortest time God will join us together as one family.
>
> Extend my warm greetings to your family.
>
> Best Regards and God Bless,
>
> TAO SAVIMBI

I spend the next few days away from my office on the trial of coke-dealers in the north of England and when I return there is a voicemail message from Tao on my phone. I play it back and note that he sounds genuinely distraught, wondering why I have not yet sent my passport details. His situation, he explains, is getting more desperate by the day and I am his last hope.

I make a note of the number that he gives me but decide not to call him back right away. Instead I decide to get some expert advice on just what to expect if I arrange to go and meet Tao. I call up the offices of the National Criminal Intelligence Service and request a one-to-one briefing on the current state of advance-fee fraud and the Amsterdam connection.

A few days later, in a bare meeting room in one of the dozen or so buildings close to the river Thames that form the frontline of the battle against British organised crime, I am introduced to 'Duncan', who proceeds to give me a crash course on everything there is to know about the 419 gangs.

'A lot of the people who get these letters and emails, they treat the whole thing as a joke and hit the delete button or throw them in the bin right away,' Duncan explains. 'They think, How could anyone be so stupid as to fall for this? Well, I have met the people who do. Some of them are stupid, others just naïve and some are plain greedy. All of them are embarrassed about what has happened to them.'

Duncan's figures show that, in 2002, British victims of 419 frauds who contacted NCIS had lost a total of £8 million. One man was fleeced of £1.4 million, another of more than £400,000. Three people were cheated out of £300,000 each while five more lost £250,000 each.

Shocking though these figures are, they represent just the tip of the iceberg. Dozens more victims would have reported their losses direct to one of the UK's forty-three police forces and hundreds of others would have kept quiet and said nothing at all. Duncan suspects that a significant number of those who get involved are criminals themselves and the money lost is the proceeds of other frauds or drug-trafficking.

'When it comes to those behind the scams, you're talking about extremely clever people. When they are dealing with their potential victims they have mastered the art of coming across as trustworthy, well mannered and well educated. The fact is that the vast majority of Nigerians living in the UK are honest and respectable: these criminals trade off the good name of their community.

'The Amsterdam thing is relatively new. A few years ago the goal was to get people to travel out to Lagos, but after a few cases of murder and kidnap many of the fraudsters realised that it was much harder to convince their victims to travel to what was seen as a dangerous third-world country. Few people have any such qualms about places like Paris, Amsterdam, Dublin, or even parts of South Africa, but the truth is these meetings can be dangerous, regardless of where they take place. All the indications are that incidents of kidnapping are becoming increasingly common.'

Duncan tells me he spends an increasing amount of his time guiding victims of 419 scams through a series of email and phone exchanges with the fraudsters and then accompanying them to a face-to-face meeting, usually in South Africa. There, working alongside the local police, the meeting is allowed to continue as long as it takes for the fraudsters to incriminate themselves before they are arrested.

It's a slow, high-risk way of dealing with the gangs and even when the suspects are caught, there is often little chance of getting back any money that has already been lost, but Duncan believes it sends an important message to them. The focus on South Africa is at least partly responsible for the increasing number of scammers basing themselves in Europe.

'So far as the latest trends are concerned, the fraudsters just get cleverer and their techniques get ever more refined. Instead of making up names at random, they are starting to use the names of real people – often staff at prominent banks or law firms – working on the presumption that people might go as far as to run the name through Google to see if the person is bona fide but are unlikely to phone them up at work, especially when the emails make it clear that all communication needs to be kept confidential.

'There are cases where the fraudsters will send out newspaper and magazine clippings to back up parts of their story about the origins of the money they need moved out of the country. More than once, the gangs have actually managed to get stories placed in genuine publications.

'When it comes to the kind of documentation that gets sent out, some of it is first class. It used to be the case that the letters were full of spelling mistakes and grammatical errors but they have really smartened up their act. They can produce government and bank letterheads with impressive-looking seals and stamps that are virtually indistinguishable from the real thing. The cottage industry that exists to support this kind of forgery is an industry in itself.

'We recently stopped a Nigerian leaving the country with a single suitcase, opened it up and found that it was full of old travel passes for the London Underground, bus tickets, stuff like that. It was all completely worthless and it took us a while to figure out what it was for. Basically in Nigeria the stuff is like gold dust. When people go to meet them wherever, they can make out they've been travelling around, that they bought things or lived in certain places. As far as the victims are concerned, it all adds to the feeling that the people they are dealing with are genuine.

'So far as the reality of you going to Amsterdam is concerned, a number of things might happen. At present around half a dozen people travel over there each week after responding to 419 emails. Some of them get picked up and driven out to somewhere in the suburbs where they are taken into the basement of a shop. If they don't hand over any money right away, they get put under a bit of pressure until they do.

'I've had calls from people who say they were told to wait in their hotel room and that they waited all day and no one turned up. Or that when the people turned up they felt a bit intimidated so they gave them all the money they had or allowed themselves to be driven to a cashpoint or bank to empty their account.

'The bottom line is that the 419 fraudsters are only interested in making money, but violence is not unknown.'

The following afternoon, my phone rings and I answer it absentmindedly. 'Hello, Tony, this is Tao.' He sounds genuinely distraught. He asks why I have not yet sent my passport number. Time is running out. Without it, he explains, he cannot put together the power-of-attorney. For a few brief seconds I forget the whole thing is a scam and find myself feeling genuinely sorry for him. I apologise and tell him I will do so immediately.

It is at this point, desperate to win my sympathy, that Tao recounts the story of the death of his father and I return to my senses. I manage to stop myself laughing out loud and instead sound sympathetic to his plight. I promise to forward my passport details by email, and explain that immediately afterwards I will book my flight to Amsterdam. I tell him the reason for the delay is that my company has just won a new contract and that I'm having to take on new staff and expand. At the other end of the line I am sure I can hear Tao's eyes widening, his hands rubbing: more business for me means more money for him to steal.

He gives me a new telephone number and also a code name, which he asks me to use whenever I try to get hold of him. 'When you call me, say the name Omega and I will respond Delta. If I do not answer Delta, hang up and call back.' Tao fails to explain the need for such a scheme but I later learn that rivalry exists even within the 419 gangs, and that if one member finds a likely mug, he will often try to exclude others working from the same office in order to keep more of the profits for himself.

The desire to cut costs means the scammers often share telephone lines and sometimes even Internet cafés, forcing them to work far more closely with one another than they would ideally like. '419s are such a popular thing in Nigeria right now,' said one high-ranking member of the Nigerian Secret Service task force, charged with investigating the schemes. 'On any given day, you may have a hundred people, ranging from amateur crooks to organised criminals, all using the same Internet café to send out 419 emails.'

I jumble up a few of the numbers on my passport – I can always claim it was a genuine mistake – and email them off to Tao. There are, according to Duncan, two possible motives for him requesting them. The best-case scenario for me is that he simply wants to make the documentation appear more legitimate and will therefore include my details on the power-of-attorney he is drawing up. The worst is that he has a contact who buys passport numbers for use in putting together forgeries. In either case it will only be a matter of time before he asks to see the real thing.

Two days later I receive scanned versions of some seemingly genuine legal documents, signed by Tao, granting me power-of-attorney over the funds lodged in Amsterdam. The email explains that Tao has sent a copy to the finance company and that they are preparing a certificate of deposit in my name, allowing me to claim the money as my own.

To my great relief, the email goes on to make the first request for money, something I had expected to happen far sooner. Tao mentions casually that when I arrive in Amsterdam I should have with me a copy of the power-of-attorney, a copy of the certificate of deposit (which he will give me on arrival), a copy of my passport (so the number can be checked against the documents) and the sum of $14,200.

The money, he explains, is to cover the 'demurrage', a kind of interest payment that has accrued because the money has been with the company far longer than was originally intended. 'I tried to negotiate with them to see if they can allow you to secure the consignment before making this payment but was categorically told that this is not permitted because of the company insurance policy. My dear friend, it was never my intention to ask you for any financial assistance but you are now the only person who can help. As a refugee I earn only a hundred and fifty dollars as a monthly allowance, which is not even enough to feed myself. Please God, I trust and have faith that you will do everything in your power to find the money so we can make this deal.'

I don't want to appear too eager so I write back and tell Tao that I had already booked a flight to Amsterdam but I was surprised to learn that I would need to bring so much cash with me. I tell him I will make inquiries and that, God willing, we will be able to proceed.

Three days later, having spoken to Tao and been told that the certificate of deposit is ready, and having convinced him that I should be able to get the money wired to me by a business associate once I'm in the Netherlands, I arrive at Luton airport in plenty of time to board my one o'clock flight to Amsterdam.

My plan is simple: I want to have one and possibly two meetings with Tao and the gang, stall them about getting hold of the fourteen grand, then get the hell out of Dodge before they realise they're not going to get anything out of me. But, having promised them a bumper pay-day, I know I'm playing with fire.

As my flight begins its descent into Schiphol airport, I can't help worrying that the fake passport number I gave to Tao may have been a dead giveaway. At the back of my mind is the inescapable fact that in every case I have examined involving violence or murder, the trigger was the victim's refusal to play along and pay up at least some of the money when asked. If the gang runs out of patience or, worse still, discovers that, far from being a new source of income, I'm just a writer trying to expose their activities, I'm going to be in big trouble.

CHAPTER TEN

According to the Dutch anti-fraud authorities there are around forty gangs made up of around three hundred Nigerians actively running 419 schemes in Amsterdam at any one time, using it as a base from which to arrange meetings with gullible victims from all over Europe.

Although Tao has repeatedly told me that he is in Amsterdam, there is no guarantee that he will actually be the man waiting for me when I get off the plane. The telephone numbers he provided may have Netherlands codes but even this means nothing. The latest digital technology means that calls can be diverted in an instant to anywhere in the world. Some of the gangs take advantage of this to make even more money by linking their numbers to premium-rate call lines. Even the most innocent inquiries can cost the hapless victim fifty pounds per minute in charges.

Instead of meeting the victims themselves many of the heads of the larger fraud gangs have team members in cities across the world who act as intermediaries. These subordinates often work hand in hand with others, who are introduced as high-flying bankers, lawyers or financial consultants but are in fact other members of the same gang. 'It's a classic good-cop bad-cop strategy,' the man from NCIS told me. 'It means one of them can sympathise about the fact everything is going wrong while the other makes increasingly desperate demands for cash. They'll pretend not to be good friends and play off one another but you'll be left with the distinct feeling that, afterwards, they'll all get together and have a good laugh while discussing their next move.'

The main discussions the gang will have will centre around just how much more money they think they will be able to screw out of me. Having already promised that I will have $14,200 on me when I arrive, and made little fuss about obtaining such an amount, I have identified myself as a man of considerable means. If they follow the usual pattern, the next request will be for two or three times as much, and if I balk at this they will slowly reduce it until they find a level I am more comfortable with.

My big fear, however, is of ending up in a confined space with two or three members of the 419 team, a situation in which they could easily apply pressure to force me to hand over any cash I have or even hold me against my will and demand a ransom.

My research has shown that, despite the supposed presence of a finance company with a vault stuffed with millions of pounds' worth of ill-gotten gains, all of the meetings between myself, Tao and others are likely to take place in my hotel room. To that end I have booked a room but have no intention of staying overnight. Instead I'll get a flight back later that same evening and escape to safety.

As I queue up for passport control I start thinking through my plan and suddenly it seems ridiculously flawed. Having made them aware that the first payment of $14,200 is just round the corner, it seems unlikely that they will let me out of their sight, even for a few minutes. More to the point, while the gangs seem to prefer to visit people at their hotels there are dozens of cases of people being met at the airport and driven to remote locations from where the deal is made.

I walk through the sliding doors into the arrivals area and scan the crowd in front of me. To the middle of the group on my left is a tall black man in a grey suit that hangs unevenly over his slightly podgy body. He holds a rectangle of paper torn from a notebook with my name scrawled on it in thin black ink. I take a deep breath and stride towards him. Then, just before I open my mouth to speak, I have a brainwave.

'Mr Thompson?' asks the man, smiling broadly.

'Actually, I'm Mr Walker, personal assistant to Mr Thompson,' I say, changing my voice slightly. 'He's been held up and asked me to meet you and apologise. You must be Tao.'

We shake hands. I feel like I'm running on auto-pilot as I explain that, due to a last-minute shareholders' meeting, my boss had to miss the flight and will be catching a slightly later one instead. In the meantime I tell Tao that if he briefs me as fully as possible about the course of events it will save a great deal of time once Mr Thompson arrives.

We make our way to the Runway Café in the foyer of the Sheraton Hotel, a short walk from the airport terminal, order coffee and orange juice and begin to speak. As I listen to Tao I try to work out whether his voice is the same as the one I have heard on the phone, but with his heavy accent it is impossible to say.

Tao seems frustrated. He keeps looking at his watch and asking me when exactly I think my boss will arrive. He says he has a number of appointments and he took time out especially to come to the airport. Deep down he seems quite angry but is struggling to control himself. 'It's all very straightforward,' Tao explains. 'When Mr Thompson arrives we will take him to the office of the security company and there, once his identity has been confirmed and the demurrage paid, he will sign the final documentation to allow the money to be released. Will he have the money with him?'

I feel a shiver pass through me as I realise that Tao doesn't intend the meeting to take place at the hotel room after all. I take a deep breath and reply, 'I believe he didn't want to bring it with him on the plane so he is having it transferred by Western Union and will collect it in Amsterdam shortly after his arrival.'

I ask where the security company is based, and Tao gives me the name of a town I have never heard of but later learn is in the southern suburbs of Amsterdam. It's an unlikely location for any kind of office, particularly a financial one, and I can't help but think that, knowing their target has access to $14,200, the gang are planning a swift kidnap.

My suspicions are aroused even more when Tao asks me about my own family – whether I am married, have children, where I live and work. It might be nothing more sinister than an attempt to make conversation but it might equally be an attempt to extract information that they could use later to work out who to approach to raise a ransom. Caught off-guard, I don't have time to lie and end up giving answers that are at least half truthful.

I am keen to have a further meeting and perhaps get to see other members of the gang but, despite racking my brain, I can't think of a single way to move things forward without putting myself in great danger. I consider asking if I can see the security-company offices for myself but dismiss it as foolhardy and pointless.

Tao looks at his watch again and sighs. It is almost three thirty and the next flight from Luton does not arrive until after six. Tao says that most of the Western Union offices close at five so the business will have to wait until tomorrow.

I apologise once more and say that I will give him a call as soon as Mr Thompson arrives, that we will collect the money first thing in the morning, meet him then and travel straight to the security company together.

Tao seems pleased by this suggestion and makes a note of the name and number of the hotel I tell him I'll be staying at. We shake hands once more and I offer to pay his fee for parking his car at the airport. He declines with a big smile. 'Do not concern yourself with this,' he says. 'We will soon be signing a deal that will make your boss a wealthy man.'

As Tao vanishes into the distance I breathe a sign of relief, turn and head back into the airport ready to catch the next flight home.

Safely back in London I track down the victim of a 419 scam who also travelled to Amsterdam and, unaware of the potential danger, took things one stage further than I was willing to. A successful businessman, but still embarrassed by his gullibility, Noah speaks only on condition that I agree not to identify him fully.

'It went on for about three months in the end. I started off being incredibly sceptical about the whole thing, just going along with it to see what happened, but then when the documents started arriving, they all looked so real that I started to believe it.

'I knew vaguely that there were some scams going around but the thing that struck me about this guy was that he never asked me for any money, not a penny. He just wanted me to go to Amsterdam and sign some papers, and then he was going to give me around six million dollars. Eventually I agreed.

'The man, he called himself Ade, said he was going to pick me up at the airport but there was no one waiting for me. I called the number he had given me and he apologised, said he was busy and that I should take a taxi to a hotel. Three hours later I opened the door of my room to find a tall and very well-dressed black man with another black guy, who told me that he was a chemist.

'Ade gave me a big hug, he seemed genuinely pleased to see me. His first email had told me all about his family troubles back in Nigeria and he kept telling me how grateful he was that I was going to be able to help, that I was "saving the lives of many people" by allowing him to get hold of the money.

'He explained that for the release of the funds the security company wanted thirty-eight thousand dollars and although he was only able to collect thirty-five thousand he said he had made an agreement with the company whereby they would bring one of the two trunk boxes, which contained twenty-four million dollars, and we would pay them the remaining three thousand directly from the funds. That seemed a perfect idea to me and, again, because it cost me nothing, made me feel completely at ease.

'He gave the chemist an envelope with the thirty-five thousand in it and told him to go to the security company for the release of the consignment. Ade and I stayed in the hotel room, waiting for the chemist to come back, and started talking about our families, religion, about his life back in Nigeria and the kind of things we planned to do once we had the money. He was good company and very easy-going. He had me convinced he was a good man, someone that I could trust.

'After around an hour and a half, the chemist came back with another man who was carrying a large silver trunk and was introduced as a representative of the security company. Ade told this man that I was to be the beneficiary. He asked me to show him my passport, which I did, and then took some papers out of his briefcase and asked me to sign them.

'The man then said he needed the remaining three thousand dollars and Ade asked if he could wait for a few minutes. The man became very upset and started shouting that this was not the agreement, that if he didn't have the remainder of the money he would have to take the trunk back with him.

'Ade started begging him to wait in the corridor for a short time and that he would be able to sort everything out. I must admit I was pretty shocked about how angry the man had been – for a few minutes it all seemed to be going horribly wrong – but once the man was out of the room Ade squeezed my arm and told me everything was going to be fine.

'He opened the case and my eyes lit up. It was full of hundred-dollar bills, stacked from top to bottom. I'd never seen so much money in my life and was absolutely transfixed. To one side of the cash was a small polystyrene box and Ade took it out and opened it and pulled out a bottle. He and the doctor then started saying something about the fact that there was only a tiny amount left and I asked them to explain.

'The chemist passed me the bottle and explained that it contained a chemical compound called Lactima Base ninety-eight per cent, which they needed to clean money. I looked at the bottle and saw that most of the material had solidified and only a small amount remained liquid at the very top. The doctor said that for security reasons all the bills had been marked with a stamp that invalidated them and that the liquid is used to remove the stamp. He planned to wash three thousand dollars to pay the balance to the man from the security company, but that there was only enough left to wash two hundred dollars.

'The chemist then pulled the first two notes off the pile in the trunk and showed them to me. Both had thick black stamps on one side which read UNDP. Ade said this stood for United Nations Development Programme and had been stamped on the money as a security precaution when his father had sent it out of Nigeria. Had it been lost in transit, the stamps would have rendered the money worthless.

'The chemist then took the notes back, spilled a few drops of the liquid on to each and began rubbing them with some tissue paper. I watched as the black marks faded away leaving behind a slightly soggy but genuine hundred-dollar bill. It was almost magical.

'But Ade was concerned. He said that because we had now run out of Lactima, we wouldn't be able to pay the courier and he would have to take the money away. He seemed genuinely worried and everything he had said earlier about just how much his family were relying on him getting money to them in order to get them out of Nigeria came flooding back to me.

'Without hesitation I said that I could probably get enough money out of my bank and credit cards to make up the balance. I was the one who suggested it, but I guess it was exactly what they had been waiting for all along. But even then the alarm bells were not ringing. The man from the security company, the forms I had signed, everything had seemed so genuine that I could see no cause for concern. And I was only taking out a few thousand dollars. It would never have occurred to me that they would get me to travel to Amsterdam, then scam me for such a small amount of money.

'The chemist offered to drive me to the nearest ATM and off we went. We got back just in time – Ade said the courier had run out of patience and was about to leave.

'We now had the trunk of money but were left with the problem of what to do about cleaning it. Ade said they would have to buy some more of the solution or try to restore the solidified material that they had but that, for obvious reasons, it was expensive and difficult to get hold of. I asked him what he meant by "expensive" and he said he would have to make some phone calls and get back to me.

'I was due to fly back to London the next morning so I told Ade he would have to finish on his own. I suggested he get the solution on credit, then pay the company once he had cleaned the money – that seemed to be the sensible thing to do.

'The next day Ade told me the Prime Chemical Company had carried out a test on the solution and managed to melt a small part of it. He then gave me an official-looking certificate, which had the results of their test. He said that they wanted forty-six thousand dollars to melt the rest. He said they wouldn't deal on credit. He said he knew I didn't have much money, and that he was so sorry to be asking me, but that it would be a shame if he had to go to someone else and make them the beneficiary of all the money because of the problems. He took me to the airport and gave me a big hug to say goodbye.

'We stayed in touch by telephone and, when I seemed reluctant to come up with any more, Ade told me that he had been able to raise twenty thousand dollars so now I "only" had to find another twenty-six thousand. The figure kept dropping and dropping over the next few days until he realised that I suspected the whole thing was a scam and he gave up.

'For a while I was really angry – with myself and with Ade and the others – but as I found out more about the kind of things these gangs are capable of, I realise that it's far more likely that I just had an incredibly lucky escape.'

Noah had fallen for the so-called 'black-money scam', which is one of the most common being run by the Nigerian gangs in Amsterdam. The exotic and expensive mix of secret cleaning chemicals, which goes by such names as SSD Solution, Vectrol Paste, Lactima Base 98%, Microtectine and Tebi-Matonic, is really just ordinary cleaning fluid that reacts with the black mixture of Vaseline and iodine that has been stamped on the notes.

Although the victim is shown a full trunk of money, only those on the very top are genuine bills. The rest of the trunk is full of pieces of paper cut to banknote size. Any attempt by the victim to make a closer inspection of the contents of the trunk will be headed off by one of the gang who will come up with a pretext as to why this is not possible.

In front of the victim the criminal will appear to select at random between two and four notes from the case. Sometimes – as with

Noah – they have been marked with a stamp. In other cases the notes are completely black. In reality, the criminal knows perfectly well which notes he is selecting and selects the only real ones there. A really dextrous criminal will invite the victim to choose notes to clean and, by using a well-practised sleight-of-hand similar to a card trick, dupe the victim into selecting the genuine ones.

The solidified-solution scam is just one variation. Another involves a specially rigged bottle of the cleaning chemical, which is left with the victim at the end of the evening. Some time during the night the bottle explodes, spraying the precious liquid all around the victim's hotel room. It is only then that the victim learns just how expensive the chemical is and is asked to shell out for a replacement.

Yet another variation involves notes that are not actually stamped or coloured. If a potential victim seems to be dragging their heels about whether the scheme is genuine or not, the gang will arrange for a trunk of money to be delivered to the person's hotel room. The sight of all that cash is usually enough to convince the most sceptical person that the transaction is genuine and that they were foolish to have any doubts. Most people are so impressed by the display that they fail to consider the reality of the situation.

The largest denomination of US currency is a hundred-dollar bill. Even when they are brand new, 500 such bills form a pile three inches high. This means that $1 million in US currency would form a pile 500 feet high. Even if it were possible to fit such an amount into a trunk, it would probably not be possible for a single person to lift it. Once again, only the top notes will be genuine.

Being shown the money is as close as anyone will ever get to it. Just before the trunk is handed over, the Nigerian playing the part of the representative of the security company will ask for the victim's certificate of something or other. In yet another round of good-cop bad-cop the members of the gang will be embarrassed or angry that this has been overlooked and tell the victim that the minor problem can be resolved for a simple payment of up to $250,000. If the money is forthcoming the victim will be the proud owner of a trunkful of blank pieces of paper.

Although the goal of the gangs is to extract as much money from their victims as possible, they will often settle for considerably less than anyone would expect. According to the man from NCIS, this is down to simple economics: 'You have to remember that the average wage in West Africa is around twenty pounds per month. They might start out asking for ten thousand but they will drop and drop, claim to have managed to raise money on their own, and keep going down in price until you stop resisting. At the end of the day they are happy to get anything out of you, no matter how little it ultimately is.'

Increasing public awareness of some forms of the scam is leading to others being introduced. Instead of money sneaked out of war-torn African nations, the emails now appear far more personal, rather than part of a mass mail shot, and give no clue of any connection to Nigeria. The authors also claim erroneously to have connections to legitimate banks and financial institutions in order to lull their victims into a false sense of security.

Dear Sir:

Good day to you. My name is P—W—. I am a senior partner in De Rosenberg Consulting, U.K. We have been engaged by Barclays Private Banking, London, UK, to carry out a search. We are conducting a standard process investigation involving a client who shares a similar name with you and also the circumstances surrounding investments made by this client at Barclays Private Banking. The Barclays Private Banking client died intestate despite investments under Barclays Private Banking management. The essence of this communication with you is to request you provide us information concerning three issues: I – Are you aware of any relative/relation, born 1st October 1930, who shares your same name whose last known contact address was Brussels, Belgium? 2 – Are you aware of any investment of considerable value made by such a person at the Private Banking Division of Barclays

Bank PLC? 3 – Can you establish beyond reasonable doubt your legal eligibility to the estate of the deceased?

It is pertinent that you inform us ASAP whether or not you are familiar with this person that we may put an end to this communication with you and our inquiries surrounding this personality. You must appreciate that we are constrained from providing you with more detailed information at this point. Please respond to this mail as soon as possible to afford us the opportunity to close this investigation. Thank you for accommodating our inquiry.

Regards, Mr————, Senior Partner, De Rosenberg Consulting.

'Although the approach is different,' says Duncan of NCIS, 'the basic idea is exactly the same. Those who respond are asked to pay certain lawyers' fees or cover tax liabilities before they can get their hands on the main payment. In some cases they will blatantly ask someone to lie and say they are a relative and share the money. When they do this, it means the victim is far less likely to go to the police when they end up being fleeced.

'Churches and charities have also been targeted. They are informed they have been left a considerable amount of money in the will of a recently deceased person. The letter goes on to say that the deceased person had attended that particular church on a visit to the UK or had an interest in the charity. If followed up by the recipient, then the requests begin for the payment of certain fees and the organisation is sucked into the fraud.'

The very latest variation often sees the victim rather than the fraudster going to prison. The key to this scam is that, rather than being asked for money, the victims are actually given it instead.

Using plants who have infiltrated the Royal Mail and other postal services, the gangs steal high-value cheques and, with the aid of high-tech forgery equipment, change the name of the payee to that of their target. Because of the size of the companies targeted and the complexities of their accounting procedures, it is not unusual for it to take more than six months for the bank to report that a cheque of this kind is no good.

This scam is also cropping up more and more with day-to-day transactions conducted in the classified-ad sections of newspapers. One woman contacted me to say that, when she advertised her car, she received a call from a Nigerian man who wanted to buy it and have it shipped over. He said that for various tax reasons, he would be sending her a cheque for £6000 more than the cost of the car and that, once it had cleared, she should wire him back the difference.

The cheque did indeed clear, and a week or so later the woman sent the Nigerian buyer the money. It was only several weeks later that her bank informed her that the cheque had been stolen and illegally altered. She found herself without a car and owing the bank some £22,000.

Although Amsterdam is a hotbed of activity, the 419 scam is alive and well right here in the UK. Prosecutions, however, are rare, as those involved tend to ensure they deal only with victims who are living abroad.

In June 2002 George Agbinone and Ovie Ukueku were jailed after pleading guilty to an advanced-fee fraud that netted them more than half a million pounds. At least eighteen victims from the USA and various European countries were called to give evidence but police suspected the pair had fleeced many others who were simply too embarrassed to come forward.

While advance fee frauds are not exclusively Nigerian, the use of such scenarios almost always is. Where other criminals are concerned the methods used to entice their victims are entirely different. In the summer of 2003 three Britons, Dennis Alexander, David Andrews and George Steen, were jailed for up to six years for defrauding hundreds of businessmen in a scam that brought them in the region of £4 million. Operating out of the resort town of Brighton on the east Sussex coast, the trio placed advertisements in various foreign publications inviting businessmen in need of additional funding to apply for commercial loans ranging from half a million to twenty million pounds.

Once the requests had been received, the company would notify the applicants that their loan had been accepted in principle and that a non-refundable administration fee of up to £7000 was required to progress it to the 'offer stage'. Hundreds paid up and were then told that further fees of up to £20,000 were payable to get access to the final loan. But in every single case, the company found a condition the applicant was unable to meet, turned them down and kept their fees.

February 2003 saw the first murder committed by the victim of a 419 scam. Seventy-two-year-old retired doctor Jiri Pasovsky marched into the Nigerian embassy in Prague and shot dead Michael Wayi, ambassador to the Czech republic.

Pasovsky had visited the embassy frequently in an effort to get Nigerian authorities to help him recoup the £400,000 he had lost in a scam involving a stake in a non-existent oil pipeline. He had borrowed thousands from his neighbours to keep the deal going and, after believing for months that he was about to become rich, finally accepted that he had been the victim of a sophisticated fraud. Pasovsky had been seeking the Nigerian government's help in getting his money back for almost a year before he met with Wayi for the last time.

Pasovsky's actions may appear extreme but there is increasing evidence to show that those who do fall victim to the scams, particularly those who lose large sums of money, can become incredibly vulnerable.

'One particularly cynical gang actually targeted people who had been caught out in the past,' says Duncan. 'They received official-looking letters from the Nigerian Presidential Task Force on Debt Repayment and were told that the fraudster responsible had recently been convicted and their assets seized. Any money lost could now be repaid to all victims – all that was needed was the recipient's full financial details so the money could be transferred into their bank accounts. Those that responded soon found their accounts drained of whatever money was left behind in the aftermath of the first fraud.'

A few days after I return from Amsterdam, acting on a hunch, I send Tao a long email. I explain that I knew right from the start that he was trying to defraud me and that I only went along with him to see what would happen. I tell him that he made the mistake of thinking I was a *mugu* – a word that roughly translates as 'big fool' and is used by the 419 fraudsters to describe their victims.

That same afternoon my telephone rings. It is Tao. But instead of being angry he is full of compliments and admiration. He congratulates me on not having fallen for his scheme and tries to justify his actions. 'In Lagos, everyone is very poor. Nobody wants to be poor, everyone wants to escape from it. There is no point in working, no man ever got rich working for a living. And there is no point in stealing it – for that they will cut off your hands and burn a tyre around your neck. The best thing is to find a scam and make your money that way. You see, any fool can steal money but to find a scam and make it work, that takes brains and intellect. In Nigeria, most people believe that if you are clever enough to make a scam work, then you should be entitled to keep the spoils.'

Tao claims to have been working the 419 scams for more than ten years and to have made more than half a million dollars during this time. 'When I first started I worked with someone else, someone who knew the business well, but now I work for myself, I am the boss.

'It's not a small operation. We have people who write the letters, people who create the documents and others who talk to clients on the phone and many more. And it's not just Nigerians. You wouldn't be alone. There are people from all races working this business all over the world.

'I have two foreigners who work for me, white guys. They lost money in this business and now they work with me. They recruit *mugu* in Europe and I send them a share of the money I make. There is a role for you if you want it, you can make money. It is good that you are in London. You can make a good business there.'

Tao explains that, if I join the scam, I would take on the role of the British manager of a security company. Tao would pass on the details of potential victims and I would then contact them to confirm that Tao is legit and that the offer is bona fide. Because I would be seen as a separate, third party, the victims would have less reason to be suspicious. Tao promises to pay me a 50 per cent share of whatever monies he receives and all but guarantees an income of tens of thousands of pounds. He advises me to set up separate fax and telephone facilities so that I cannot be traced. 'There is plenty of money out there. You would be surprised at how many people want something for nothing. Greed makes them foolish. About one in three who comes to Amsterdam give us money. They may be cynical when they first receive the email but once they are given a telephone number and get to speak to someone in person, they always start to believe it is real. Some of them even know about the *barawo* [criminals] but believe that because they have a telephone number, they are safe.'

I tell Tao that I will think about it and end our phone call. I do not hear from him again and I am not surprised. I feel certain he would have found a way to force me to pay something upfront before I could begin working with him. The truth is that, even if I were another criminal, I wouldn't trust Tao at all.

In the latter part of 2003 customers of all the major high-street banks were hit by a new kind of email fraud asking them to log on to their banks' website for a security check. In each case the criminals had constructed a fake but convincing-looking email using the official logo and included a link to take the customers through to the website.

The link appeared to be genuine – for example www.barclays.-co.uk, which is Barclays' real web address – but although the page they were taken through to looked identical to the real thing, it was a fake website set up by the fraudsters. Customers were then asked to type in their user names, passwords and membership numbers –

information that went straight to the fraudsters and allowed them to begin raiding accounts.

All the high-street banks constantly monitor Internet traffic to pick up on potential rogue activity. Measures include the use of special-service devices that trawl through cyberspace and look out for any incidents where a bank's name is being used out of context. Thanks to this, only a few dozen accounts were attacked but the raiders still stole tens of thousands of pounds.

Incidents of 'phishing' and 'spoofing' (two forms of online fraud) rose by more than 400 per cent during 2003, according to the National High Tech Crime Unit. And while only a tiny proportion of customers will ever fall for the scam, no one believes the problem is going to go away.

The very first credit-card fraud was attempted one day after the launch of Barclaycard. It was inevitable that, as people became more used to the Internet and felt more comfortable using it for all aspects of their finances, the weakest link in the technology chain – the people – would be attacked. Willie Sutton, the notorious US bank robber, was once asked why he always went for banks and famously replied, 'Because that's where the money is.' With more and more money circulating around the Internet and computerised banking systems, it comes as no surprise to find the latest generation of criminals setting their sights there.

'The banks brag about their firewalls and virus protection and say that customers can trust them online,' says one officer with the National High Tech Crime Unit. 'The trouble with that is that once one person trusts another they create the perfect opportunity for the criminals to move on in.'

HI-TECH CRIME

CHAPTER ELEVEN

The first time I meet her, tucked away at the back of the public gallery of Hendon magistrates' court, she tells me her name is Elaine. A week later, when we meet for a drink in Mill Hill, she apologises for lying and tells me that her real name is Suzanne, pulling out her photocard driving licence to prove that, this time, she is indeed telling the truth. Later than night, when the barman of her local pub refers to her as 'Julie' she simply looks at me and bursts out laughing.

The truth is that Mary – the name she uses most often – is an élite member of a team of high-tech criminals taking advantage of the latest technology to empty people's bank accounts through dozens of cutting-edge schemes and scams. Being able to switch identities at a moment's notice – enabling her to walk into every shop or bank along a particular street and pretend to be a different person with a different credit card each time – is one of her key skills and something she likes to practise even during her spare time. 'I like the idea of people in different places knowing me by different names and having to remember them all,' she confides. 'It keeps me on my toes. There are so many times that shop assistants have gone off to check whether something is in stock, then come back and called me by the name on the card from across the room. I can't afford to hesitate for even a moment in case I make them suspicious. It was hard at first but now I'm used to it.'

Mary was in court after being arrested with ten false passports, all with different names and all with her picture inside. She was upset, not because of what will happen to her, not because for the first time the police have a good-quality picture of her to use on *Crimewatch* (the last time round no one realised it was her and she has never been charged) but because the passports were linked to a job that would have netted her a major share of £80,000.

Mary is well-spoken and immaculately turned out. Born to successful white middle-class parents, Mary is a million miles away from the age-old image of the 'kiter' – the name given to women who walk into shops and buy high-value goods with stolen credit cards. Once upon a time kiting was a good way of making money. The credit-card companies simply swallowed their losses and never worked too hard to pursue those involved. In the early days the window of opportunity between a card being stolen and a report being made to the issuing bank was wide. Thieves had days, sometimes even weeks, before their purchases drew even the slightest suspicion.

These days, the chances of getting caught with a stolen card have increased greatly – as have the penalties. 'Back in the eighties lots of shops still had those machines that imprinted the card details on a piece of carbon paper. There was no connection to the credit-card company at all, apart from a book with a list of stolen cards that no one ever looked in.

'Nowadays it's all electronic. If someone reports their card stolen it can be blocked from the system in a matter of hours, sometimes minutes. If the card's hot then as soon as you use it you're setting off a chain of events that brings you closer and closer to getting caught.

'Virtually every high-street store has CCTV cameras fitted and it's just impossible not to get caught on them. But even the biggest stores only keep their tapes for a week or two at most so the way to get round it is to make sure no one realises that you're using a stolen card.'

The first solution Mary's gang came up with was to move into cloning. Rather than stealing an existing card, they would copy its details and imprint them on to a perfect replica. Mary would then be 'employed' to pose as the original card-holder and go out on major shopping sprees. 'With a stolen card you're always worrying about the window of opportunity,' says Mary. 'With a cloned card you can pretty much relax. It hasn't been stolen so no one is looking out for it. The first time most people realise their cards have been cloned is when they get their monthly statement through. The only thing you have to worry about is the credit limit.'

By the dawn of the new millennium, card cloning had become a massive industry worth more than £150 million each year. Hundreds of waiters, petrol-station attendants and hotel staff have been caught using hand-held scanners to 'skim' details from the cards they are given. Sold at the end of each working day for around fifty pounds each, the numbers are then used to produce cloned cards. Many of those involved had links to the Russian and Eastern European Mafias, who are heavily involved in this sort of activity.

ATM cards are equally at risk, particularly if the criminals are able to get hold of the PIN number. There are numerous incidents of scanning devices being attached to cash machines to record the details of the magnetic stripe while a member of the gang hovers nearby to catch sight of the PIN.

In October 2003 a gang of four men and two women from Romania was jailed for running a high-tech scam that introduced a new level of sophistication to credit- and debit-card fraud. Micro scanners were fitted to the doors of indoor cash-machine lobbies so that when customers attempted to gain entry, their card details were recorded. The gang also fitted tiny cameras to the top surface of the ATM machines and beamed pictures of the customers typing in their PIN numbers to other gang members waiting nearby.

Although the gang refused to talk, detectives believe they were part of a far wider operation. All six were illegal immigrants and one theory is that they were being forced to carry out the fraud to pay off their passage to the UK.

But, lucrative as it is, card cloning is in decline. One reason is that most of the credit companies have automated computer systems in place that detect unusual patterns of spending. These can sometimes trigger alarm bells almost as soon as the cloned cards are used. Furthermore the old-style magnetic-stripe cards – perfect for cloning – are set to be replaced by more secure 'chip and pin' cards, a move that cut fraud by 80 per cent when it was introduced in France five years ago. Impossible to copy, the chips fitted to the front of all cards carry all the information that is currently on the magnetic strip but in a far more secure form. Rather than being swiped, the cards are read in special terminals, and rather than signing a receipt, customers will simply input their PIN numbers to authorise their transactions.

The move will raise the stakes for the fraudsters, but they have already made a start on taking things to the next level. Instead of merely stealing the details of someone's credit card, the best high-tech gangs go a step further and attempt to steal their entire identity.

'People just don't realise how important their identity is, and how vulnerable it is,' says Mary. 'I know house burglars who say that people will buy safes and ensure all their cash and jewellery is well out of sight but think nothing of leaving old credit-card bills or passports lying around. It's become so valuable that, for some of the guys I know, it's all they go after. The beauty is that they can break into your house, take a few bits and pieces and half the owners will never even know. When the police arrive they will say the gang must have been disturbed because they didn't take anything.'

Many people fail to take even the most basic security precautions. One survey of 2000 people found that one in three did not destroy bank and card statements, which contain account details.

But burglary isn't the only way to get hold of such information. The computer whiz-kids working for Mary's gang say any computer logged on to the Internet is a rich source of information from credit-card and bank-account numbers to passwords and billing addresses. Using this as a starting point for getting hold of personal details, the gang has made more than £300,000 in the past year.

And Bevan should know. In 1996 he and a friend were accused of almost starting the third World War from his bedroom after hacking into secure computer systems belonging to the US Air Force and defence manufacturer Lockheed. Bevan, who used the name Kuji, hacked into a research centre at Griffiss Air Force base in New York state and allegedly planted a sniffer programme to obtain further passwords. He was arrested and charged, but the case was dropped. According to former hacker Matthew Bevan, if the information is not there right away, you can install a pro-gramme called a 'sniffer' to find it. 'A sniffer will sit there in the background and monitor the computer, recording everything that someone types into it, including all their password and address information.' He now uses his skill to expose the shortcomings of computer companies around the world. 'Websites that request bank details carry a padlock sign denoting a secure socket layer [SSL], but although they claim it is safe, that's just not true. All it means is that the link between you and the company is encrypted. With a lot of companies, we hack over their SSL – the expectation that this is secure is a really stupid assumption. No one I know has an online bank account.

'Although significant steps have been taken to try to combat online fraud, it is increasing at around thirty per cent per year. As we eliminate opportunistic fraud, we are left with a highly skilled "professional" class of fraudster, often linked to organised crime.

'In the old days, there would be groups of kids using specialist programmes which generated random credit-card numbers,' he adds. 'Since the introduction of tighter security, the methods of obtaining numbers have also evolved. Today the criminals will set up a bogus but professional-looking website offering desirable goods at well below normal high-street prices. The would-be buyers will input all their details – including their billing address and security numbers – but when they try to purchase something, the site will tell them their card cannot be processed. People running the site will have collected the information they need. They sit on it for six to eight weeks, then use it fraudulently.'

Dozens of chatrooms and specialist sites exist where thieves and hackers swap the personal details of card-holders. The numbers are exchanged for cash or given in return for passwords allowing free access to websites that normally require payment. 'Virgin' numbers – those that have not yet been used fraudulently – are highly prized.

While some fraudsters try to get the maximum amount of money from the card in the shortest time, others adopt a more sophisticated approach. Knowing a large transaction will quickly be reported as suspicious, they use a number of cards and make small debits from each. Most bills are issued weeks after a debit is made and the criminals hope that, during that time, the victim will not recall all they have bought and assume the transaction is legitimate.

Another online option is to go 'phishing', the practice of getting individuals willingly to submit their genuine ID to bogus sites. One of the first companies to be attacked in this way was the Internet auction company eBay. Hundreds of thousands of emails were sent out at random, telling customers that they needed to re-enter their credit-card information or risk their accounts being shut down. Both the email and the website that was linked to it looked like the real thing and thousands complied, losing thousands of pounds in the process.

Another, more sophisticated means is to masquerade as a legitimate online bank with irresistible interest rates and reel in customers. Dozens of lookalike sites including barclays-private.com and eurocitibank.com – neither of them anything to do with existing banks – were shut down, having been used to garner ID details for fraud.

'But there is only so far that you can get with basic credit-card information,' says Bevan. 'What we're seeing more and more of now is people moving into creating whole new identities loosely based on an existing person or completely from scratch.

'Often it's a case of searching around on the Internet and picking up bits of ID on the way. If you have someone's name and account number, guessing the password to their online bank account is often relatively easy. People most often use their date of birth as their numerical password, and their mother's maiden name – the most common security question – is printed on everyone's birth certificate and you can get a copy of that for just a few pounds.

'With this kind of information it then becomes easy to pretend to be someone else. You can call the automated bank service and transfer money from their account. You can set up a whole new account in the same name and, provided it is kept in credit for a few months, apply for loans and credit cards. When the bailiffs come knocking it is on the door of some ordinary Joe who never even knew his identity had been stolen.

'The Internet has changed everything but not in the way many people think. The information available through online sources was always available. There is nothing available now that wasn't available years ago. It's just that gathering the information is now much faster. You can do in a day what used to take weeks.'

The net also offers a host of opportunities to obtain bogus documents. High-quality fake passports, driving licences and birth certificates are all relatively easy to come by online. For anyone willing to spend a short amount of time looking there is a range of websites where you can buy duplicate documents on literally anything. The sites are shut down regularly by the authorities but reappear elsewhere in another guise.

Identity theft is believed to be the fastest-growing crime in the world – worth an estimated £1.3 billion in the UK alone – and Mary is a master of it. Armed with nothing more than a few bits of paper she boasts that she can walk in anywhere and convince people that she is who she says she is.

'The store cards are the best, especially in the run-up to Christmas when they're really busy. Normally these sort of places are strict about the sort of ID you need to sign up, but they know for a fact that most of the people who go shopping had no intention of getting a card when they left home. That means they are a lot more flexible. If you've got a couple of utility bills and a credit card with your name on it, you're away with up to two thousand pounds of instant credit. You just go from one shop to another, sign up in every one and max out your limit. I've spent more than twenty thousand pounds in the space of a few hours like that. You go for digital cameras, portable DVD players and laptop computers – stuff you can sell on. It's easy.'

Stealing a whole new ID is a slow and intricate process. The starting point is to get hold of some form of identifying document such as a bank statement or utility bill, which will also provide a name and address. Such things are by no means difficult to come by. A survey by the Experian credit-reference agency found that two-thirds of local authorities around the country had a problem with 'bin raiding' and that it was getting worse. In a further analysis of four hundred domestic bins, the agency found that almost three out of four contained a full name and address, four out of ten contained a credit-card number and expiry date linked to an individual, while one in five held a bank-account number and sort code alongside a name.

As well as earning money for themselves, identity thieves can cause havoc for the individuals whose details they steal. Credit can be rejected, bank accounts shut down and enormous debts run up all without the individual ever knowing. It can take years and cost literally thousands of pounds to put everything back in order.

In a bid to stamp out the problem, the Home Office has announced plans to introduce ID cards to the UK. But many fear that the cards themselves could become targets for ID theft. It would also mean that a thief would have to obtain only one item rather than a range of items to acquire absolute proof of identity. In the US, where ID is linked to one single point, a social-security number, there are now instances where identities are so thoroughly compromised that their true owners have to go so far as to declare themselves legally dead – a practice known as 'pseudocide'.

Although identity theft mainly affects individuals, they are not the only targets for computer criminals. Finance companies and online banks are also being hit hard, often by hackers who threaten to cause havoc unless they receive substantial sums of money. Although such activity is believed to be commonplace, it rarely attracts publicity.

Soon after its launch in 2001 the police National High Tech Crime Unit commissioned NOP Research to survey leading organisations in the UK on hi-tech crime. The report confirmed what the police had known for some time – that businesses were reluctant to report online attacks to their systems because of concerns about their reputation with customers and shareholders.

Although almost all of the companies in the survey had experienced at least one incident of serious computer-related crime in the previous twelve months, only half had involved the police, typically where there was a need for an insurance claim or if a successful prosecution was likely. The police were usually a second choice to having outside security consultants fix the problems, and one in ten said they would not involve anyone outside the company at all. When Russian hacker Vladimir Levin tricked Citibank's computers into paying out more than $10 million the bank was initially reluctant to allow the matter to become public, calculating that the media coverage would cost them even more in shares and customers.

Catching those working at the highest levels of high-tech organised crime calls for specialist skills and techniques. Security companies employ people to pose as hackers, hanging around in chatrooms and trying to pick up the latest gossip – hackers are notorious for their love of bragging. As well as being experts in computing many such operatives also have a background in psychology to enable them better to understand group behaviour and the mindset of those they are dealing with. They will create a series of net personae – up to twenty or more – which they use to gain the confidence of other hackers on the web. It is a long, slow process. It is not unknown for the teams to spend more than a year just listening in to conversations before they join in.

Although reports of successful hacks will be made to the police, the teams are far more concerned with prevention. Their Holy Grail is to get hold of a piece of computer code that a hacker is working on before he has a chance to try it out. This enables them to add preventive measures to the systems they are working on, ensuring their safety.

Similar techniques are now being employed to catch another group of computer-savvy criminals who do most of their work in Internet chatrooms: paedophiles. When I visited the offices of the Child Protection Command of the National High Tech Crime Unit at Scotland Yard, a nine-year-old girl, a twenty-seven-year-old stockbroker and a forty-eight-year-old geography teacher were quietly surfing the Internet. The girl was bored, lonely and looking for pen-pals; the stockbroker was looking to add to his collection of hardcore, sado-masochistic child pornography; while the teacher was looking for someone who shared his interest in sex with pre-pubescent blond boys. The girl was typing slowly, misspelling some words and abbreviating others. She made passing references to her favourite television programmes, complained about her lack of pocket money and told silly jokes.

In reality the girl, the stockbroker and the teacher were just some of the dozens of fictional characters created by the unit's under-cover officers.

'Some of the paedophiles out there are the best hackers in the world,' Detective Inspector Brian Ward told me. 'They have the ability to examine the hard disk of someone online to check whether they are who they say they are.'

This means that if an officer is going to pose as a nine-year-old girl, he has to ensure that everything on the hard disk fits in with that. There will be certain types of music files, emails to and from friends about problems at school and home. All this information has to be created simply to ensure the deception is complete. Stacks of hard disks containing the different identities are spread around the room.

Child pornography – or, rather, the threat of it – also features in the latest crime to emerge from the growth of computer technology in the home and the office. Cyber blackmail is on the rise, with dozens of computer users receiving emails from criminals who threaten to delete essential computer files or install pornographic images on their work PCs unless they pay a ransom.

The extortion scam, which first emerged early in 2003, indis-criminately targets anyone on the corporate ladder with a PC connected to the Internet. It usually starts with a threatening email in which the author claims to have the power to take over a worker's computer. It typically contains a demand that unless a small fee is paid – at first no more than twenty or thirty pounds – they will attack the PC with a file-wiping program or download on to the machine images of child pornography. As is the case with the 419 gangs, the scam works even if only a handful of the countless recipients follow through and pay up.

But high-tech crime doesn't only revolve around the Internet. Former paramilitary gangs in Northern Ireland are using the latest computer technology to run a sophisticated, multi-million-pound counterfeiting and smuggling operation, whose tentacles reach across the globe. Forsaking politics for profit, loyalist and republican terror gangs have linked up with the likes of the Russian and Italian Mafia and the Chinese Triads to reap huge rewards from a wide variety of criminal activities. Up to a hundred criminal gangs are operating in Ulster and at least two-thirds are linked to the Provisional IRA, the Ulster Defence Association and other paramilitary organisations. The province has become a major UK hub for the sale and distribution of counterfeit goods, which is believed to have earned the gangs more than £150 million last year.

Law-enforcement agencies in Northern Ireland seize more counterfeit goods than all other UK police forces combined, but still believe they stop only five per cent of the total market. 'Pubs, clubs and taxi firms who operate in districts influenced by paramilitary groups are known to facilitate a lucrative trade in counterfeit goods. Door-to-door sales are also undertaken. The most popular goods include clothes, computer games, DVDs, CDs and videos.'

Much of the counterfeit clothing is believed to originate from factories in the Leicester area, while a raid on a fair in Ballycastle last year was tracked back to an operation in Glasgow.

Counterfeit currency produced and printed in Northern Ireland has been discovered all over the world. In addition to copies of sterling – complete with watermarks and foil strips that only experts can tell from the real thing – the gangs are also producing dollars and euros. They make use of sophisticated scanners and digital cameras to take close-up photographs of real notes, then manipulate them electronically to allow them to be reproduced more accurately.

Customs officers have uncovered a trade in counterfeit cigarettes, made in factories in the Far East with only a minimal amount of tobacco and harmful fillers. Fake vodka, made from watered-down industrial alcohol, has also been found.

One up-and-coming development, straight out of the pages of a science-fiction novel but enough of a reality to be a major cause for concern, is the development of so-called 'cyber narcotics'. Rather than being taken orally or via injection, these digital stimulants would involve hooking up to a special machine that would then directly stimulate the pleasure centres of the brain. The technology is in the early stages of development but the FBI believes such products have the potential to be more addictive than heroin and cocaine. Furthermore, they could be transmitted across the Internet or using radiowaves, and could be taken without anyone ever needing to possess them.

Such products may still be some way off, but there is no doubt that the web is increasingly replacing pubs or nightclubs as the favourite criminal forum for exchanging useful information. The simplest of searches will produce dozens of sites dedicated to providing details and descriptions, often including the registration numbers, of unmarked police cars operating across the country. Many of the lists are compiled by youngsters employed by criminal gangs to stand outside their local police station and note every vehicle entering and leaving. Most experienced undercover officers now prefer to park their vehicles some distance away and walk to the station when attending briefings.

More sophisticated searches reveal the existence of sites where specific information about suspected police informants and the identity of officers working on covert operations is disclosed. The information is often found within anarchist sites alongside tips for manufacturing explosives, picking locks and creating false identities.

The largest and most sophisticated gangs now employ technicians and engineers, and subscribe to trade journals to keep up with developments in forensic and technological science, helping them counter the threat from law enforcers. They also have their homes and vehicles swept regularly for bugs following convictions in which police have gained crucial evidence after breaking into a suspect's property and planting listening devices. These gangs keep up to date by sending representatives to court to listen to detailed evidence of how rival gangs were tracked down. Increasingly aware of this, the police will often seek a public-interest immunity certificate, or even drop a case rather than disclose the technology used to gather the information.

But for all the power and versatility of the Internet and the speed and flexibility of credit- and debit-card payments, one fast-growing area of crime revolves around nothing more sophisticated than the humble cheque book.

Although cheque use is falling each year – we wrote 2.8 billion cheques in 1999 and the figure is expected to drop to 1.7 billion by 2009 – the amount of money lost to cheque fraud is rising dramatically. Intercepted in the post or stolen during house burglaries, cheques with crudely forged signatures are used to pay for millions of pounds' worth of goods each year and no amount of technology seems able to defeat the problem. In 2002, losses from cheque fraud involving forged signatures increased by a third to £23 million.

All of which goes to show that, no matter how sophisticated and computer-savvy society becomes, some criminals will always prefer the low-tech approach.

BIKERS

CHAPTER TWELVE

If it had been any other Stephen Cunningham, there would have been little cause for concern. By the end of the second week of September 1997 the family of the forty-six-year-old civil engineer from Swindon had not heard from him in almost five days. After contacting a few of his friends and confirming that they, too, had heard nothing, his daughter decided to file an official missing-persons report at her local police station. On average, around four thousand such reports are made each week, and middle-aged men are one of the groups most likely to disappear – a way of temporarily escaping concerns about careers, debts and growing old. The vast majority simply return of their own accord, but from the start this case was different.

This particular Stephen Cunningham was a man better known to the police as 'Grumps', a leading member of the Nomads chapter of the Hells Angels Motorcycle Club. Cunningham had achieved a dubious level of notoriety in April 1991 when he travelled to Southampton and attempted to plant a bomb under a car belonging to a member of a rival biker gang. As Cunningham moved the device into place it detonated early, tearing off his right hand.

The car-bomb attack came in the midst of a fierce battle between the Nomads and the Southampton chapter of the Satan's Slaves. The fighting had begun a few months earlier when Nomads chapter president Stephen Harris, a motorcycle salesman, and fellow member Barry Burn, a mechanic, were shot at during a trip to Bristol. Harris was hit in the arm but Burn escaped without injury. A few months later another member of the gang, David McKenzie, was stabbed eight times in an attack outside a Gloucester pub. Rescued by fellow Nomads, McKenzie was taken to the grounds of Gloucestershire Royal Hospital and stripped of his 'colours' – the patches that identified him as a Hells Angel – before being taken in for treatment. Within a few days McKenzie had discharged himself.

With no sign of Cunningham the fear was that the war between the two gangs had claimed its first life. 'Both the police and his family have grave concerns for him,' Detective Sergeant Jerry Butcher said at the time. 'It is rare for him to go for more than a couple of days without making some form of contact. It means you have to consider that he may have come to some harm.'

His daughter, Michelle, seemed to accept this. 'Whatever may have happened, my family needs to put it to rest,' she told the *Swindon Evening Advertiser*. 'Not knowing anything is worse; we are in a state of limbo. Even if it is just to confirm our worst fears, we would like to know.'

But the more the police probed, the more the mystery deepened. Their inquiries showed that Cunningham had left his Swindon home early on 9 September, driven to Ramsgate in Kent and boarded the four p.m. Sally Lines ferry to Ostend as a foot passenger. Video footage showed him arriving in Belgium at around six p.m. UK time, and records show that he used his mobile phone an hour and a half later to get it switched to a network that would allow him to make calls across Europe. Although Cunningham had booked a return passage on the ferry for 11 September, he never used it.

In accordance with the rules and regulations of the Hells Angels, the other members of the Nomads chapter refused to give the police any assistance, not making so much as a single statement. The message was loud and clear: whatever reason Cunningham had to travel abroad, whatever he planned to do while he was there and whatever trouble he had got himself into, it had absolutely nothing to do with the club.

According to its one-time spokesman, the late Ian 'Maz' Harris, Ph.D: 'The Hells Angels Motorcycle Club is a loosely based organisation of motorcycle enthusiasts who own bikes of 750cc or more. We are primarily and exclusively a motorcycle club. That is all.'

The Memorandum of Association for Hells Angels Limited, registered at Companies House in October 1976, adds the following objectives: 'To foster, encourage and advance the sport and recreation of motor-cycling and to promote the acceptance of the ethical code of morality of the Hells Angels club; to encourage, promote and hold race meetings, happenings, rallies, reliability trials, exhibitions and shows and give entertainments of all kinds related to motor-cycling.'

Indeed, every year the club's 250-odd members, along with hundreds more associates, attend a number of exclusive rallies and conventions, stage huge, highly profitable shows where customised bikes are displayed, and donate thousands of pounds to various charities. In June 2002 it was a Hells Angel, Alan 'Snob' Fisher, who led a cavalcade of fellow bikers in a Jubilee procession past the Queen, raising money for the anti-child bullying charity Kidscape in the process.

However, according to the police, the Hells Angels are a major international criminal organisation, a 'pure form of organised crime', who 'have accomplished in twenty-five years what it took the Mafia over two hundred years to do'. Interpol describes outlaw motorcycle gangs as 'one of Europe's faster-growing criminal networks' and closely monitors their activities. Not surprisingly, the bikers disagree: they insist that the police are simply paranoid and that, because they live an alternative lifestyle yet remain highly visible, they are the ideal soft target.

'We're so prominent it's untrue,' Dr Harris told me. 'We ride about on big bikes and wear patches on our backs to say who we are and where we're from. I mean, if you're hell bent on collective criminality, it's hardly the way to go about it. We'd have all been arrested years ago. We're not trying to claim that we're all perfect. Nobody ever is, but to suggest that we represent a significant threat to the peace and prosperity of Britain is taking things too far.'

So when, as happens periodically, an Angel is arrested, charged and convicted of crimes ranging from murder and mortgage fraud to drug-dealing and assault, the usual excuse is that their ranks might contain a few bad apples but that doesn't make them a new Mafia. 'The club,' said Harris, 'cannot be held responsible for the actions of individual members.'

There are many things the Hells Angels don't like to talk about. The exact meaning of the many patches and badges that they wear comes near the top of the list. One Hells Angels website features a handy code of conduct for members of the public wishing to fraternise with members: 'Don't ask what a patch or insignia means on any Motorcycle Club member's vest. It's club business! It's okay if you're talking to a club member to ask/say, 'That's a great-looking pin, is it ivory?', but not 'What does that stand for? It's not that it's anything mystic or cryptic, it's just that it's for members, and members only, to know.'

As soon as he had recovered from the injuries sustained in the car-bombing, Cunningham was back on the Angels social circuit, attending rallies, parties and runs, and generally living the hedonistic biker life. Almost immediately the denim cut-off and leather jacket that bore his colours featured a new patch: two Nazi-style SS lightning bolts below the words 'Filthy Few'. According to the biography of legendary Hells Angel Ralph 'Sonny' Barger, president of the Oakland chapter, the Filthy Few patch is a piece of harmless fun. 'It means that someone is the first to arrive at a party and the last to leave,' he says. In reality the patch is only awarded to Angels who have murdered on behalf of the club – usually in the presence of another member for corroboration – or who are prepared to commit a murder at a moment's notice. Despite failing to complete the task he had been assigned, Cunningham's willingness to plant the bomb had been judged sufficient to enable him to join the Filthy Few.

Such a reward was necessary for Cunningham because activities of this kind are not undertaken lightly. When the Angels go to war with rival gangs (and occasionally among themselves) outsiders can be forgiven for thinking it revolves around nothing more than club pride and maintaining the hedonistic fighting and drinking traditions of the biker lifestyle.

The truth is that the primary reasons the Angels do battle is to protect their business interests. And these days, almost exclusively, that means the drugs trade. Across the world biker gangs are involved in drug-dealing and trafficking on a massive scale. Estimates from the FBI and the Bureau of Alcohol, Tobacco and Firearms suggest the Angels and the other biker gangs collectively earn up to £1 billion a year from the drugs business.

'The Hells Angels particularly are very involved in the drug-dealing scene in the UK,' says a spokesman for the National Criminal Intelligence Service. 'Traditionally their commodities were cannabis and amphetamine, but they are moving more and more into Class A drugs.'

Stephen Cunningham was a major amphetamine and cannabis dealer and the man whose car he attempted to blow up was not just the member of a rival biker gang but also the head of a rival drugs outfit that had been attempting to flood Cunningham's turf with cheap supplies of cannabis, amphetamine and cocaine.

Virtually every fight, every shooting, every stabbing and every bombing that has taken place between biker gangs in the UK and further afield in the past twenty-five years is ultimately connected to a desire to protect the highly lucrative drugs business from which the gangs derive the vast majority of their income. Although they are also involved in several other areas – prostitution, theft and extortion among them – drugs are considered the core business.

The Angels in particular are super-cautious, rarely carrying the product themselves, preferring to bury it then tell customers where to find it. One amphetamine dealer supplied by the Angels complained to police how they regularly drove him half mad with his weekly delivery. When he had deposited the money earlier in the day at a 'safe' drop site, they would call him in the early hours of the following morning and simply tell him, 'It's in your garden.' The dealer's neighbours reported how he could regularly be seen in his underpants at four a.m., armed with a torch and a spade, searching frantically for the goods.

One police surveillance team followed a pair of Angels (who were not wearing their colours so as not to attract attention) to a local park and watched as they sat about for around two hours feeding the ducks and exchanging pleasantries with passers-by before leaving. It was only later that it emerged the two had been supervising the pick-up of a kilo of amphetamine. The drugs had been concealed in a rubbish bin earlier in the day and the Angels were there to ensure that no one but their customer picked it up.

Failure to stick to protocol leaves the bikers open to prosecution as was the case when a Thames Valley Angel was stopped on his bike during a routine check. He was found to have a half an ounce of amphetamine sulphate inside his glove, and later privately admitted that the only reason he had been caught was because a sale had been cancelled; rather than taking the product to the stash site, which would have involved a longer journey, he decided to risk keeping it with him.

But even when caught red-handed, many Angels are bolshie enough to beat the rap. When one senior member was stopped in his car soon after leaving a rally and found to have a bag containing nine kilos of high-quality cannabis resin beside him, he didn't hesitate to tell the police officers the truth. 'What a coincidence,' he told them. 'I was just on my way to the police station to hand this in. I found it at the rally. I think it might be drugs.' The Angel's fingerprints were found on the outside of the bag but not on the packets of drugs inside. It meant it was impossible to disprove his story – no matter how unlikely – and the charges were dropped.

It was a similar story when another Angel was stopped and found to have half a kilo of cocaine and a loaded handgun hidden behind a door panel of the vehicle. 'You've got me bang to rights,' he told the officers. 'I stole the car.'

Indeed, the vehicle was not registered to him or anyone else within the gang (though it wasn't until some hours later that the registered owner reported it stolen). With no fingerprint evidence, even the owner could not be charged with possession. All those connected to the vehicle were acquitted of all charges.

The Angels and the other biker gangs involved in the drugs trade protect themselves from police 'buy and bust' operations by restricting themselves to selling to those on a list of 'approved' customers. Particular deals are co-ordinated and run by individual bikers using a few associates, mostly prospects or hang-arounds (the two ranks below full membership of the club) to do the legwork. That way, even if they're caught, the club is unlikely to be implicated.

For this reason prosecutions involving large numbers of bikers or attempts to prove the club as a whole is involved in a conspiracy are rare, but the case against the St Austell-based Scorpio gang, jailed in the mid-1980s, shows the level of sophistication the trafficking can reach. The Scorpio had earned themselves more than £1 million by cornering the market for cannabis, amphetamines and LSD in the West Country, and Plymouth in particular, by using strong-arm tactics to drive other suppliers out of business.

Under the guidance of president Mark 'Snoopy' Dyce, gang associates purchased large quantities of amphetamine powder and cannabis resin in Amsterdam, paying for them using Thomas Cook money orders. Packets of drugs were then concealed in false compartments of specially adapted Ford cars and driven through Customs. Then, from a safe house in Rainham, Essex (deliberately far away from the gang's home turf), the drugs were wrapped in brown paper, labelled 'motorcycle parts' and sent to customers around the country using British Rail's Red Star parcel-delivery service. Ever conscious of police surveillance, drug deals were never spoken about but negotiated on paper. Like the Angels, they kept many of their drug supplies hidden away. Amphetamine worth £20,000 belonging to the gang was found buried in Southway Woods.

The Scorpio gang were relatively small and isolated so had to run every aspect of the smuggling operation themselves, but the Angels and the larger clubs are able to take full advantage of the fact that they have representatives in countries around the world to help ease the passage of narcotics from one border to another.

In 1994 detectives swooped on London's Hilton Hotel and arrested two Canadian Angels, Pierre Rodrigue and David Rouleau, who had travelled to London to supervise a planned shipment of more than a tonne of cocaine. Rouleau in particular, clean-cut and fresh-faced, looked far more like a city stockbroker or accountant than a member of a biker gang and typifies the way the Angels have adjusted their image to blend into the background rather than stand out from the crowd.

It was for this reason that Cunningham was freshly scrubbed and wearing a smart business suit the day he boarded the ferry to Ostend and vanished from the face of the earth. His final destination was Amsterdam where he was due to meet with Dutch Angels to pay for a consignment of cannabis that would be shipped to Britain later. There were also discussions to be had about future drugs deals and deliveries of ecstasy to enable the Angels to move into the club drugs market.

The Angels already control much of the cocaine, amphetamine and ecstasy trade in the Netherlands. They work closely with the Kampers – the Dutch gypsy community – who in turn are closely connected to members of the Colombian Cali cocaine cartel, and Cunningham is believed to have been promised an introduction.

'That part of the trip went smoothly,' one source close to the Nomads told me, 'but the problems began when he started heading back. Grumps had always been a popular member of the club, but a few months before he vanished, he had a big falling-out with some of the other Nomads. They unanimously voted to get rid of him and when the Angels do that, they mean something more than just kicking you out of the club.

'He had been involved at the highest levels and knew all their secrets and that meant he was a liability. When they decided to take him out, they knew it had to be done on a permanent basis. Members of the Dutch Angels agreed to do the job. They say

Grumps is at the bottom of some canal now. I don't think his body is ever going to be found.'

The legend that was to become the Hells Angels was born on 17 March 1948 when Second World War veteran Otto Friedli formed a new bike gang out of the remnants of two notorious fighting and drinking clubs.

Dozens of loose-knit biker groups, with names like the Booze Fighters and the Pissed Off Bastards of Bloomington, had sprung up across America in the mid-1940s. Motorcycles were cheap – many were sold off as military surplus – and appealed in particular to the hundreds of former soldiers and airmen who found it hard to cope with uneventful lives following the end of the war. They came together at weekends, riding hard and drinking even harder. For those who had nowhere to go when Monday came, the club turned into a surrogate family.

In 1947 at an American Motorcycle Association drag-racing meeting in the quiet town of Hollister, California, the Pissed Off Bastards rode in drunk and created absolute mayhem, fighting anyone and everyone and ripping the place to shreds. The local sheriff later described the scene as 'just one hell of a mess'. Quick to control the public-relations damage, the AMA denounced the Bastards, saying it was unfortunate that one per cent of motorcy-clists should ruin it for the law-abiding 99 per cent. To this day, outlaw biker gangs wear the '1%' badge with pride.

In the months following Hollister, internal tensions rose among the Bastards and the Booze Fighters so Bastard member Friedli broke away and took a few like-minded souls with him. Basing himself in San Bernadino, Friedli adopted a name favoured by fighter pilots – Hell's Angels – structured the gang along military lines and continued the theme on the gang's crest: a grinning, winged death's head wearing a pilot's helmet. (Friedli's seamstress forgot to include the apostrophe and it has been officially omitted ever since.)

The Angels continued the drinking, fighting and terrorising

tradition that had started at Hollister and their exploits reached a new level of public awareness following the release of the 1953 Marlon Brando film *The Wild One* (based loosely on the Hollister incident), which proved a Hollywood hit. That same year, the original Hells Angels chapter merged with San Francisco's Market Street Commandos to spawn the club's second chapter, and soon more popped up along the California coastline. Although the numbers were growing there was no real organisation among the groups, no single vision. All that changed, however, in 1957 when Ralph 'Sonny' Barger helped establish the Oakland chapter.

Charismatic, intelligent and willing to lead by example, it was under Barger's guidance that the Hells Angels chapters came together, hammering out bylaws, codes of conduct, and harmonising patches, colours, tattoos and clubhouses. When Friedli was sent to prison a year later, Barger took over as president. Although Barger insists he is not the leader of the Hells Angels, he is widely considered so by both law-enforcement officers and club members, and undoubtedly wears an unofficial crown.

The tales of violence and destruction culminated in 1964 when four Angels were accused of rape in the oceanside town of Monterey. The high-profile case not only saw the first of many, many headlines demonising the biker gang but also allegedly marked the beginning of the Angels' move into international drug-trafficking. In order to pay legal bills, so the legend goes, the Hells Angels made a few drugs deals, selling methamphetamines coast to coast.

The defence was successful and the rape suspects were acquitted, but the Angels saw no reason to stop their money-making ventures. Chapters were added in Zurich, Hamburg, Amsterdam and Montréal. George Wethern, a leading American Hells Angel, said at the time, 'The additions were designed to contribute to our image and business concerns, by providing a drug-route link, manufacturing a drug, supplying chemicals or distributing drugs to an untapped area.'

Infamy bred notoriety, and in the mid-1960s *The Nation* magazine sent a young Hunter S. Thompson to write about the Hells

Angels. Thompson returned to the bikers after completing the article, riding with the Hells Angels for a year while researching his book, *Hell's Angels: The Strange and Terrible Saga of the Outlaw Motorcycle Gang*. Soon afterwards Hollywood came calling again and Barger starred next to Jack Nicholson in the 1967 release *Hell's Angels on Wheels*. Rock stars such as Jerry Garcia of the Grateful Dead struck up friendships with the bikers, which Garcia admitted was a bit scary because the Hells Angels were, as he put it, 'good in all the violent spaces'.

That was proved beyond doubt on 6 December 1969, when the Hells Angels were hired – for $500 worth of free beer – to act as security guards for a Rolling Stones concert at Altamont Speedway outside San Francisco. Armed with pool cues, they attempted to keep order while drinking, smoking marijuana and dropping acid.

At one point a black, eighteen-year-old Stones fan named Meredith Hunter rushed the stage, just as the band finished playing 'Under My Thumb' and was beaten back. He rushed again, was pushed back, pulled a gun, and shot a Hells Angel in the arm. Barger later laid all the blame for what happened next firmly at Hunter's feet: 'When he fired, people started stabbing him. The guy killed himself by pulling the gun and shooting it into a crowd. And, to me, that's just part of everyday life in the Hells Angels – somebody shoots you, you stab him.'

But the idea that Hunter provoked the attack is only one version of the event. One eyewitness, Tony Sanchez, described the scene thus: 'A great six-foot-four grizzly bear of a Hells Angel had stalked across to Meredith [Hunter] to pull his hair hard in an effort to provoke a fight . . . A fight broke out, five more Angels came crashing to the aid of their buddy, while Meredith tried to run off through the packed crowd. An Angel caught him by the arm and brought down a sheath knife hard in the black man's back. The knife failed to penetrate deeply, but Meredith knew then that he was fighting for his life. He ripped a gun out of his pocket and pointed it straight at the Angel's chest . . . And then the Angels were upon him like a pack of wolves. One tore the gun from his hand, another stabbed him in the face and still another stabbed him repeatedly, insanely, in the back until his knees buckled.'

When the Angels finished with Hunter, several people tried to come to his aid, but an Angel stood guard over the motionless body. 'Don't touch him,' he said menacingly. 'He's going to die anyway, so just let him die.' It was never proven that Meredith actually had a gun. Later, arrests were made but the Angel concerned was acquitted. Although hundreds of people had witnessed the event – including the band, who had seen it from their stage – and although the whole grisly affair had been captured on film hired to document the gig for the band, no witnesses were willing to come forward.

Now, with their bad-boy reputation squarely in place and undeniably earned, the Hells Angels began to emerge as a more sophisticated outfit. They formed a corporation to protect their legitimate business interests, trademarked the infamous death's head logo and opened more chapters around the world.

The first British chapter of the Angels was formed in London in mid-1969 and it took only three years for the gang to achieve the same kind of status as their American brothers. In late 1972 eighteen-year-old Ian Everest, along with two others, abducted a fourteen-year-old Girl Guide off the streets of Winchester and dragged her along to an Angels party where he raped her in front of cheering clubmates. At the subsequent court case the girl told a horrified jury that Everest had laughed throughout the assault.

Sentencing him to nine years, Mr Justice Waller launched a thousand tabloid shock-horror headlines telling Everest: 'We have heard of Hells Angels as an utterly evil organisation, evil and corrosive of young people. I do not sentence you for being a Hells Angel, but no doubt the evil nature of that organisation has led you into this situation.'

Every few years something new happened to keep the image alive, often helped by the media's inability to tell the Hells Angels apart from other biker gangs. In 1980 a group of Angels ambushed members of the 'bootleg' Windsor chapters and shot its leader,

Richard Sharman, in the head three times. Miraculously, he survived.

The attack had come about because, despite dressing themselves in close copies of the official Hells Angels colours, the Windsor chapter had never applied for an official charter. Started up by local rockers they were only accepted into the official fold in 1985 shortly after one of the members, John Mikklesen, died in police custody. The fact that Mikklesen was black – an official Angels taboo – had played a significant part in the club failing to be sanctioned earlier.

In 1983 a Hells Angels party in Cookham ended in violence after a fight broke out in a queue where bikers were lining up to gang-rape a woman who had been staked out in a corner of the tent. The ensuing battle, chiefly between six members of the south London gang the Road Rats and some twenty-four members of the Manchester-based Satan's Slaves, involved axes, knives, shotguns and chains. Two Rats were killed but the remaining four fought on, stabbing and beating the Slaves and eventually herding around twenty into an old barn. They had just managed to set the building alight when the Angels intervened, wanting to know what was being done for the dead and injured.

Two years later the Angels made headlines again after terrorising a family living next door to the Windsor clubhouse. The bikers famously held axe-throwing competitions and, after complaints, first offered to buy the family out, then changed their minds. 'They had a meeting and we could hear them deciding it would be easier to kill us. They were shouting, "Kill them, kill them,"' said then neighbour Pat McSorley. The family decided to move.

It soon occurs to me that if I want to find out more about the dark side of the world of biking, I'm going to have to go to rallies, runs, biker pubs and do my best to blend in, something I won't be able to manage in my fifteen-year-old Vauxhall Astra. I briefly toy with the idea of buying a helmet and a set of leathers but quickly come to the conclusion that I'm going to have to get myself a bike.

I spend four days on a Direct Access course in north London, which allows you to go from novice to Easy Rider in a matter of days. I spend the first day on a Honda CG125 before moving on to a 500cc Kawasaki ER-5, driving around for hours on end practising my turns, manoeuvres and road craft in readiness for my test. Almost as soon as I begin the training I'm hooked. The sense of freedom, the element of danger and the whole Steve McQueen thing are there right from the start. Even at such a rudimentary level the appeal of the biker lifestyle is clear.

The day of the test comes all too soon and, though convinced I had messed it up, I'm surprised to find the examiner passing me (my first words when he told me were 'Good grief,' and I only just managed to stop myself adding, 'Are you mad? Have you lost your mind?') But although I am now legally able to ride a bike of any size, I'm still a long way from becoming a Hells Angel.

Joining the gang is out of the question. Even the God's Squad Motorcycle Club say that gaining membership to their organisation, which does nothing more sinister than extol the virtues of Christianity to bikers the length and breadth of the UK, takes on average around three years.

But there is no difficulty in obtaining a ticket to the Angels' most celebrated annual event: the Bulldog Bash.

From its humble beginnings in the mid-1980s when a couple of thousand bikers gathered in a field to drink and show off their customised machines, the Bulldog Bash has grown into Europe's premier biking event, attracting around forty thousand bikers from all over the world for a non-stop, four-day party. It all takes place at the Shakespeare County Raceway, one of Britain's premier drag-racing tracks, just south of Stratford-upon-Avon. Inside the grounds there is a massive beer tent, open twenty-four hours a day, of course, hundreds of food stalls, a shopping village, bungee-jumping, mini-motorbike tracks and tattoo parlours.

For those who find the heat too much one way to cool down is to submit to the topless bike wash where four young women, cropped T-shirts pushed up over their breasts, use sponges, buckets of soapy water and their bodies to put a smile on the face of the lads who have paid five pounds for five minutes of mammary delight.

In the evening there is a giant musical stage with top rock and heavy-metal bands – the Fun Lovin' Criminals were the headline act – as well as an all-night trance and dance tent. Up on stage the grinning death's head skull is replaced by a far more family-friendly image – a cute bulldog sitting astride a Harley, its little paws up on the handlebars.

After midnight that is the first of the Bulldog's famous 'novelty acts', which are suitable only for those with strong stomachs. Bands like the Impotent Sea Snakes and Kamakazi, who practise self mutilation and blood-letting on stage, push back the boundaries in keeping with the Angels traditions. By the time one of the women is threading syringes through her breast and upper thigh and attaching yet another clothes peg to her labia the tent is almost empty.

But one of the biggest attractions is the 'Run What Ya Bring' event, where bikers can run their machines on the quarter-mile-long drag strip. With some road-legal bikes achieving times of less than ten seconds on the mile strip, reaching speeds close to 160 m.p.h., you quickly understand why the RWYB is so popular. It provides the only opportunity for bikers to find out just how fast their machinery really is. Eager participants will line up for hours waiting for their chance to race while hundreds of spectators sit on the grass banks overlooking the track and enthusiastically cheer them on. More than once I saw racers complete their run and simply rejoin the queue.

The event is policed by the Angels themselves and, despite the vast numbers attending, in all the years it has taken place there has not been a single reported crime. The event is now recognised by Warwickshire Police as their least troublesome public event. Teams of Angels make regular 'security' patrols in customised black Ford Escorts that have had all the glass removed and large white swastikas painted on the sides. It's a menacing sight at the best of times so it's little wonder that there are dozens of tales of people losing wallets or purses full of money and finding them in the lost-property office with all their cash intact.

GANGS

It was at the Bulldog Bash that I first met Colin, an associate member of a leading back-patch gang – he has asked me not to say which one – who later agreed to be my guide to the inner workers of the biker world. I was parking my hired Honda VT750 Shadow, essentially a Japanese copy of a Harley, while Colin glided in on a heavily customised kit bike based on the genuine article. Colin's bike had been 'chopped' – fitted with extra long front forks – and the brightly painted Dayglo green and orange surfaces reflected around the gleaming chrome-covered engine. It was a remarkable machine, and he was clearly enormously proud of it. He soon lost me in a blur of technical detail as he explained how he had taken a 1984 Harley-Davidson FXRS 1340 V2 Evo and transformed it with a new swinging-arm section, ported cylinder heads, yokes, drive sprockets and hypercharger filters.

Although I had not initially told him that I was a writer researching a book about the Angels and other biker gangs, our conversation slowly moved on to the topic as we sat in the corner of the beer tent and heard someone complain about the price of the tickets for the Bash – thirty-five pounds in advance and forty-five on the gate. 'That's the trouble with this lot,' said Colin, nodding towards two patrolling Angels on the other side of the marquee. 'They're all about the money, these days. A couple of years ago I was leaving the bash and I saw some of the Angels collecting up some of the takings. There must have been at least ten bin liners, all of them stuffed with cash that they were putting in the back of this van. God knows what they do with all the money. They're making stacks of it from this place.'

The best estimates suggest the Angels earn at least £1.5 million from the bash, and they're not the only ones making money. Later in the afternoon I spoke to a hot-dog stall owner, told him I was thinking of getting into the business and ask him how much the Angels charge for a pitch. He smiled and whispered, 'Eight hundred quid a day.' I whistled and asked if it was worth his while. 'I'm still here, ain't I? And I keep on coming back, so something must be going right.'

*   *   *

Away from the bike shows, Colin and I meet up for a few drinks. At first he is shocked when I reveal my true motives for wanting to talk to him but, after being assured that his true identity will never be revealed, he agrees to fill me in on what he knows about the current back-patch gang scene.

He has never been a member of the Hells Angels but was once a prospect for a different biker gang and got to know several Angels as a result. He decided not to continue with the recruitment process after realising that he simply didn't have the time or the energy to commit fully to the lifestyle. He laughs at the idea of me thinking I could join any of the clubs, let alone the Angels. 'You're talking about a long, long process,' he says. 'You start out as a hang-around. That's a chance to get to know the club and for them to get to know you. That's before you can become a prospect, and that stage can last for at least a couple of years.

'You've got to be able to fight or you're not going to get anywhere. Your face has to fit. All that stuff about biting the heads off chickens, eating dogs and the like, some of it used to happen but it was never club policy. The hardest part is knowing how to deal with having a family. You always have to put the club first.

'It's a real commitment. You can't hold down a full-time job, because if the club needs you and calls on you, you have to be there. Most of the members will be self-employed because that gives them the flexibility they need. If you're single, you're expected to be there most evenings and weekends. If you have kids, you might get away with just the weekend but you'd still be expected to be around for any important meetings, etc. Or if there is a big party, you shame the club if you don't make it along.'

As for the criminality, in particular the links to drug-trafficking, Colin says it is an open secret within the biking world that members of the Angels and other gangs are heavily involved. 'You have to remember that when it comes to the Angels, the organisation is basically controlled from America. The guys here might say they are not the same and, in many ways, they are a few years behind, but if

America says jump, they all jump and know that if they don't, they're gonna get kicked out.

'When you look at the Angels in America, in Canada and across Europe, the evidence of their involvement in drug-trafficking is absolutely fucking overwhelming. A lot of the money that gets made is funnelled back to the US and that's what keeps it ticking over. The British Angels have to do their part. Most of the legwork is done by the prospects and hang-arounds so it never gets back to the club, they just keep a cut of the profits.'

Colin lights a cigarette as he casts his mind back to his own time as a prospect. His voice grows quiet as he tells me he did some things he was ashamed of, things that he would now rather not talk about.

'The whole point of being a prospect is that you have to do what you are told and that's how you show commitment. It doesn't matter how stupid, how insane or how distasteful the thing is, you have to do it and you can't question it. I know one guy, a former member of the Satan's Slaves, who decided to join the Angels. He did everything that was asked of him and finally they said they would allow him in on one more condition. He had to square it with the Slaves.

'The Angels insisted it would be okay but of course it wasn't. The Slaves put him in hospital for six months and when he came out the Angels gave him a patch. I know of cases where the Angels have been beating the shit out of some biker, two or three of them on one, and at the end because the guy has put up a good fight, they've offered him a patch too.

'Whenever there is trouble or something to be done, it's usually the prospects who are first to get involved. Sometimes it's because they are told to but more often it's because they volunteer. They know if they do something good for the club, it means they are more likely to get their patch sooner.

'When you go to something like the Bulldog Bash, you've got pretty much everyone in the biker fraternity all in one place, from the rich white-collar workers on their Harleys to despatch riders to the back-patch club members. It's hard to believe there is any tension but, of course, there always is. There are tensions and there are political pressures. Outsiders don't realise the ties and commitments members have to each other, it's like family but more so. And what would you do if someone messed with members of your family?

'The Bulldog Bash may be one of the most peaceful big events around, but that hides a lot of problems. So far as the Angels are concerned, there is always a war to be fought somewhere.'

CHAPTER THIRTEEN

No one can remember quite how it began and few can recall exactly what it was all about but, by the early 1990s, the vicious fighting between the Wolverhampton chapter of the Hells Angels and the Birmingham club known as the Cycle Tramps had reached its bloody peak. There had been literally dozens of assaults, numerous stabbings, the odd shooting and a number of mass rumbles in which huge groups of both gangs would rush one another, armed with motorbike chains, baseball bats and meat cleavers. Many predicted the Cycle Tramps – the only remaining outlaw gang in Birmingham – would soon be extinct.

Biker battles were nothing new in the West Midlands. A few years earlier the Pagans and the Ratae had fought a bitter six-day war that started with a series of raids by Pagans on members of the Ratae deemed to be living on their territory. Two days later more than thirty members of the Ratae and reinforcements from Humberside and Norfolk drove in twelve vans to the Pagans' headquarters in Leamington Spa, Warwickshire, and laid siege. After a brief stand-off the quiet street was engulfed in flames as both sides threw petrol bombs and the clubhouse began to burn. Shotgun blasts rang out and a team of Ratae 'commandos' made a frontal assault, firing a gun through the front door before storming the building. The first two to enter made it only as far as the hall before they were beaten back by knife- and sword-wielding Pagans. One was scalped Red Indian-style, while the other was stabbed in the neck. Both were dragged to safety by other Ratae and the rest of the gang hastily withdrew. By the time the police arrived they met an all-too familiar response: no one had seen or heard anything.

Three days later the Pagans visited Brackley, Northamptonshire, and attacked the home of the then vice-president of the Ratae, who managed to keep his attackers at bay using repeated blasts of a .410 shotgun. One of the attackers fired back with a weapon of his own, but accidentally hit fellow Pagan Stephen 'the Rabbi' Brookes, killing him instantly. Nine Pagans were eventually convicted of manslaughter; eight Ratae were convicted of conspiracy to cause grievous bodily harm.

But in early 1993 a delegation of bikers from the Cycle Tramps, visited first the Pagans, then the Ratae. Exactly what was said has never been made public but within the space of a few hours the rifts of the past seemed to have been forgotten. Representatives of all three clubs then travelled to Derby to visit another gang: the Road Tramps. At the time the Road Tramps ran the Rock and Blues Custom show held each summer and it was the largest event of its kind in the Midlands. The show has been going since 1983 and is well respected in the biker community as well as a solid money-spinner. The Road Tramps, like the Cycle Tramps, had been involved in a long-running dispute with the Wolverhampton Angels, who had expressed a considerable interest in taking over the Rock and Blues Custom show, with or without the Road Tramps' blessing.

A few weeks before the opening of the July 1992 show, Derbyshire police received a tip-off that the Hells Angels would mount an attack at some point during the proceedings. The police promptly forbade the Road Tramps to allow any Angels on to the site and unwittingly cleared the way for the most crucial development of the biker war to proceed unhindered.

A few hours after the show had opened, members of the Road Tramps, Cycle Tramps Pagans, Ratae and several other gangs, including the Stafford Eagles and the Road Runners, appeared and slipped on new jackets. Emblazoned on the back were colours that no one had ever seen before. The logo was a skull with a kind of Indian headdress made up of different-coloured feathers. One was blue and white – the colours of the Pagans. Another was red and blue, the Road Tramps, and yet another red and yellow, the Cycle

Tramps. There were seven feathers in all, each representing a different gang. The rivals had come together to form a brand new gang: the Midland Outlaws.

In August, a week after the show, there was a bungled attempt to nip the new alliance in the bud. A former member of the Cycle Tramps narrowly avoided death after answering a knock on his front door. As he walked down the hall, someone pushed the barrel of a sawn-off shotgun through the letterbox and fired. He survived and was later rehoused for his own safety.

Two weeks later at the Bulldog Bash, two Angels kidnapped a member of a neutral outlaw gang who was known to be friendly with members of the Midland Outlaws. He was tortured until he told everything he knew about their reasons for formation and their plans for the future. The Angels, it seemed, were running scared.

And with good reason. On an international scale, the second largest biker gang after the Hells Angels is known as the Outlaws. With upwards of forty chapters, mostly in America and Australia, they have a no-nonsense motto – 'God forgives, Outlaws don't' – and wear colours that are a close copy of those worn by Marlon Brando in *The Wild One*, depicting a skull sitting above a pair of crossed pistons.

Although for the most part the two clubs leave one another alone, there has been bad blood between them since 1974 when three Angels were murdered by two Outlaws in Chicago. Periodic violence has flared up ever since. The Midland Outlaws, it seemed, were 'prospecting' to join the ranks of one of the Angels' worst enemies. Throughout the biker world, the talk was not so much of whether the Midland Outlaws would launch an attack as of when it would be.

For a club to join *en masse* it must prove itself 'worthy' of wearing the colours. Exactly what this proof entails is not known, though past experience shows that a major attack or act of violence will often suffice. The Rowdies Motorcycle Club in Trondheim, for example, spent ten years hoping to be granted a charter to enable them to become the first Hells Angels in Norway. Then, one July, they launched a vicious knife and chain attack on a rival club, putting several of its members in hospital. Two weeks later the Rowdies received their Angels patches.

But then another gang came into the frame. The following summer Interpol tracked the movement of dozens of members of the third biggest of the international back-patch gangs – the Texas-based Bandidos – entering Britain and visiting members of the Midlands Outlaws. The Bandidos are one of the world's fastest growing outlaw clubs, whose battles with their rivals have been characterised by extreme acts of violence. Sometimes referred to as Bandido Nation, their colours depict a gun- and machete-toting Mexican cartoon character, and clearly state that they are an MG – motorcycle gang – rather than a club. Their motto is equally brash: 'We're the people our parents warned us about.'

For the Angels, the prospect of either club on British soil was bad enough (the Outlaws and Bandidos have a non-aggression pact and members of one often tattoo themselves with one other club's colours as a mark of respect) but tensions with the Bandido Nation in particular were at an all-time high.

The latter had announced their intention to open a chapter in Denmark, using former members of the Bullshit Motorcycle Club, which had broken up after their leader was gunned down by a Hells Angel in 1985. The Copenhagen chapter of the Bandidos opened in early 1993 and within six months the Bandidos had expanded into Sweden, Norway and Finland, and had numbers rivalling those of the Scandinavian Angels. Not only that, the Bandidos were becoming increasingly active in the local drugs scene, taking valuable sales away from Angels-sponsored dealers. Tensions between the two groups increased until the inevitable happened.

The fighting began in 1994 when a Hells Angel was shot dead in the southern Swedish port of Helsingborg during a fight that also saw a Danish Bandido wounded. In March a Finnish leader of the Bandidos, Jarkko Kokko, was shot dead in Helsinki. Days later Bandidos leaders were attacked at airports in Oslo and Copenhagen. In July a Danish Bandido was shot near Drammen in Norway.

A week or so later an anti-tank missile – one of a batch of twelve stolen from a Swedish army base – was fired at the empty clubhouse of a Finnish Hells Angels affiliate. The building was reduced to a smoking pile of rubble. Days later two similar rockets slammed into Angels clubhouses in Copenhagen and Jutland.

In October 1995 several Hells Angels were dining at the Stardust restaurant in Copenhagen when they were set upon by a group of Bandidos. Two Angels had to make a humiliating escape via the women's toilet. The incident prompted the Angels to obtain missiles and explosives of their own and go about seeking revenge.

Within a few weeks they had fired an anti-tank grenade at a prison in Copenhagen housing a Bandido accused of an earlier missile attack against the Angels. The Bandido was wounded but survived.

In October 1996, during the annual 'Viking Party' of the Hells Angels in their heavily fortified headquarters in Titangade, central Copenhagen, the Bandidos fired an anti-tank missile from the sloping roof of a nearby building. It tore through the concrete wall and exploded in a ball of molten metal. Louis Nielsen, a thirty-eight-year-old prospect for the Angels, was killed, as was twenty-nine-year-old Janne Krohn, a local woman who was only at the party because the Angels wanted to improve their image by opening the event to neighbours.

Shockwaves from the attack were felt throughout Europe and beyond, and as a result a bill was rushed through the Danish Parliament giving police sweeping new powers. The 'Biker Law' was used to prohibit gang members gathering in residential areas, and allowed police to close down many of the bikers' clubhouses. At the same time they introduced round-the-clock surveillance of the remaining biker strongholds, and kept a close watch on the key players in the conflict.

Yet, despite the clampdown, more violence followed.

In January 1997 a Hells Angel was shot dead in his car in Aalborg, Denmark, and six months later a car bomb exploded outside the Bandidos clubhouse in Drammen, Norway. A woman was killed as she drove past. The blast flattened the heavily fortified building, set nearby factories ablaze, and shattered windows three-quarters of a mile away.

That attack was followed by another three days later, in which one Bandido was killed and three wounded by a Hells Angels associate who opened fire at them outside a restaurant crowded with holidaymakers in the Danish resort town of Liseleje.

By this time both gangs were increasingly aware that the feuding could not be allowed to continue. The massive amount of self-imposed security, as well as the high cost of arms and explosives, had put a major financial strain on both groups. Soon, feelers were being put out in an effort to restore peace.

Officially, the last violent confrontation occurred on 7 June, 1997, when a Bandidos 'trainee' was shot dead by a Hells Angel in northern Zeeland. The toll stood at twelve dead and around seventy seriously injured. Shortly afterwards, live television coverage captured the emotive image of high-ranking Hells Angel Bent 'Blondie' Svane Jensen shaking hands with Bandidos leader Jim Tinndahn. The pair announced that, following a summer of negotiations, a truce was now in place. 'We have agreed to co-operate to stop what has been happening,' said Tinndahn.

The truth was that the two former enemies had drawn up an agreement in which every town and city had been systematically split up, right down to specific pubs, discothèques, and striptease clubs, in an effort to control their lucrative criminal activities. The 'contract' states that Hells Angels have 'sovereignty' over Denmark's three biggest cities – Copenhagen, Århus, and Odense – while Bandidos have control of the rest of Denmark. Major holiday locations in Jutland, which have a flourishing drugs trade every summer, have been divided on a town by town basis, while Randers, Aalborg and Horsens have been declared 'open', giving both gangs the right to operate.

'This deal not only gives the two groups a monopoly on crime in their respective territories, but also relative peace and quiet, and freedom from outside competition,' says Troels Jørgensen, head of the National Investigation Centre, which keeps bikers under surveillance.

But Kim Jenson, a spokesperson for the Angels, denied the contract covered any criminal activity. 'This agreement simply exists to prevent constant confrontation between our two gangs.'

Meanwhile, back in England, the Midland Outlaws (who had repeatedly and publicly declared their support for the Scandinavian Bandidos) and the Angels both focused on increasing their numbers and recruiting new members, seemingly gearing up for the inevitable clash.

In June 1997, just three months before the truce in Scandinavia had been announced, the Hells Angels heard that a small but notoriously violent London-based club called the Outcasts were attempting to absorb an equally small Hertfordshire club called the Lost Tribe. Concerned that such a move would make the Outcasts too great a force to be reckoned with, the Angels jumped in and made the Tribe honorary members. They made approaches to several Outcasts and invited them to become Angels. 'It was more like a threat than an invitation,' one Outcast said later. 'The Angels had received orders direct from the United States which said that unless they maintained their position as the premier biker gang in the country they would lose their charter. They made it very clear that if we didn't join them, they would destroy us.' A couple of Outcasts took up the offer but the vast majority remained determined to stand up to the might of the Angels.

But the Outcasts didn't see it that way. In November 1997 two members of the club were arrested in east London in possession of loaded shotguns, seemingly on their way to confront the Angels. There followed a series of minor clashes between the two gangs and it was clear that it was only a matter of time before things came to a head.

January 1998 saw the annual Rockers Reunion in Battersea. About 1700 people attended the concert, which has traditionally been regarded as an Outcasts event and had been trouble-free for fifteen years. But this time up to twenty Hells Angels were involved in a brutal attack on two Outcasts.

According to eyewitnesses, the Angels attacked 'like sharks', going in small groups, kicking and stabbing before retreating and another group taking over. Groups of four or five Angels, armed with knives, axes, baseball bats and clubs, swooped on their victims in wave after wave of attacks. Unarmed bikers equipped with headset microphones helped pick out the Outcasts from the crowd.

The first victim was thirty-three-year-old David Armstrong, a father of one, known as Flipper because he had lost his right leg while serving with the Royal Irish Regiment. He was dragged from his bike and hacked to death with axes and knives. He was stabbed four times in his abdomen and left leg. His lungs were pierced and he suffered severe internal bleeding. Armstrong's friend, Malcolm St Clair, raced to his aid but soon became the next target. Italian photographer Ramak Fazel, who was passing by, watched in horror as a bearded biker laid into St Clair with an axe. 'He was bringing his axe up over his head. The victim was lying with his head between his knees.' Fazel then saw another man pull out a ten-inch knife and continue the attack. 'The knife was thrust in on both sides. Then they calmly walked away. It was cold-blooded.'

Fazel then saw two of the attackers climb into a Volvo and made a note of the registration number on a napkin. The car was traced to Ronald Wait, vice-president of the Essex Angels – known as the Hatchet Crew. He was arrested after Mr Fazel picked him out at an identity parade.

Wait initially said he was drinking at a bikers' clubhouse in Reading, Berkshire, at the time of the killings. The alibi was supported by several members of the club, but dismissed. Wait, who has had triple heart bypass surgery and suffers from angina and diabetes, then said he was too ill to have taken part in any attack. Despite this, he was taken to court to face trial.

During a brief spell in the witness box Wait, who gave his occupation as security guard, refused to talk about the incident, explaining the Angel code of silence thus: 'The rules state that you are not allowed to make a statement to police, or speak to them if it involves another club member. You have to seek permission to speak to the police.' Wait was initially charged with murder, but the prosecution decided not to proceed with the charge and he was eventually found guilty of conspiracy to cause grievous bodily harm and jailed for fifteen years.

The weeks that followed the deaths of Armstrong and St Clair saw more clashes between the two gangs. In March a fertiliser and petrol bomb was found at the clubhouse of the Angels' Lea Valley chapter, in Luton, Bedfordshire. A Kent motorcycle shop owned by members of the Hells Angels was the target of an attempted arson attack. Then two Outcasts were shot close to the clubhouse of the Outcast Family chapter in east London. Both victims survived but refused to co-operate with the police.

In June 1998 Outcast Richard 'Stitch' Anderton was arrested after officers from the National Crime Squad found a massive haul of guns and ammunition in his home. They believed the weapons were intended to be used as part of an assault on several properties owned by members of the Hells Angels. Detectives stopped Anderton in his car and found a loaded Smith & Wesson .45 revolver tucked into the waistband of his trousers. A search of Anderton's flat uncovered weapons, including an Uzi submachine-gun, an AK47 rifle and a rocket launcher.

After his arrest Anderton claimed he had been told that the Angels had drawn up a 'death list', containing the names of several Outcasts who were to be 'killed on sight'. Anderton had previously been a 'prospect' member of the Angels. He left for unknown reasons and was believed to have been placed on the death list because he was considered a traitor. (The two men murdered at the Rockers Reunion were also former Angels associates.) Fearing for his life, Anderton moved from Essex to Dorset and armed himself with the handgun. He claimed the other weapons and the drugs were merely being stored at his property.

The Outcasts subsequently disbanded and joined forces with the Midland Outlaws who, in early 2000, were awarded a charter by the US Outlaws and officially welcomed into their fold. The multi-feathered headdress has gone, replaced by the skull and crossed pistons.

Since the start of the new millennium the biker world has been relatively quiet. But there are stormclouds on the horizon. And the biggest battle of all might be waiting in the wings. While the Nordic Biker War was raging and even when it was over, the big question was when the hostilities would reach the UK. 'You guys in Britain are sitting on a delayed-action timebomb,' warned Sergeant Jean-Pierre Levesque of Canada's Criminal Intelligence, one of the world's experts on biker gangs. 'I think what is happening in Scandinavia will have to happen in the rest of Europe. I'm surprised that Britain hasn't been hit yet.'

At the time the main reason given was that the Bandidos had no representation in the UK. Even with the Midland Outlaws (subsequently the Outlaws) pledging support, the situation was never going to be as tense as it would be if there were bikers riding around with Bandidos colours on their backs on British soil. Even with their numbers dwindling, the combined might of the Angels would still outnumber any single prospect club, making it impossible for the Bandidos to get a foothold anywhere in the UK.

However, in early 2003 the Bandidos opened chapters on two of the most southerly parts of Great Britain, the Channel Islands of Guernsey and Jersey. The Bandidos arrived in Guernsey after absorbing an existing gang, the Islanders, who were made prospects soon after their clubhouse was raided by police and a significant number of drugs and weapons were found. Guernsey also supports a small branch of the Bandidos' 'sister' club, the Outlaws.

Nearby Jersey also has branches of both the Bandidos and the Outlaws. The current membership of both gangs throughout the Channel Islands is unknown but, with no Hells Angels on either island, many within the biking world believe this is just the beginning.

'The Bandidos are one of the most formidable and violent biker gangs in existence,' says the outlaw biker specialist at the National Criminal Intelligence Service. 'They have strong links to the drugs trade and have shown themselves more than willing to defend their turf with violence. They have been responsible for dozens of murders, many of them committed in broad daylight with no regard for public safety. They have access to military-grade weapons, including rocket launchers and assault rifles. In September 2003 they punished their former leader in Copenhagen for leaving by planting a massive bomb under his car. The blast was so huge it could be heard miles away. The Bandidos have been expanding ever since the sixties and show no sign of slowing down. It is unlikely they will stop at one or two British chapters. The significance of seeing the first Bandidos chapter on UK soil cannot be understated.'

Detectives in Britain and across Europe are watching events on the Channel Islands with great interest.

CANNABIS

CHAPTER FOURTEEN

Jason points a stubby finger across the street as a heavily laden tram passes by. 'Just through there, you see it? That's where it is,' he says softly. 'I'm telling you, that's the Piccadilly Circus of drugs dens. It's where just about every major gang in the South-east gets their gear from.'

Jason should know. He spent a frantic eight months working for a major cannabis-trafficking gang based in Essex before deciding to retire. During that time he helped to import more than a tonne of high-quality cannabis and never once got caught.

Jason and I are in Amsterdam, standing just off the Damrak on the edge of the red-light district looking at a small coffee shop on a corner a few streets away. Jason, who has no desire to see the owners again, waits elsewhere while I go for a closer look. Inside, the smoky interior is tastefully laid out with dark-wood booths and mirrors. A menu at the counter shows that Thai grass is available at four euros fifty per gram, skunk at five euros and the subtly named AK47 at seven fifty while Nepalese hash weighs in at ten euros. The crowd is made up mostly of tourists, some American, most British, whose eyes have glazed over as they enjoy the delights of being able to smoke a joint without fear of arrest.

Cannabis was first decriminalised and coffee shops introduced in Holland in 1976. The experiment was introduced to reflect what the Dutch see as a fact of life: most young people experiment with illegal substances. If you let them buy and use 'soft' drugs in a regulated setting, you can keep them away from street dealers pushing highly addictive 'hard' drugs like heroin. The approach appears to be working so far as drug use among the Dutch is concerned – only 26 per cent of the Dutch will use cannabis in their lifetime compared to 66 per cent of Britons – but Amsterdam has become a centre of organised crime.

In the early days, coffee shops sold mostly imported cannabis resin but now the market is increasingly being dominated by Dutch-grown grass. Although Holland's climate is not particularly conducive to growing marijuana, the use of artificial lighting for indoor growing has become highly advanced. There are now hundreds of named varieties of seeds available and large-scale cultivation supplies the coffee shops with a good range of exotic herbs.

As part of a scheme to reduce criminal infiltration of the cannabis market, Dutch law allows anyone to grow up to a dozen plants in their home for their personal consumption. Commercial growing, however, remains illegal, so the vast indoor greenhouses that supply most of the coffee shops keep their locations as secret as possible.

Today, coffee shops can sell up to five grams of cannabis per transaction, as long as they obey five rules: no minors, no alcohol sales, no hard-drug sales, no advertising and no 'public nuisance'. They are also limited to holding no more than 500 grams of stock at any one time, but this rule is almost always broken, particularly at the bigger shops.

Because cannabis is decriminalised rather than legalised, it creates a bizarre *Catch-22* situation: coffee-shop owners can sell small amounts of cannabis to customers but it is illegal for them to purchase the bulk supplies they need to keep stock. It's known as the front-door/back-door problem: if the Dutch government tolerates people going in at the front door of the coffee shop, what about the back door, the supply? Unofficially police authorities allow 'ethical dealers' – individual small-scale suppliers supposedly untainted by international trafficking rings – to handle transactions. But the truth is that more than 90 per cent of Amsterdam's coffee shops are controlled by organised crime.

Huge quantities smuggled in from abroad or grown on the secret farms are distributed to the coffee shops by gangsters, who sell off the excess to anyone who can afford it. Certain coffee shops – like the one Jason had pointed out to me – are particularly well known for this. Providing you know the owner, you are allowed to enter via the rear door and make your way up to the office above the main bar where you can negotiate for as many kilos as you like of whatever you fancy.

Living on the edge of criminality, Jason first got involved when he started selling puff for a notorious local villain, Syd. 'Selling the stuff had shown me how easy it was to make a little bit of money at that end and I knew that the profits from smuggling were going to be much higher. Syd seemed to be doing very well out of it and I wanted some of what he had.

'But Syd had doubts. He was worried about the fact that, at the time, I'd never been abroad in my life – I'd only got a passport for the first time a week or so earlier. He'd decided to stick to his usual team but then Fate lent a helping hand. One of the crew, a guy called Paul, got himself arrested for breaching a warrant banning him from entering Belgium. He had just been caught out by a routine Customs check as he was getting off the boat and they discovered he was the subject of a ten-year ban. It all meant that the gang was one man short for the next trip so Syd called on me.

'We met up with another member of the team, Peter, and made our way to Folkestone. On the way Syd told me that he wanted me to go to Amsterdam with him to meet John, his main contact over there because, with Paul in prison, I'd be making the trips over there to complete the first stage in the smuggling process.

'All I had to do was to pick up the drugs in Amsterdam, having negotiated a good price, then drive them all the way to Belgium – there's no border between the two countries so I didn't have to worry about being stopped unless I did something really silly or I was just plain unlucky. Once in Belgium, Syd would meet me at the beach in his specially adapted speedboat. I'd load the drugs in and he'd set off back to England where he would make for a secluded beach and meet his friend Jack, who would help to unload the drugs. Once Syd was on his way, I'd be free to make my own way back on the ferry and, even if I did get stopped and searched, there would be nothing to incriminate me. I have to admit, it sounded like a pretty good plan and the two grand a time he promised me for the work sounded even better.

'We got to Folkestone and Syd pulled out a bundle of cash from his bag to cover the cost of the tickets. "How much you got in there anyway?" I said, as a joke, really. Syd looked at me. "Eighty grand." He said it so casually, I tried not to sound like I'd never seen that much money before in my life. "Oh. Right. Drinks are on you, then." I guess until that point I hadn't realised the scale of his operation.

'We finally got to Ostend in the early hours of the morning and I drove all the way to Amsterdam along the coast road. By the time we pulled into the centre of the city and Syd told me where to park, I was absolutely knackered.

'We walked to the café, which is on a road that runs parallel to the Damrak and nearly opposite a police station. When we arrived John wasn't there and we waited in the bar. The place was full of English blokes just like us, none of whom were smoking. And in every group, there would be one bloke holding a bag just a little bit too carefully. And slowly I realised that everyone there had come to do a deal.

'This tall blond guy with a pushbike arrived and put his head through the door. He saw the three of us sitting there, stared at us for a minute, and then came over and introduced himself. Syd and John were being really friendly – over-friendly. It was obvious that they hadn't actually met before. John had been in prison in Britain at the same time as Syd and they had been put in touch with each other through a mutual friend.

'John invited us all upstairs to the flat above the café. The place was full of masses of video equipment with loads of cameras trained on the café below. Apart from that, the room was very basic with a large table, one big corner sofa, a couple of chairs and a ski-machine for exercising.

'We all sat around drinking coffee and chatting about drugs and exchange rates because everything there was bought in guilders. He also explained that he had no drugs for us to buy and could not say when there might be some as there was currently a shortage across the whole of Amsterdam. He simply didn't know whether it would be soon or not. Syd decided that he couldn't take the money with him back to England so he decided to leave it with John – I guess he trusted the guy completely by then. It was left that John would contact Syd, and I would go over and do the deal with John to ensure the exchange rate was correct.

'A couple of days later, Syd rang to say that the drugs were ready to be picked up. It was time to go abroad again. I drove over to Syd's and then followed him in his car to the pub where we had met Pete the last time round. The three of us then went to a cashpoint in Clacton where Syd took out two hundred and fifty pounds – money to cover our expenses.

'It was another overnight ferry so it was nearly ten a.m. the following morning when we met John in Amsterdam. We agreed a price of £1150 per kilo, which gave us just under seventy kilos of top-quality cannabis resin. The drugs themselves weren't kept at the café so we had to wait for them to be brought to us. One of John's business partners pulled up outside the café in a brand new Merc about three hours later with the drugs in his boot. Rather than just taking them there and then, I asked him to guide me to the main road out of the city so I didn't end up driving round in circles for hours. Once I knew where I was, he pulled over and we swapped the drugs over from the boot of his car to mine and then I set off towards Belgium.

'We only made one stop on the way – at a payphone to call Syd and let him know that we were on our way to Blankenberg. He had a four-hour journey across the English Channel and wasn't particularly keen to leave unless he knew we definitely had the goods. I could hear the excitement in his voice as I told him that everything was fine and that we'd meet up with him as planned. It was the first time he had done any proper smuggling since he'd been sent to prison back in 1990. As far as he was concerned, the good old days were back again.

'We made really good time and got to Blankenberg about three hours early. The area had been chosen because it had a perfect ready-made smuggling spot that Syd had taken advantage of many times in the past. If you stand on the pier and look out to sea, on your left is a beautiful, ten-mile-long sandy beach. On your right there are three or four really ugly great concrete pipes, which take sewage or something into the sea. The pipes stick up out of the water a good few feet and Syd was planning to bring the boat up by the second pipe on the right. That way he'd be hidden from the beach and the pier.'

The pair had been given a Marine Band radio to communicate with Syd once he got within range. Although he had a satellite-navigation system on the boat it was only accurate to within twenty metres and he would need guidance for the final approach. Jason and Peter planned to flash a torch out to sea to help Syd find their position.

'We soon saw the silhouette of the boat come into view, packed all the drugs in and then Peter climbed on board. Syd turned to me, a big grin on his face. "Call Jack, tell him that it's all going to plan." The boat had come so far into shore that it had virtually been grounded, I had to push it back out to sea and the water was coming up to my chest. I pushed the boat as hard as I could but it just couldn't seem to break free of the waves that were pushing it back to shore. Then suddenly, the propeller caught and it shot off into the darkness. I was soaking wet and walked slowly back to the car where I changed into my tracksuit bottoms and trainers. It was absolutely freezing and so was the water, but I was so worked up with the adrenaline that I couldn't feel the cold at all. I was shaking, but it was with excitement. All my nerves and fear had gone and all I could think was, Fuck, I've done it. I've got away with it. I've got to admit, it was a great feeling.'

Jason made the short drive from Blankenberg to Ostend, arriving just in time to learn that he had missed the last ferry. The next one didn't leave until seven the following morning, which in turn meant he would not be at home until the middle of the following after-noon. Not wanting to spend the night in his car he decided instead to drive to Calais where a ferry to Dover would be leaving at two thirty a.m.

'When I reached the French-Belgian border, I got pulled over by one of the guards and asked where I was going. They searched my car and found my wet clothes in the boot and asked what I'd been up to. I was feeling confident and cocky – after all, there was nothing to link me to any kind of drug-smuggling. I had nothing to fear. I told the guard that I'd been playing around in the sea earlier that day and I'd missed the last ferry home from Ostend so I decided to go back via Calais so that I'd still be home the following morning. He looked a bit suspicious but checked my passport, ran my name through the computer and let me go.

'I got to Calais and, on my way to the boat, I got pulled over by French Customs. "Fucking hell," I said. "I've already been searched once tonight." The guy's face didn't even break into a grin let alone a smile. "Not by me you haven't." He proceeded to give the car a really good going-over but, of course, couldn't find anything so he let me get on the boat. I tried to get to sleep on the ferry but I couldn't because the crossing was so rough. Once we got to Dover, the only thing on my mind was getting back home and going to bed as quickly as possible.

'I drove the car off through Customs and, as sod's law would have it, I got pulled over again. I was so tired, so totally exhausted, that I just couldn't handle it. I freaked out. I was swearing and shouting and going on about the fact that I must have some kind of guilty sign stamped on my forehead because I'd been pulled over twice already. In the end I think they felt sorry for me. They just photocopied my passport and let me go home.

'We did another run a few weeks later, then another, and before I knew it I felt like a veteran. When it came to the fifth time Peter was off on holiday so Syd wanted me to find someone to go to Amsterdam with me – I'd be running the whole thing. It also meant I'd be the one going back in the boat. For my trouble I'd get double the usual fee.

'The next day Syd gave me seventy grand and strict instructions to try and get grass rather than resin, even though it was bulkier and a lot harder to handle. There was, of course, method in his madness. Syd charged three hundred pounds per kilo to import drugs. It didn't matter what he was importing, that was the amount he charged. Because grass was a bit cheaper per kilo than resin, it meant we came back with an extra thirty or so kilos, which meant that Syd earned an extra nine thousand for taking exactly the same risk. Clever boy, old Syd.

'I took my mate Christian and we got the overnight ferry from Felixstowe to Zeebrugge, then drove to Amsterdam. Syd had phoned John a couple of days earlier to tell him to expect me, and within a couple of hours I was heading to Blankenberg with three nylon laundry bags full of grass in the boot of my car.

'Syd and the boat arrived at the rendezvous at dusk, sticking out like a sore thumb because it wasn't as dark as it had been the time before. But Christian and I loaded the boat and I got in. I was trying to pretend that I was really cool about it but the truth was I was really excited about being in the boat. I wasn't disappointed. When we sped off it was the most incredible sensation. There was loads of noise and spray flying up all over the place, and because we were so low down, it felt like we were going at a million miles an hour. Syd was in front and I was directly behind him. The sea was really calm, as flat as a pancake, and in the half-light, you could see for miles. It was like being on some gigantic pond. Absolutely fantastic.

'After about ten minutes, when we were well out of sight of Blankenberg beach, Syd stopped the boat and started fishing around in a bag. "Here, put this on," he said, handing me a buoyancy aid. "The weather's not too clever ahead so you'd better wear it. Unfortunately, I've only got the one life-jacket and I'm wearing it." As I put the buoyancy aid on, I had a good look at Syd. I saw that, as well as the life-jacket, he was wearing a full dry suit – proper boating clothing. He also had a safety line attached to the console so if he fell in, he wouldn't end up separated from the boat. If I fell in, my waders would fill up with water and I'd sink to the bottom in seconds. All I could do was hold on. And pray.

'We set off again and Syd told me that, rather than sitting down, I should straddle the seat directly behind him. That way, if the boat left the water for second and came down with a bang, my legs would act like suspension springs. After about half an hour, the land behind me was vanishing fast – and so was my excitement about my first-ever trip in a speedboat. The waves were getting quite rough now and we were bouncing up and down like a trampoline. We'd started out speeding along at about thirty-three knots but now we were down to about twelve knots. I decided the best policy was just to keep my eyes shut and use my ears instead. I knew that when I heard the engine note change it meant the boat had come out of the water and the whole thing was airborne. That was my signal to hold on extra tight and brace myself for the landing.

'I was concentrating really hard but one time, I don't know, I must have just lost my focus for a second because I slipped. I just managed to grab the edge to stop myself going over. I was rolling all over the place and I was bawling like a baby until Syd stopped to have a look at what was going on. He switched on a torch and saw immediately that the main fuel tank had split. We couldn't see the hole but we could see the fuel slowly leaking out. Naturally, I started to panic. After all, I didn't have Syd's experience – this was all new to me. But what really freaked me out was that Syd started to panic as well. He said we'd have to sit on the seats – even though it was more dangerous and made the boat less stable – and that we'd have to go as fast as possible to make sure we hit the shore before we ran out of fuel altogether. He reprogrammed the GPS so that we headed for the nearest bit of land rather than the intended landing site. If we could get close enough, he explained, Jack, the man he used to help unload the drugs at the other end, could always come out and get us in his speedboat, but if we ran out of fuel where we were, we'd have to call the coastguard and that would mean dumping seventy grand's worth of drugs over the side.

'We were flying along and I was absolutely terrified. Syd was trying to work out where we were but the GPS was playing up. He reset it to read the depth of the water rather than location so he could try to work out how close we were but somehow he fucked it up. The whole screen went blank.

'So there we are in the pitch black with no guidance system, totally fucking lost and with a boat that's pissing away fuel going round and round in circles. Then Syd perked up and pointed to some poxy little light he could see in the distance. He said it was definitely Clacton pier, or maybe Walton pier, and that he knew where we were, probably. Either way, he reckoned we were only four miles from the coast. I was just gearing myself up to feel a bit more confident when, right on cue, the engine died and we ran out of fuel completely.

'We switched to the reserve tank but that was empty too. We primed the carbs on the engine by hand and it started up, went about fifty yards and then stopped again. We kept on doing it and I had to rock the boat from side to side – the last thing I wanted to do – to try to get the last remaining splashes of fuel into the pipes.

'Then Syd managed to get the GPS working again. I don't know what he did. I don't even think he knew what he did. I just heard him say, "Fuck me, it's working again," and at last we were going in the right direction. We had to kangaroo hop all the way with the engine firing and dying every few yards, but when we got about half a mile from the spot where Jack was, we realised it was just about shallow enough for me to get out and push the boat to the shore. So I did.

'I'd never been so happy to see Jack as I was when I saw him sitting on the beach waiting for us. I could have kissed him. He helped us drag the boat up to his Range Rover and we started unloading the drugs.'

It was to be Jason's last trip. Syd hooked up with a new partner – a petty criminal called Russell and found a new, more profitable route. There, cars would drive down to Spain where, using his contacts, Russell was able to buy cannabis for just £750 per kilo. (Cannabis, like all drugs, gets cheaper the closer you get to the source country. Falling prices mean that today, bringing it over from Amsterdam is barely worthwhile. The extra risk of bringing it all the way from Spain, or better yet Morocco, produces a far higher return.) The three cars would then head back north in convoy. The drugs would be in the middle car and the other two vehicles would be spaced out, one a mile or so ahead and the other a mile or so behind. That way, if either car thought they saw anything suspicious or that they were being followed, they could radio the middle car and give them a chance to change the route or dump the drugs.

'The really clever part was that Russell's gang included a couple of women,' says Jason. 'Rather than a bunch of single blokes travelling on their own, which always looks suspicious, each car in the convoy looked like a couple off on their holidays. The cars would come up through France and then Belgium where the drugs would be driven up to the beach at Blankenberg and Syd would meet them on his boat.

'It sounded good but by then I was glad I was out of it. Customs had been watching them and they all ended up getting nicked. I'd left it alone just in time.'

Jason's experience of cannabis-smuggling as something of a *Boy's Own* adventure is typical of the way many see what is by far the most popular drug on the planet.

Derived from *Cannabis sativa*, a plant related to nettles and the hop that is believed to have originated in India, cannabis still grows wild in many parts of the world reaching heights of up to five metres and flowering between late summer and mid-autumn. It is the leaves and flower heads that contain delta-9 tetrahydrocannabinol (THC), the main psychoactive chemical component; however, THC potency varies considerably. The average for resin is between two and eight per cent while herbal 'skunk' or 'sinsemillia' can have as high a content as 24 per cent. Cannabis oil, distilled from resin and rarely seen in the UK, contains up to 70 per cent THC. (The stem of the plant provides hemp, a fibrous substance that was, and continues to be, used to make ropes and sails. Low-THC varieties of cannabis used to be widely grown throughout England: both

Hampstead in north London and Hemel Hempstead in Hertford-shire were named after the acres of hemp fields that for years were cultivated there.)

Cultivation dates back thousands of years. The first written accounts of cannabis use can be found in Chinese records dating from 2800 BC. However, experts widely accept that cannabis was being used for medical, recreational and religious purposes for thousands of years before that, relieving the pain of childbirth in Roman Palestine and putting a smile on the face of Greek philo-sophers.

When it first came to Britain in the nineteenth century, and was sold by an Oxford Street pharmacist, one of its benefits, recorded in the *Lancet*, was 'restoring the appetite which had been lost by chronic opium drinking'. Although it was made illegal in 1928, its popularity has grown ever since. Thanks to advances in genetic engineering and careful blending of brands, the average cannabis joint available today is around ten times stronger than those that were being passed around in the 1960s.

This increase in strength has led to an increase in associated health problems. Although most cannabis-users find the drug helps them to relax and chill out, others find themselves feeling paranoid, or, worse, violent and aggressive. An American study of 268 murderers showed that almost a quarter of them had been under the influence of cannabis when they committed their crimes and that many claimed they would not have killed had it not been that their inhibitions were lowered by the drug. In Britain the president of the Coroners Society has declared that cannabis is increasingly the factor behind deaths recorded as accidents or suicides. He estimates that in 2003, cannabis was a significant contributory factor in about ten out of 100 deaths with which he dealt.

Cannabis consumption has been linked to depression, paranoia and other mental-health problems. But any health problems linked to cannabis pale alongside those caused by alcohol and tobacco. For this reason the Government has bowed to pressure from the pro-cannabis lobby and, in January 2004, reclassified the drug from

Class B to Class C. Although supply and trafficking remain illegal, possession for personal use is no longer an offence for which the police can make an arrest.

Britain now has the highest rate of use in Europe and the annual market is worth at least £1 billion. There are an estimated 1.5 million regular cannabis smokers in Britain, spending around £800 a year each on their drugs. Another 1.5 million count themselves 'occasional' users and the numbers of both are steadily growing. Beloved of ageing hippies, rebellious teenagers, and the middle-aged – men and women with equal enthusiasm – it is the only drug that truly transcends generations, with many households where parents and children share the same stash.

Most regular users obtain their supplies from small neighbourhood dealers, who often conduct their business from their own living rooms, or directly from friends, all of which adds to the sense that smoking cannabis has little to do with organised crime.

This could not be further from the truth.

CHAPTER FIFTEEN

Martin agrees to talk only on condition that I do not use his real name and say nothing about his current location other than that it is a high-security British prison. A well-spoken, middle-aged business-man, he recently allowed his greed to get the better of him when he dabbled his toe in the waters of high-level cannabis smuggling. Within a few weeks he found himself working alongside some of the most notorious villains in the UK and, following a police bust, is now in fear of his life.

'I'd been working in the import/export business but all legitimate. I was doing okay but not as well as I'd have liked, and word must have got out to a friend of a friend who suggested a way I might make a lot more money.

'Initially I thought they were talking about cigarettes but I soon found out the truth. If it had been anything other than cannabis I would never have got involved. I'd smoked a bit of dope when I was younger, mainly during my student years, and had this romantic notion that the people in charge of bringing the stuff into the country were all a bit like Howard Marks – well-educated, well-groomed sorts with hippie tendencies, who felt it was part of their mission in life to help people to chill out. I guess it might have been like that once, but it certainly isn't any more.

'The people I was working for threw me right in at the deep end. I was working for gangs in Nottingham, Cardiff, Liverpool, Man-chester, Birmingham, London, Kent and Southampton. They were big-time dealers ordering hundreds of kilos at a time.

'I collected the money for these shipments and arranged for it to be sent back to the leaders of the gang who were in Spain and

CANNABIS

Gibraltar. I guess I always knewthat somewhere up the supply chain cannabis was big business, but the scale of it astonished me. In the space of a few weeks I had dealt with more than £75 million.

'I'd fallen in with one of ten or so gangs operating at the top level. They were bringing in twenty tonnes of cannabis each month and could bring in a further ton of cocaine or heroin at the same time. It took only three weeks of involvement for me to realise I was in way over my head and that I had to be out, but by then it was too late.'

Following a tip-off, officers from Customs and the National Crime Squad followed one of the gang's lorries and raided it as it pulled into a shopping centre in Southampton. They found three tonnes of high-quality cannabis resin. Martin was arrested soon afterwards – more than £700,000 in cash was found at his home – and that was when his problems really began.

'A lot of people got arrested but, as is always the way, the main organisers had managed to get away clean. I'd never been in trouble with the police before. As soon as they locked me in the cell I had pretty much decided the best thing was to plead guilty. They had made it pretty clear in the initial interview that they had all the evidence they needed against me. It had all taken place in such a short period of time that I hadn't had a chance to get rid of any paperwork or anything.

'But everyone else in the gang was pleading not guilty. I didn't think it was going to be a problem – I wasn't planning on saying anything – but they didn't see it that way. Because my plea was different the police took me to court separately from everyone else. When I got up into the dock I had a quick look around the public gallery to see if my friends and family were there. They were, but so was another man. He was the chief bodyguard of the man who was at the head of the gang, one of those who had got away. I'll never forget the look he gave me. His eyes were so cold, so dead. I felt like I was going to pass out.

'Once I'd been sentenced, officers from the National Crime Squad came to see me in prison to see if I could tell them anything.

They wanted to know about large quantities of Class A drugs that the gang had been bringing in. They said they knew I had been working for some extremely serious people, and that if I helped them, they could arrange a huge reduction in my sentence. I told them I had nothing to say, but they told me to think about it and that they would come back.

'A few days later I was told that my solicitor had come to see me. I was surprised – I wasn't expecting him – but made my way down to the meeting room anyway. When I arrived I saw that it wasn't my solicitor, it was the solicitor of the leader of the gang. He got straight to the point. He knew all about my meeting – I have no idea how – and said that if I talked to the police, I would get a bullet in the head. He said that he'd be keeping an eye on me during my time in prison and that he'd been authorised to send me a little money every now and then.

'He knew so much about what had been said it was almost as if he'd been sitting in the room when I had the meeting. He even knew the number of my prison cell. By the time the meeting was over I was a nervous wreck. I became completely paranoid. I felt I couldn't trust anyone. I felt the only way I could possibly be safe was if I co-operated with the police and got them to agree to protect me. I knew the gang I was dealing with had a great deal of power, I just didn't realise how much I had underestimated them.

'The police said they could only help if I made a statement against the gang leader, which I did. They then began discussing proposals for placing me in the witness-protection programme and moving me to a special prison unit where I would be beyond the reach of the gang. They said they would make inquiries and get back to me.

'Two weeks later I had another legal visit and this time I was astounded to see a solicitor for one of the other members of the gang waiting for me. I had never met the man before but I had seen him making his way in and out of the visit room. He had a reputation for dealing only with wealthy, guilty criminals and almost always managing to get them off. My day went from bad to worse. He explained that he had seen the transcripts of the interview I had given to the police and wanted to know what I was planning.

'At that moment the prison staff came in and explained that I had been shown into the wrong room by mistake. A few doors down, the officers from the National Crime Squad were waiting for me. They explained that a Customs officer had been arrested for corruption and that they suspected he may have been passing information about me onto members of the criminal gang. They were concerned, distraught, saying it was the first time anything like this had ever happened to them. I was absolutely terrified, too terrified even to tell them what the solicitor in the other room had told me.

'The police said that for my own safety I was immediately being moved to another prison and that they would have to carry out the interviews once again. This time I refused point-blank.

'I know that I am being watched. Prison is not a safe place to be and I will be here for at least ten more years. Not a day goes by that I don't worry about being maimed or killed. Even though I never gave evidence against anyone in the gang, they know I once said that I would. I'm going to spend the rest of my life looking over my shoulder.

'I feel so ashamed and terrified of what might happen to me. Even though I was involved for such a short time I dealt with some very serious criminals. They had connections to Colombians and Russians, and to people like Kenny Noye [a notorious gangland figure linked to the Brinks Mat gold and currently serving life for a brutal road rage murder on the M25]. They were not scared to have someone shot if he talked or stepped out of line. I don't want that person to be me.'

The link between British organised crime and the business of drug-trafficking is relatively recent. Up until the mid-1970s the old-school criminals saw all drugs, even cannabis, as something to be avoided, the stuff of hippies and junkies. But as the decade came to a close, gangs of former armed robbers – many of whom had experienced cannabis in prison – began moving in on the scene and taking it over. Between 1977 and 1980 the amount of cannabis resin seized by British customs officials trebled.

One of the first to get involved in the trade was none other than George Francis, the armed robber and Brinks Mat gold handler, who was shot dead in May 2003. In late 1979, Francis was a prominent member of one of Britain's first large-scale criminal drug-smuggling gangs. Specially converted containers were sent to a shoe factory in Pakistan, where millions of pounds of cannabis were hidden among legitimate goods and shipped back to the UK. The first four runs went like clockwork. Francis and other members of the gang began living the good life, buying cars, jewellery and making a show of lighting their cigars with twenty-pound notes in the south London pubs they frequented.

But when the fifth drug consignment arrived, Customs officers were watching. Lennie 'Teddy Bear' Watkins, driving a lorry filled with £2.5 million worth of cannabis, spotted the surveillance team, prompting Customs investigator Peter Bennett to move in to make the arrest. Watkins opted not to come quietly and promptly shot Bennett dead.

Watkins was sentenced to life and the rest of the gang were put on trial. Rather than spend time inside, Francis let it be known that he would pay £100,000 to anyone who could nobble the jury in his trial.

The contract was supposedly taken up by the A team, a notorious north London criminal clan, and turned out to be money well spent. At his first trial the jury failed to reach a verdict. At the retrial Francis was acquitted, even though several other members of the gang who had been faced with exactly the same evidence had pleaded guilty.

At the time Pakistan was the main source of cannabis coming to the UK, but shipping it in was a long and expensive high-risk process. The market didn't really take off until the summer of 1978 when the Spanish government ended its hundred-year extradition treaty with Britain. Originally drawn up by Benjamin Disraeli with the specific intention of preventing British runaways finding sanctuary in the sun, the Spanish decided it was unworkable, paving the way for the birth of the infamous Costa del Crime.

Over the next three years more than a hundred of Britain's most-wanted men beat a retreat to a luxurious exile. Few became homesick. The weather was warmer, the houses were bigger, the cars were always convertible and the police didn't recognise you, let alone trouble you. There were British pubs selling British beer, restaurants serving double egg and bacon for breakfast, scampi and chips for lunch and roast beef and Yorkshire pudding for Sunday dinner. There was even a British tabloid paper linked to the *Sun*. The expats who weren't ready for complete retirement also had an ace up their sleeves. With Morocco just a fast speedboat ride from the Costa del Sol, Spain soon became the biggest port of entry to Europe for North African hashish.

In the charmless town of Ketama, high in Morocco's Rif mountains, growing cannabis, or *kif*, as it is known, is an industry that supports more than a million families. The area is renowned for its beauty but the soil is too harsh for wheat or olives. Cannabis, on the other hand, flourishes.

Fondly referred to by the locals as 'green petrol', the export of up to two thousand tonnes of *kif* per year earns Morocco around £2 billion a year in hard currency, albeit illegally. In 2001 the Moroccan government announced that it planned to eliminate all hashish production within seven years, but in Ketama there are few signs of any change, with cannabis plantations spreading as far as the eye can see. It is a business everyone wants to be in. Even the lowest grade pickers and weeders can earn thirty pounds a day in a country where the average weekly wage is less than fifteen.

But the real money is in exporting and trafficking. The Moroccan drugs barons, powerful landowners who control Ketama, quickly forged a close relationship with the British expat criminals.

At first the British took a purely financial interest, putting up money as a stake and doubling their investment in a matter of days. But then they started to get more involved. The biggest 'firms' employed Moroccan middle-men, who would haggle for a good price in the Rif mountains where the marijuana grows on discreet farms, hidden from prying eyes by cedar forests, or meet representatives of the growers in plush Tangiers hotels. There would also be a team of boatmen, drivers and heavies. Rarely would quantities of less than half a tonne be considered.

To stay one step ahead, the method of smuggling would be varied. Sometimes small boats would be used, sometimes panels of hashish would be stashed inside lorries in 'friendly' Moroccan warehouses. The vehicles would be loaded with perishable goods, such as oranges or fresh flowers, then sealed shut with Transport Internationale Routière (TIR) bonds, which ensured they would speed through Customs checkpoints with little or no interference. Other teams would simply fly their consignments direct from the Rif to small airfields in quiet Spanish provinces while others would rely on visiting friends and relatives to strap a few kilos to their bodies and breeze through Customs with the holiday crowd.

By the early 1980s, there was an efficient, British-controlled cannabis-smuggling network moving approximately four tonnes of high-quality resin back to the UK each year. The local police had little chance of infiltrating the network – few of the firms hired Spaniards – and it took years for the investigations to make any progress. In the late 1990s, the trade was at its height and a kilo of cannabis resin was worth around £2200 in the UK.

Today, users have become more discerning. As Baz, a Manchester-based dealer who imports direct from Spain, says, 'People are getting a lot choosier about what they want from a smoke. Ten years ago they were happy to take whatever was available. Now they'll actually put in orders for certain brands, certain varieties, and if you don't have what they're looking for they'll just go elsewhere. They've started to realise how good skunk can be and that's why the price of resin has fallen so much.

'There's talk about them legalising it but that's never gonna happen and even if it does, it still won't affect me. If they legalise it, they're going to have to tax it. If they do that, it means that people who buy in bulk on the black market will still be able to undercut the official price. Cigarettes and alcohol are legal, but people still make millions from smuggling them for just that reason. People seem to think that you can get rid of crime just by making something legal but that's never been the case and it never will be.'

Baz has one more trick up his sleeve. He has formed an alliance with a group of local 'home growers' in the Salford area and gets some of his supplies direct from them.

Research carried out by the Joseph Rowntree Foundation in 2002 found there had been a sharp rise in domestic cultivation, particularly in home-grown cannabis for personal use. Most of the crop is produced hydroponically – without soil and using special lights and heaters for the best possible environment. The foundation found that yet another reason the price of imported cannabis had fallen was because for the first time the amount of domestically cultivated product had overtaken the level of imports.

Although growing plants are illegal, the paraphernalia that surrounds them, even the seeds (until they germinate), is not. With two hundred shops and several websites catering exclusively for those who want to grow their own, advice and equipment is always at hand. For an investment of just £500, it is possible to grow plants that will produce £1000 worth of high-quality cannabis every three months.

After putting in a request with Baz, I receive a phone call from David, one of his new suppliers: 'It started because me and a few of my mates who like a smoke were getting fed up with the way our dealers were behaving. Everyone knows the price is going down, and every time we went round, they'd start putting us under pressure to try this or try that. We don't want anything else, we just want to enjoy a nice smoke every now and then. This way we get to have weed without any of the hassle.

'It's a high-risk operation. We're lucky because our room is based in a loft and we've got plenty of room for the lights and heaters. We've got about forty plants on the go at the moment and they'll mature in a couple of weeks. The smells are a problem – it's so distinctive that if someone happens to be walking past and the wind is going in the wrong direction, you're fucked. We got some carbon filters in the other day and that seems to be helping a lot. But then there's the heat and the lights. It's pretty bright up there when everything is on so you have to make sure you don't have any gaps in your roof tiles otherwise it looks like a fucking Christmas tree when they come on in the middle of the night.

'But everyone I know who has ever been busted, it was because they got grassed up, no pun intended. They do stupid things at parties like passing joints and asking what people think because "a friend of a friend" grew it. That's why it's good having Baz around. We don't have to go out and find customers, we just give him our excess and he gives us back the money. Very few people know what we're doing.

'Most of the time I feel like I'm wandering around with a stick up my arse. I don't drink and drive, I help old ladies cross the street, I even pick up bits of litter. It's mad. The thing is, though, you can't be seen to be doing anything wrong. The last thing you want it to get picked up for something that gives the plod the chance to search your place.

'In Amsterdam it's legal to grow up to twelve plants as long as they're only for your own personal use. It would be great if they would do something like that over here. All this cloak-and-dagger stuff, sometimes it's exciting but most of the time it's just a pain in the arse.'

Ironically the increasing market for home-grown cannabis has emerged at a time when cannabis being smuggled in from overseas is less likely to be intercepted than at any time in the past thirty years. Both Customs and Excise and the National Criminal Intelligence Service admit that, since the start of the new millennium, their efforts have been focused almost exclusively on Class A drugs. Large shipments are seized whenever they are found but all intelligence efforts have been redirected towards heroin, cocaine and ecstasy. Since the introduction of the new policy, cannabis seizures have fallen by almost half.

CANNABIS

With more of the drug flooding into Britain than ever before, the price has also fallen dramatically, particularly in the case of resin. (By the time it was reclassified, the price of resin had fallen by around 60 per cent from the mid 1990s high.) For major traffickers, like the gang Martin worked for, this hasn't been too much of a problem. They import in such vast quantities that sizeable profits are always guaranteed. Not so for the middle-ranking smugglers. Some are leaving resin aside to focus more on herbal varieties, which still command high prices, others are bringing in Class A drugs alongside their cannabis to maintain their level of income.

Some have found a more novel way to make up the difference: they are forsaking Morocco and tapping into a brand new source where rock-bottom prices mean they can enjoy profit margins as high as 4000 per cent. In many cases the new gangs are making more money than those trafficking cocaine and heroin.

Cannabis from South Africa and neighbouring countries is some of the most potent in the world and now accounts for the vast majority of seizures in the UK. In Britain, high quality 'skunk' cannabis sells for around £3500 a kilo. In South Africa the same product – known locally as *dagga* – can be bought for twenty pounds a kilo, less if bought in bulk. In some areas, *dagga* is said to be on sale for only forty pence a kilo.

The rapid growth of this market is creating overnight multi-millionaires, who invest their new-found wealth in other areas of criminality. Those running the trade rely on a network of couriers to bring suitcase-sized loads of the drug to the UK, often via France, Germany and, in particular, Ireland.

During the summer of 2003, eight out of ten drug smugglers detained at Dublin International airport were South African. The gangs have since switched tactics and are flying into other airports. Customs officials at Birmingham have dealt with a string of cases involving South African couriers in recent months. Authorities in South Africa have also seized shipments bound for the West Midlands.

Most of the mules are white Afrikaners who have fallen on hard times. They are given a plane ticket and paid around five hundred pounds to carry a suitcase holding up to twenty-five kilos of marijuana. The drugs are wrapped in plastic and covered in coffee and carbon paper to avoid detection by sniffer dogs and X-ray machines. The couriers, usually women, are given telephone numbers to call on arrival in Dublin, then get tickets to complete their journeys to the UK.

One Garda detective told me, 'A lot of what is going on involves testing out routes. Because the amount of money invested is low, the traffickers can afford to lose a shipment or two. The average amount the couriers carry is twenty-five kilos. That costs just five hundred pounds at the South African end, but is worth seventy-five thousand when it gets to the UK.'

Interpol now rates South Africa as the fourth-largest cannabis producer in the world. Around a quarter of worldwide seizures involve South African cannabis. The trend is confirmed in a report by the Institute for Security Studies in Cape Town, which says that most of the marijuana seized in the UK, and a third of that seized globally, is now of South African origin.

The potential for vast profit from South African cannabis was highlighted in late 2003 when five members of a gang led by unemployed twenty-four-year-old Robert Beal were jailed for varying terms totalling thirty years. Beal was arrested at a north London flat along with two South African accomplices, businessmen Aaron Reichlin, fifty-three, and forty-year-old Katiso Molefe, when police carried out a search in connection with a robbery. They found 25,000 ecstasy pills, 5.2 kilos of cannabis and a cache of firearms, including a submachine-gun and two semi-automatic pistols.

They also found details of a shipment of two electrical transformers from South Africa, which were awaiting collection in Ipswich. When police searched the transformer units at the dockyard they found 825 kilos of high-quality herbal cannabis. They resealed the empty containers and put them under surveillance as they were taken to an industrial estate in Wembley, north-west London, where police arrested the three other gang members. Beal had paid £65,000 for the cannabis concealed in the transformer units. In the UK, its value was £4.5 million.

In early 2003, when the Government first floated the idea of making cannabis a Class C rather than a Class B drug, critics of the scheme pointed out that, if this were the case, the maximum penalty for trafficking, regardless of quantity, would be just five years' imprisonment. The penalty for trafficking has since been increased to fourteen years, but studies have shown that confusion reigns, particularly among the young, about the implications of the change in the law. Many teenagers mistakenly believe that cannabis is now legal but, although police are now more likely to confiscate the drug than make arrests and no longer target those using cannabis in their own homes, the personal use and possession of the drug is still against the law.

The confusion echoes that seen in the initial pilot scheme that took place in Lambeth in south London in 2001. Designed to give local police the chance to focus their attention on Class A drugs, like heroin and crack, the scheme led to a three-fold rise in consumption, with dozens of Londoners travelling to the borough in the mistaken belief that they could buy the drug there and not be arrested.

The increase was blamed on the fact that the experiment had been carried out in Lambeth in isolation creating a 'goldfish-bowl' effect as the curious travelled to the area to see for themselves what was happening. While this was true to some degree, the early feedback from a rolling-out of the experiment on a national basis is that consumption is rising rapidly. Once it has settled down, the value of the UK market for cannabis is expected to double to £2 billion as a direct result of the change in the law.

One thing is certain: for great numbers of people cannabis is already a way of life. For them, the only question that matters is, 'Is the price right?', and that seems unlikely to change – whatever happens to the law.

MONEY LAUNDERING

CHAPTER SIXTEEN

I'm sitting in a quiet corner of the ZiZi pizza restaurant on George Street in the heart of Oxford, tucking into a huge plate of mushroom ravioli with chilli and spring-onion sauce. Opposite me is the well-tanned face of Laurence, a forty-something company director with a glowing smile and flowing blond locks, whose various business enterprises show a seven-figure annual turnover.

The meeting has been arranged by a series of intermediaries on the basis that I have a problem that Laurence might be able to solve. As far as he is concerned, I am a mid-ranking drugs-dealer with just short of three hundred thousand pounds in cash that I somehow need to make legitimate. Laurence, whose real wealth has been made though laundering millions of pounds' worth of criminal gains for top drug-dealers and associates of some of Britain's most notorious family firms, has offered to give me an initial consultation.

In the old days when armed robbery was king, money-laundering didn't enter the picture. If you did a successful job you simply spent the cash as and when you needed, storing the rest in a safety-deposit box or, for the ultimate discretion, in a hole in the ground at some secret location. If you opted to deposit the money in your bank account, you could simply say you'd had a good day at the races and no one would ask too many questions. Banks were under no obligation to pass on details of suspicious transactions to the police and were unwilling to do anything to alienate 'good' customers, regardless of the source of their income.

Today, thanks largely to the growth of the global drugs trade, all that has changed. The sums being earned by even modestly successful criminals are simply so vast that the old methods will no longer suffice. A mid-ranking dealer, like the one I am pretending to be, would be selling grams of cocaine to street dealers who would pay them out of the profits of their own sales. That means the money would come to them in small-denomination bills – mostly five and ten-pound notes. Although they could easily use this money to purchase flashy jewellery, and perhaps a nice car or some fine antiques, new banking regulations and the fact that we live in a largely cashless society would mean they could do little else.

Few estate agents would be happy about accepting payment for a house in cash; most hotels and all car-hire companies would rather have a credit card than a wad of notes and even rental companies would rather receive their funds by direct debit. Paying the money into a bank account would immediately cause suspicion. All banks and other financial institutions are legally obliged to report all transactions of £10,000 or more if the customer cannot adequately explain the source of the income. All of this and more has made those with expertise in the field of money-laundering among the most powerful figures in the modern criminal underworld. Rarely drawn from the traditional criminal classes, the best launderers are successful businessmen, accountants or lawyers, who enjoy the thrill of beating the system almost as much as they do earning money.

Money-laundering consists of three phases: placement, layering and integration.

In placement, money derived from criminal activities is introduced into the financial system. In many money-laundering schemes, the biggest 'problem' here is handling cash.

In the layering stage, the money-launderer manipulates the illicit funds to make them appear as though they were derived from a legitimate source. This always involves transferring money from one account to another, and even though this may be done as carefully as possible, it still creates problems in the traditional banking system. First, there is the possibility that a transaction could be considered suspicious and reported as such. Related to this is the paper trail created by these transactions. If any portion of the laundering network is examined, the related paper trails could lead investigators directly to the source of the criminal proceeds and unravel the money-laundering network.

In the final stage of money-laundering, integration, the original supplier of the money finally gets the chance to get their hands on the loot. The launderer either hands over the 'cleaned' cash, invests in other assets or continues to invest in additional illegal activities on behalf of the client.

Wary at first, Laurence soon opens up and tells me about his life. He explains that he has no criminal convictions – his background is that of twenty years as a legitimate businessman, working first in the aerospace industry and later in diamond mining in Africa. 'Over the years I built up a lot of trust and started dealing with lots and lots of cash because the diamond business is like that. I'd fly from Freetown to Brussels with a suitcase containing two or three hundred thousand pounds and I'd be doing that at least once a week. It was all completely above board and the bank had no problem with it.

'I got to know a few people in the course of my business who were involved in slightly less legitimate enterprises, and once they found out that I had the ability to funnel large amounts of cash into the system, they asked if I could attach some of their profits into my turnover. That's how it started and it grew from there.

'You have to have a contact with a cash economy of some kind otherwise you're fucked. This business of banks and accounts and lawyers having to report anything over ten thousand pounds only applies if the transaction is suspicious. There is no law saying you cannot go to your bank and pay in a million pounds in cash just so long as it is in the normal course of your business. Otherwise half the businesses in the high street would be getting reported every Friday afternoon when they took their takings down to their local branch of NatWest.

'So, what you have to do is create a sequence of events that legitimises the transaction or provides enough of an explanation for the bank to feel confident and not have to ask for any more information. In my experience, banks don't really care what the source of the money is just so long as they can say they had no reason to suspect it was suspicious. We have an account with a high street bank and put a lot of money through them. They look back at our accounts and see that, in the line of our business, we always put through a lot of cash. That means they're covered under the laundering act so they feel a lot better.

'How you proceed is down to you. If you give me the three hundred thousand now and say you want it turned round in seven days, I'm going to have to say no. Trying to launder that kind of money and get it into the system in such a short time is going to be a huge risk. I'll do it, but it will cost you seventy-five per cent commission because that's the risk I'm taking. What I prefer to do is take the money and come back to you in a month or so.

'We could tag it on the back of second-hand car sales. We've got a few dealers who trade Bugattis, Bentleys and the like and they do a lot of cash work. Cars like that, you can easily be looking at seventy-five thousand. They can claim to be making an extra sale a week and put the money through their books. In a couple of months, your money is all sorted.

'It all depends on how quickly you want the money and how much work you're prepared to do. For example, you could go to Scotland, rent a warehouse and a yard and spend three weeks going out to auctions and buying big pieces of plant equipment. Some of those diggers and big earth-movers go for fifty or sixty thousand a time, sometimes even more. No one is going to blink an eye if you pay cash, but you couldn't spend the whole three hundred thousand at once, you'd have to spread it out.

'After a month or so you can put the stuff on the market and adjust the price according to how quickly you want to sell it. If something is worth a hundred thousand and you put it on the market for seventy or eighty, it's going to sell right away. Okay, you're making a twenty or thirty per cent loss on your original money, but for a lot of people in your situation, that's acceptable.'

I ask about commission, and Laurence sits back in his chair and lights a cigarette. 'That completely depends. It goes from zero upwards. I dealt with one company who wanted to clean up three hundred grand. We took the money and bought plant in Europe, then shifted it out to Africa. Over there we actually managed to get a lot more money for the gear. It took three months but at the end of that I gave them back the exact sum they had given me. I didn't need to charge commission because we'd made about sixty thousand profit on the sales.

'It's a gamble in case you lose the money but for me it's a gamble worth taking. Normally, on cash, the commission varies between two and five per cent. If you have things like Scottish currency – especially the hundred-pound notes they issue – they're a pain in the arse to get rid of. With that and small denominations, the commission goes up to ten or sometimes fifteen per cent, but that's still a pretty good rate.

'I guess I'm used to it now but at first it always surprised me that, especially in this day and age, the diamond business still revolves around cash. I think the reason it's not well known about is that the Jewish community in Antwerp keeps a very tight rein on it. But once you get out to Africa, they no longer have control. That's where our contacts are and these are the people who help us get the rough stones. Once you get them back to Europe it's a whole different ball-game. You're dealing with a whole new business community and you don't trust them and they don't trust you.

'We have our own polisher. If you try to sell rough stones in the UK, you're talking about maybe ten buyers in the whole country. And that means they're going to spend just that bit more time checking the paperwork because they know they're in the frame. If you have polished stones, then you can sell the things at every jewellery shop in the country. For cash.

'It's perfect because it's one of the few areas left in the world where you can trade cash for product. The most difficult thing to do when it comes to money-laundering is to get the cash into the system. It's still relatively easy to exchange the notes from one denomination or currency to another. If you gave me half a million in ten-pound notes and you want to change it into Swiss francs, no problem, I can do that at the airport. I'll hire a bunch of guys, give them a few thousand each and they'll hit every booth in Heathrow and get it changed.

'If you had the money in Europe, then it's just a case a driving around to every *bureau de change* you can find and changing a couple of thousand here, a couple of thousand there. That's not a problem. You work hard for two weeks, change maybe thirty grand a day, and at the end of it, it's done. Doing that won't bring you any problems – you can even do it on your own passport.

'If you gave me your money right now, and you had a bit of time, what I would do with it is go out and buy diamonds. Simply because with diamonds, more than with any other commodity, no one can disprove where they came from. If Customs turn around and ask where you got them, you say they came from a mine in Sierra Leone and there's nothing they can do about it.'

Diamonds, as Marilyn Monroe once sang, are a girl's best friend but they are also, increasingly, the best friend of criminals, international terrorists and money-launderers the world over. Infinitely more manageable than gold or cash, as well as being far less easy to trace, diamonds have become the chosen currency of the global underworld.

Apart from a recent commitment to avoid trade in what are termed 'conflict diamonds' (uncut diamonds sold by various guerrilla movements and corrupt governments in Africa, in return for arms) by authenticating and certifying rough diamonds, the industry imposes few restrictions on the identification and movement of cut diamonds. Such distinguishing marks that are put on some diamonds – like the hallmarks put on gold – are easily polished off, making cut diamonds untraceable.

According to Hatton Garden jeweller Joel Grunberger, stolen and illegally smuggled diamonds do end up in the hands of the shops there. 'Hatton Garden has a number of people whose history is not exactly squeaky clean.' Grunberger was a consultant on the Guy Ritchie gangster film, *Snatch*, which begins with the robbery of an Antwerp diamond dealer. 'Honest dealers work cheek-by-jowl with the villains. I don't mean that they sell to the villains, but there are unscrupulous people. Everyone knows the Brinks Mat gold haul came to Hatton Garden,' he says.

Like Rick the cocaine dealer, Laurence finds moving the money from one place to another one of the most difficult aspects of his work. One of the many tricks up his sleeve is to use something called *hawala*, an ancient system developed in India before the introduction of Western banking practices. A similar system exists in the Chinese community where it is known as 'chit' or 'flying money'.

Hawala works by transferring money without moving it. If a man in London wants to send money to his family back in Bombay he simply approaches a *hawala* dealer and hands over his cash. The dealer gives the customer a password, then makes a call to an associate in Bombay who, on being given the correct password by the family, hands over the equivalent sum of cash – minus a fee.

'It's all done on trust and it works like a charm,' says Laurence. 'It was never intended as a system for laundering money, but a lot of people are using it just for that because it's so good. You don't have to worry about getting the cash over to Europe or into a high-street bank, you just walk into one of these places. They're everywhere, in the back of little cafés, travel agents – places like that.

'It's quick and efficient, and the real beauty of *hawala* is that if someone is trying to follow a money trail and you bounce money from one bank account to another to try to lose them, they're still going to catch up eventually. Taking it out of the banking system and putting it into *hawala* means it's lost for good. There's no way these transactions can ever be traced.'

As the waitress appears to take our lunch things away, Laurence asks if I want to make use of his services. I tell him that I'll need to think about it, that I've worked hard for my money and I don't feel I know him well enough to hand it all over.

He nods and tells me he understands. 'A lot of people, especially some of the older ones, long for the days when they could just stuff it in their mattress and spend it as and when. But those days are gone. If you want to be able to spend the cash, you need to get it professionally laundered. At the end of the day, you need to find someone you can trust.'

And that trust goes both ways. Launderers enjoy many of the benefits of criminal activity but have a better chance of staying out of the police spotlight. Those who are caught, however, can often provide rich detail about the dozens of criminal gangs for whom they work.

In 1998 diamond merchant Solly Nahome was shot outside his north London home. A professional hitman pumped four bullets into him before escaping on a waiting motorcycle. As well as having an office in Hatton Garden, Nahome was financial adviser to the notorious A team.

Nahome was known to the police as an international criminal specialising in fraud and money-laundering. He was said to have met with the A team three or four times a week and arranged for £25 million to be hidden in property deals and offshore accounts. It is thought that he was shot after rumours surfaced that he had been seen talking to police officers.

Although they may be some of the wealthiest criminals around, money-launderers always play a dangerous game. Some more dangerous than most.

CHAPTER SEVENTEEN

I'm sitting on a hard wooden bench just behind the witness box of Woolwich Crown Court in south-east London.

Some seventy-five feet below me is a tunnel leading directly to HMP Belmarsh, which occupies the land alongside the court. Belmarsh is, by all accounts, the most secure prison in the country. It features a special unit used to hold high-risk prisoners, and also houses suspected terrorists who are detained without trial under emergency legislation. There has yet to be an escape. Or an attack.

The whole building has been designed with security in mind. There are ranks of metal-detectors and X-ray machines at the main entrance, and once more at the entrance to the court building. Inside, high Perspex screens around the dock eliminate the possibility of any prisoner making a break for it. For reasons like this and many more, Woolwich is fast taking over from the Old Bailey as the best venue for trials that need to take place under the strictest security possible.

Behind me, a number of police officers with flak jackets and Heckler and Koch carbines held against their chests are on patrol. Grey-wigged barristers wait eagerly and the judge sits at his bench, his hand resting on his chin. One other journalist and I are the only reporters there. Everyone in the place turns and looks as the door swings open and the main prosecution witness – the reason for all the extra security – swaggers in. Overweight and ungainly, dressed in a sharp business suit with his lank hair swinging above his shoulders, this is Michael Michael, chief money-launderer of a £150 million international drug-smuggling operation.

Constantine Michael Michael was born in Brighton on 25 November 1957, the eldest son of Greek-Cypriots who had travelled to England in search of a better life. By the time his brother, Xanthos, came along in 1962, Michael's shoemaker father, John, and mother Maria had moved to north London to run a small fish-and-chip shop.

Michael attended the hard Highbury Grove School in Islington and quickly dropped his 'sissy-sounding' first name in favour of something more conventional. His teachers remember him as an affable, well-mannered boy who, despite an obvious talent for mathematics, showed little interest in studying. None were surprised when he left school without gaining a single qualification.

His parents insisted he make something of himself so Michael enrolled at Southgate Technical College to study fashion – 'like a good Greek boy' – but found the subject tedious. He began missing more and more of his classes and, after falling in love with Georgina, a Greek-Cypriot girl from Leicester, he dropped out altogether. Within six months, Georgina had become Mrs Michael.

The newlyweds moved to the Midlands and set up home with Georgina's parents, who also ran a fish-and-chip shop, but almost immediately the marriage fell to pieces. Within eight months Michael had returned to London and was living with his own parents again. 'I had to come back,' he told them. 'I couldn't stand her. We weren't compatible.'

Michael started work as a driver for a local VW dealer, doing little more than moving vehicles about. Keen to boost his earnings, he did a little buying and selling in his own time but soon came a cropper. He was given a Porsche 928 and sold it for a tidy profit, only to discover it had never belonged to him. Charged and convicted within the space of a few weeks, Michael spent four months at Brixton prison.

It was his first brush with the law and, initially, the experience left him shell-shocked. But at the same time Michael found himself irresistibly and inexplicably drawn to the characters that populated the criminal underworld. He made a number of firm friends and would later brag that he had lost all three elements of his gangland virginity – first arrest, first charge and first time in prison – in one fell swoop.

Soon after his release he met and married another Greek-Cypriot girl, Alexandra, following a second whirlwind romance. Around the same time he joined forces with a friend who was launching an accountancy business and set up a dual partnership, trading under the name Michael & Co and specialising in arranging mortgages and pensions.

The firm was legitimate, but Michael's private clients were not. Using some of the contacts he had made while in prison he began keeping the books of businesses that operated just on the wrong side of the law. There were pubs and bars that got their alcohol off the back of lorries from the continent, car dealers who sold more ringers than anything else, and brothels masquerading as saunas or massage parlours. He also specialised in giving references and providing fake paperwork for people who didn't have legitimate jobs but needed to show banks that they had a steady income before being granted a mortgage. From there it was a short leap to arranging mortgages for people who didn't exist. In 1989 Michael set up a scam in which he helped arrange £3 million worth of bogus loans, earning himself a commission of around thirty thousand pounds.

Before long the second Mrs Michael got sick of it all and left. Michael promptly took up with Lynn Baker, a former vice girl, whom he had met while keeping the books of a Highgate brothel. Blonde, busty and cocky with it, Lynn had many childhood friends and acquaintances who had grown up on the edge of the world of organised crime. Despite this and the fact that, to his mother's horror, she wasn't Greek, Michael was smitten.

Within three months they were living together and Michael became more and more involved in the day-to-day running of the sauna that Lynn co-owned. Seeing an opportunity for expansion and even greater profit, the pair soon went into business together, pooling their resources to buy more saunas and start their own little empire.

GANGS

Then it all started to go wrong. The mortgage fraud was uncovered, and just as Lynn announced she was pregnant, Michael was arrested again and that was when he began travelling down the path that would make him a multi-millionaire and one of the most powerful figures in the British underworld.

With dozens of detectives poring over his financial records in the aftermath of the mortgage-fraud case, Michael was terrified that the police would soon shut down all his saunas – fast becoming his chief source of income. Out on bail, he arranged to meet up with the police officer who had first arrested him. 'Even though he was the one who nicked me, I didn't bear a grudge. I thought the guy had been fair to me. I actually quite liked him.'

The feeling proved mutual and, as the pair talked and a cautious friendship developed, Michael saw a way of striking a bargain. Through his work and his time in prison he had got to know a number of high-ranking criminals – armed robbers, drug-dealers and the like. He would often get to hear about raids that were being planned, drug shipments that were arriving, and even underworld murders that were being set up. It was all because Michael was seen as a man with good connections, the gangland equivalent of the *Yellow Pages*. If you needed a fake passport, a stolen car or a few kilos of cocaine, Michael was a good man to ask. He didn't get involved in anything, but he always knew someone who did and was happy to make the introduction.

Although most people imagine the underworld is very secretive and closed, that's not always the case. If, for example, you come into possession of a large quantity of gold bars, the only way to convert them to money is to find people willing to buy them. And the only way to do that is to put the word out. Once you achieve a certain level of trust and credibility, usually by having been in prison, the underworld becomes awash with requests for information, buyers, drivers for robberies and so on. It meant Michael had access to the kind of information any policeman worth his salt would give his right arm for, and Michael knew it.

A deal was soon struck: Michael would become an informant,

passing on details of the criminal enterprises of those around him. There would be occasional payments for the information but his main reward was that the saunas would be allowed to flourish.

A top-secret file was opened and, working first under the codename 'Andrew Ridgley' then later 'Chris Stevens', Michael talked. As the information flowed, it soon became clear that, far from being a nuisance, the brothels were a valuable source of intelligence. Whenever Michael met big-time drug-traffickers he would get them drugs and then, 'I'd introduce them to the girls and make sure they had a good time,' he says. 'The saunas were a very good cover. When people are totally relaxed in a steam bath, they drop their guard and tell you things they'd never tell you anywhere else.'

Michael threw himself into his new role with surprising enthusiasm. In his first few weeks he gave the police details of the people who had laundered the proceeds of his mortgage-fraud scam; he told them about being approached to nobble a juror in a high-profile trial, about a group of burglars who were committing violent robberies, and the men believed to have killed a prostitute whose body had been found in Epping Forest.

Also, he continued expanding his chain of brothels and broadening the range of financial services his company offered. 'Maintaining the saunas and the accountancy office was an integral part of my ability to provide. The way the police viewed it was that I lived the right sort of lifestyle, drove the right sort of cars. I could converse with criminals on their level so it was a good opportunity for me to get bits and pieces, which I would then pass on to the police.'

Right from the start he demonstrated a considerable talent for deceit and a remarkable ability to get people to do his bidding. When two of his accountancy clients, who made their living from drug-smuggling, lost their supplier, they asked Michael if he knew anyone who might help. He told them he would set up a meeting with some friends of his, but insisted it should take place at his office. The gang met and Michael sat there. Only he was aware that the police had placed hidden microphones all around the room and were monitoring every word.

The flow of information continued for eight months while Michael awaited trial. Then, when the time arrived and, eventually, the case was drawing to a close, it was payback time. The public and press were sent out of court and the police made private representations to the judge about what an important asset Michael had become. Despite the serious nature of his crime, and that it was his second offence, he served just two months in prison.

By the time he was released and their first child was born, Lynn and Michael's sauna business was flourishing. They now had several branches spread out across London and, with no police interference, were making profits of tens of thousands of pounds each year. Some of the money they spent on property, buying ever bigger and more elaborate houses. The rest they spent on luxuries.

Michael continued to sing like a canary at every opportunity. Every little piece of information he came across he would pass on. If the police felt they could make an arrest or prevent a crime taking place without compromising the source of their information they would do so.

As the months ticked by, many of Michael's underworld associates suffered occasional spates of bad luck. Vehicles carrying shipments of drugs would get pulled over by the traffic police because of a faulty light or broken mirror, only for the officer to notice an 'odd smell' and uncover the booty; gangs who had spent weeks casing out a location for an armed robbery would arrive to find the cash truck was taking a new route; budding contract killers would find their homes being searched on a pretext and all their weapons being confiscated.

On other occasions, when approached and asked if he knew of any prospective customers for shipments of heroin or cocaine, Michael would agree to find someone, then introduce the gang to a man who would later turn out to be an undercover police officer. This first officer would then introduce the gang to another and then another so that by the time they were arrested it was impossible to link it back to Michael, and his position as an informant was not compromised.

But not every tip led to an arrest or a raid. Most of the time the police simply added the information Michael had provided to their intelligence files, using it to help give them an unprecedented insight into the workings of the country's top gangsters.

To Michael, the concept of 'honour among thieves' was a mystery. In May 1991 he gave information about a flat in Northolt where up to a thousand ecstasy capsules were being made each day. The police report recorded the name of the suspect and noted: 'Ridgley is in a position to assist us heavily with info in this matter and it would appear the Northolt address is a major outlet.' It was many years before anyone realised that Michael had informed on his own brother-in-law.

In the offices of senior police officers up and down the country, Michael was soon being talked about as one of the best and most reliable of their informants. He was proving an absolute gold mine. No other informant had access to or was so trusted by the senior figures in the British underworld. So when the police wanted to run an undercover sting operation against the A team, Michael seemed the obvious candidate to help. The police were desperate to find out what the family did with their money so they transferred tens of thousands of pounds into Michael's own bank account and told him to approach the family to see if they could help him to launder it.

Michael told the family that the money was profit he had made on drugs deals and, with their assistance, transferred it to a bent solicitor who often acted on their behalf. He in turn transferred the cash into an offshore company. Behind the scenes the police quickly became hugely excited – it seemed they might be able to pursue the family for tax evasion, the same method the FBI had used finally to bring down Al Capone.

But the scheme fell apart when Michael himself came under the scrutiny of the tax office. 'They said they had information that had been passed on by the police that I was involved with the A team, that I owned a yacht in Cyprus, which I never did, that I was a front man for the A team, which I never was. Then they said that I owed them seven hundred and fifty grand in taxes. The police tried to sort it out and tell them to forget it because I was part of an operation, but they wouldn't listen. In the end I became an informant for the Inland Revenue as well and they agreed to reduce the amount to a hundred and twenty-five thousand of which I paid off around twenty thousand.'

Although the débâcle temporarily soured his relationship with the police, things were soon back on track and the tip-offs flowed once more. It was around this time that Michael started providing information about a shadowy underworld figure known as the Pimpernel, a.k.a. Mickey Green.

Originally hailing from north London, Green switched from bank robbery to the drugs trade in the late 1980s and never looked back. He is said to have amassed a £100 million fortune from his global drug-smuggling empire, appears in the top ten most-wanted list of at least a dozen countries and has spent almost half his life on the run.

Green got his nickname from his ability to evade the best efforts of law enforcement to track him down. When the police in Britain got a little too close, he fled to Spain, leaving behind speedboats, yachts, Rolls-Royces, a Porsche, a Ferrari, gold bullion, cash and cocaine. The loss seemed to have little effect on his wealth and he soon became a well-known figure in Marbella, driving around in a white Rolls-Royce and enjoying the millionaire lifestyle.

He then travelled to France and made millions more smuggling cocaine, fleeing just before the police raided his apartment in Paris. He turned up next in America where he had extensive contacts with the Mafia and the Colombian cocaine cartels. Green was lounging by the pool in Rod Stewart's former home in Beverly Hills when he was arrested by the FBI.

Imprisoned in San Francisco, Green needed someone to sell one of his properties in Spain to help fund his escalating legal bills, which could only be paid with money that was shown to come from a legitimate source. His estranged wife, Ann, was a childhood friend of Lynn and, having heard all about Michael's formidable accounting skills, asked if he would be interested in helping out. Michael readily agreed and was soon working on behalf of one of the most dangerous criminals in the world.

It took two years and a dramatic escape from custody – Green was being flown to France to face trial there but slipped off the plane during a refuelling stop and fled to Ireland – before they could finally meet in person. By then the relationship between the two had developed into a firm friendship.

By now Michael had all the trappings of the successful criminal. He and Lynn had moved into their £1 million house at Radlett; Michael had a Porsche and a Rolls-Royce. Their two sons attended private school. No expense was spared. To Green, Michael seemed to be cast from the same mould as himself. Of course, Green had no idea that details of everything he said and every new criminal enterprise he planned were being reported to the police. Michael was playing an increasingly dangerous game, but he loved every minute of it. And he was about to become one of the most successful money-launderers in Britain.

The link with Green boosted the value of Michael's stock even higher. In the words of one detective he was 'one of the best, if not the best informant ever . . . providing information against arguably some of the most notorious British criminals'. As a result the bigwigs of police intelligence were so impressed that there was talk of him being the central figure in a sting that would be carried out jointly with the FBI. The idea was for Michael to travel to Chicago and link up with some of his Mafia contacts. He would be provided with thirty kilos of cocaine and use it as a lure to get the Americans to agree to make a deal while being secretly filmed.

That particular deal fell apart but the stakes were dramatically raised in the mid-1990s when, due to his old contacts being promoted, Michael was given a new 'handler', Detective Constable Paul Carpenter, who worked at Scotland Yard's élite Criminal Intelligence Branch and was responsible for handling top-secret information between informants and undercover officers. Carpenter explained that he wanted Michael to take an even more active role in the criminal activities of his new associates in order to gather more detailed information.

But while previous officers had played things strictly by the book Carpenter, according to Michael, spent all his time pushing him to get more and more involved.

It wasn't the only change. Rather than simply guaranteeing a quiet life for the saunas, Michael's tip-offs were now generating cash rewards, often several thousand pounds at a time. The money would be shared with Carpenter and soon the relationship between the two had become what would later be described in court as 'completely corrupt'.

The basic deal was that Michael would do pretty much what he wanted – sell drugs, launder money, trade in guns, anything – and Carpenter would make sure the police never went anywhere near him. In return, Michael would provide Carpenter with enough titbits of information to create a few arrests and make him look good in front of his bosses, but also share the vast wealth his criminal activities were generating.

The arrangement suited both parties down to the ground and when Green invited Michael to Spain in order to meet some friends of his, he did not hesitate to go. Then, when Green offered Michael the chance to become the British head of his new drug-distribution ring, he accepted right away. He didn't worry about not knowing how to run a drug-smuggling operation, Carpenter promised he would give him all the help he needed.

Michael's first drugs job for Green was to arrange the collection and storage of several hundred kilos of cannabis resin, which had been imported to Britain hidden in soap-powder boxes. It was the first of several shipments that would arrive in this way. The money for the drugs came back in sterling but Green wanted payment in Dutch currency so he could pay his suppliers without having first to change the money over. Michael spoke to a friend about the problem and was soon introduced to a man called Housam Ali, who liked to be called Sam for short.

They met in the central London office from where Ali conducted his finance business and hit it off immediately. Michael then handed over £76,000 in cash, taking Ali's Lebanese passport as security, and waited.

Ali returned, having changed all the money into Dutch guilders. His contacts in the world of international finance meant he was able to do so without arousing suspicion. The process was repeated several more times until the £250,000 Michael had made selling the cannabis had all been exchanged. Ali had made a small commission on each transaction but, knowing that Green would soon have more business for them, he and Michael soon realised that the best way to maximise their profits would be to set up their own *bureau de change*.

Michael and Carpenter then sat down to address the problem of how to get the money out of the country and back to Green. One technique they devised was to place up to £400,000 in a car's spare tyre and drive it to Spain. For smaller amounts, they decided to use couriers. 'What you need to do,' explained Carpenter, 'is recruit a bunch of pretty girls but don't let them know what's really going on. That way they can stroll through Customs and no one will be any the wiser.'

As their experience grew, they adjusted elements of the scheme. They worked out that it was best if as few couriers as possible knew about the existence of the others. That way, the suspicious among them would be more likely to believe they were part of a small scam rather than some massive international operation.

Another rule was that the couriers were not allowed to know how much money they were carrying. There had been a disaster early on when a courier had vanished with £150,000 after discovering just how much those funny foreign notes were worth.

Michael changed tactics. By wrapping the notes tightly in clingfilm he found he could squeeze huge sums into a package only two inches thick. The wrapping also meant there was little chance the money could be interfered with.

The couriers mostly travelled to Spain. On arrival in Marbella they would make their way to the four-star Hotel El Fuerte. All their bills – hotels, meals, car hire – would be paid. The money would usually be handed over later that evening at a Chinese restaurant near the hotel. They would stay overnight and fly back the next morning, receiving £800 a trip.

With authorisation notes from a *bureau de change* Michael had set up showing where the money had come from, the couriers believed that – at most – they were simply helping to carry more currency out of the country than was normally allowed.

One such courier was former page-three girl Tracy Kirby: 'I met Michael through a friend and he told me he ran a *bureau de change* and employed couriers to take small bundles of cash to affiliated branches throughout Europe.

'With hindsight it seems obvious, but at the time there was little reason to be suspicious. The bureau had an office on the Edgware Road, Michael's wife helped out by taking money abroad and every time I went away I was given a letter of authorisation explaining what I was doing and that the money belonged to the bureau. On my first trip I went to Dublin and took five thousand in sterling.

'On later trips to Amsterdam and Spain I assumed I was taking the same amount of money but I'd actually been carrying more than a quarter of a million pounds each trip and over six months had moved more than four million. I did start to get suspicious, but every time I questioned it, Michael would say something to reassure me. He was incredibly charming and could make you believe anything. If he said black was white, you'd believe him, that's how convincing he was.'

With the courier business under control, Michael turned his attention to finding new and better ways to smuggle drugs. Green put him in touch with a man called Richard Hannigan, who claimed to have a foolproof method of bringing cannabis into the UK. The drugs would be placed in blue barrels, which would be hidden inside tankers carrying paraffin wax or other products. The paraffin wax would hide any odour from the drugs and, because the tanker still appeared to be full, there was nothing to draw any suspicion. Hannigan's claims proved to be right on the money. Of the twenty-one cannabis-laden tankers that came into the UK, only one was ever discovered.

Michael didn't stop there. He hatched a plan with a gang based in Spain to buy a typical tourist bus and build in a secret drug-carrying compartment. The coach would be filled with tourists and even have a guide. It would be the perfect cover. As regular shipments of cannabis with the coach began, Michael dubbed it the 'fun bus'.

Michael made money from all aspects of his business with Green but most of his wealth came from the money-laundering. He would charge between one and five per cent of the total amount laundered to hand the money back to the European dealers. Within months he had become a millionaire many times over.

Carpenter observed his promise to keep away the police and was rewarded accordingly. At least once a week he would arrive at the house in Radlett and Michael would hand over up to £10,000 in cash. The money would be brought down from the loft where Michael kept a cash stash of between £30,000 and £1 million. In all, Carpenter is said to have received more than £250,000. However, he has never been convicted.

Michael lied to everyone in order to keep his laundering business working. To his friends, his couriers, even members of his own family. Even the NatWest bank was taken in. When the money-laundering scam got too big for their own *bureau de change*, Housam Ali struck a deal with one in the Lebanon, where he already had an account.

Ali would phone through an order to Beirut for batches of foreign currency and then Michael would meet the courier at an airport or hotel to swap the foreign notes for the sterling he had received from drug deals. The couriers would deposit the money at a London branch of NatWest as if it had come directly from Beirut. It meant that, to all intents and purposes, the money seemed to be coming from a legitimate source.

At one point a manager at NatWest raised questions about why some of the cash coming from Ali did not resemble the rest that was coming from the Lebanese *bureau de change*. Michael reacted by importing the same wrappings used by the Lebanese office to wrap his own cash. The questions stopped.

A few weeks later Customs officers detained some couriers carrying cash from Beirut on Michael's behalf. But he had done such a good job of convincing NatWest that the money was legitimate that the bank itself intervened and reassured Customs that there was no problem.

Between January 1997 and April 1998, Ali and Michael successfully laundered £28.2 million through NatWest right under the bank's nose. The bank had done nothing wrong. It had followed its own rules and regulations and made genuine efforts to check the source of the cash.

Michael was living in style. He celebrated his fortieth birthday by hiring a ballroom at the Dorchester. Fifty guests toasted his health and happiness with seemingly endless supplies of vintage champagne and fine wines. The highlight of the evening was the unveiling of a cake made to reflect Michael's lifestyle: alongside a bright red '40' were icing-sugar copies of the three mobile phones he always carried, his silver Porsche, the stacks of fifty-pound notes that bulged in his wallet and the Silk Cut cigarettes he constantly smoked. 'Michael loved it, and we all thought it was a great joke at the time,' says Tracy Kirby, 'but looking back you feel a bit stupid for not having worked out what was really going on.'

Operation Draft began on 23 January 1998 when officers from Customs and Excise began a routine investigation into the Hatfield industrial warehouse unit after receiving a tip-off that it was being used to store drugs. Within a few days they had identified Michael Michael as the principal mover behind the organisation and placed him and all his associates under close surveillance. For four months they watched as tankers, tourist buses and cars, all laden with drugs, moved in and out of the unit. They saw Michael meeting with some of the biggest names in organised crime and then, to their horror, with DC Carpenter.

They listened in on telephone calls, planted bugs in hotel rooms (at one point catching Michael with his lover) and recorded the comings and goings of more than a hundred people. They filmed and photographed Tracy and other couriers making their way to and from the continent with their bundles of cash and they identified Michael's suppliers in France, Amsterdam, Ireland and Spain.

The knock took place on 25 April. Dozens of Customs officers surrounded the house at Radlett and moved in to arrest the main man. Michael, out of his head on coke, believed he was being robbed by rivals and grabbed a loaded gun, pointing it at the first man in through his door. Only when the intruder identified himself as a Customs officer did he drop the weapon and give himself up.

Inside Michael's house, the investigators were staggered at what they found. It wasn't the £800,000 in cash or the original paintings worth £1 million hanging on the walls. It was the fact that, like a good bookkeeper, Michael had kept precise and detailed records of every drug transaction he had ever taken part in. The paperwork told who had bought what and how much they had paid. It listed each courier, where they had travelled to and how much money had been taken. It listed cash due from drugs sales across the country and who owed what. 'We had absolutely everything,' said one Customs officer, 'all the evidence we could ever want.'

For a short while Michael said nothing except that he was glad it was all over. The strain of living a double life was starting to get to him. He had been telling so many lies to so many people that he could no longer separate fact from fiction. He believed that, at any moment, Paul Carpenter would walk through the door and apologise and that he would get the chance to give up the life of an informant. After all, that was exactly what he had been paying him for.

Then he was told that Carpenter had been arrested. Furthermore, he was told that whatever arrangement he might have had with the police (at the time Customs were unaware of the allegations of corruption that would later surface), it did not cut any ice with Customs. He was the head of a major drugs gang and that was all there was to it.

And that was when Michael decided to talk to customs. And talk and talk and talk. During the course of 250 taped interviews Michael told customs absolutely everything. He told them about the suppliers, the traffickers, the smugglers, the money-launderers, and the 'money mules'. Most of all he told them about the money he had paid Carpenter and the information he had received in return.

'Even to my family I have had to tell lies and be deceitful,' he said, in one of these many interviews. 'I have become a polished liar. There were occasions when I informed on my family. Because of my statements my friends, my family and my lover are all awaiting trial. It is part of the business of informing and dealing – being disloyal goes with the territory.'

During a series of trials lasting for more than two years Michael gave evidence against everyone he had ever worked for and with, including Lynn and his mother. His testimony resulted in more than thirty convictions, though the operation failed to snare any of the bigger fish. Green was arrested and held for extradition, but charges against him were dropped and he remains a free man.

Although Michael is said personally to have made more than £58 million from his money-laundering and drugs-smuggling operation, the courts ordered him to repay just £69,000. He, Lynn and their children now live under new names courtesy of the witness-protection programme. The contract on Michael's head is said to be worth £4 million.

Operation Draft helped uncover the fact that vast sums of money were being smuggled out of the country by couriers to pay for drugs and led to a massive crackdown by Customs. Ports and airports are now patrolled by specially trained sniffer dogs who detect stacks of currency instead of drugs.

Since then huge sums of cash have been found concealed in

hollowed-out shoes, electrical goods, bicycle tyres, nappies and specially constructed body-suits. A woman leaving Heathrow airport hid £418,000 in boxes of Persil washing powder.

Although there are no limits on what quantities of cash can be brought in or taken out of the country, Customs officers have the power to seize amounts greater than £10,000 if the owner cannot explain its origin and there are suspected drugs-trade links.

'Everyone we stop has the option of staying and convincing us that the money is legitimate, or simply continuing on their way,' says one Customs officer. 'More than ninety per cent leave the money. In many cases we never hear from them again. The only thing they make sure they have is a letter from us stating the money has been seized. That way they won't get into trouble with the people who have employed them.'

The best estimates suggest that at least £1 billion is smuggled out of Britain each year. The couriers travel to countries all over the world but one country stands out as being something of a magnet for the trade: Turkey.

A survey of flights leaving London for Istanbul discovered more than £150 million in cash being flown out in just three months. Customs officers and senior detectives alike believe the money was destined to pay for supplies of a hugely popular and highly addictive drug, which, despite the rise of crack and cocaine, is still regarded by many as the most dangerous substance in the world.

HEROIN

CHAPTER EIGHTEEN

It was just before four p.m. on Saturday 22 June 2002 and I was sitting at my desk at the *Observer* waiting patiently for it to get close enough to six o'clock for me to leave without being too conspicuous.

I'd spent the morning putting the finishing touches to a story about a 200 per cent rise in crack-cocaine seizures across Britain and, apart from keeping an eye on the breaking news bulletins to ensure I didn't miss anything, had little else to do.

For most of the day the office had been alive with World Cup fever but, not much of a sports fan, I'd paid little attention to that day's game between Turkey and Senegal. Then the paper's news editor, Andy, appeared at the side of my desk and suggested that, as Turkey had won, I should take a trip to Green Lanes in north London and write a small piece about the victory celebrations.

Anxious to finish work at a reasonable hour I tried to point out that, notwithstanding my lack of knowledge about the beautiful game, this hardly fitted in with my usual line of work. Andy was having none of it. 'I wouldn't be so sure,' he told me, in his soft Scottish tones. 'Some of the decisions that ref made . . . I'd say they were pretty criminal.'

Green Lanes stretches from the edge of Bush Hill Park to Stoke Newington but a single one-mile section, from Turnpike Lane to Manor House, has become famous as the business and cultural centre of Britain's Turkish, Kurdish and Cypriot community.

Both sides of the street are lined with cafés and clubs, foreign banks and shops selling a wide variety of specialist foodstuffs and supplies. Everywhere there are signs and posters in Turkish and

Kurdish and many residents consider the area a little piece of home.

I arrived at the corner of Finsbury Park just as a massive victory parade was setting off and spent the next hour joining the flag-waving crowd as they cheered, sang and stopped traffic to share the good news. The atmosphere was straight out of a carnival and I carried out dozens of interviews, filling my notebook with multiple exclamations of joy from the ecstatic fans and predictions of victory against Turkey's next opponents – Brazil.

The atmosphere was jolly and carnival-like, but as the section of crowd I was moving with passed a small grocery store, words were exchanged and all hell broke loose. Weapons, including knives, cricket bats and staves of wood, were produced and a mass brawl developed.

I watched, horrified, as one man, armed with a thick piece of wood, used it to batter another to the floor, leaving his face a bloody pulp. Across the road from me two other men were having a heated argument. When the taller of the two tried to throw a punch I saw the smaller man draw a large knife from his belt and lunge forward. The tip of the blade only just missed his opponent's belly. As the crowd around me gasped, the taller man used his long legs to turn and run like hell.

All around me the crowd fought viciously, running back and forth in waves of spectacular attacks. Outnumbered, the men in the grocery shop retreated and used their own produce as weapons, throwing whole melons and potatoes as the crowd surged forward around them. This only made things worse: the mob surged forward and smashed the shop display to smithereens as the owners cowered inside behind a flimsy wooden door.

Then, from nowhere, reinforcements seemed to arrive and the crowd gathered around the shop found themselves caught in the middle of a brutal mêlée. The fighting continued until more than fifty police officers arrived in riot gear and acted as a human barrier in order to keep the warring sides apart.

The scene I had witnessed had left me shocked and speechless. I tried to speak to a few locals and find out more about what had prompted the battle but the answers I received were conflicting and confused. All I could discern was that the shop-owners were Kurds and that several members of the Turkish procession said they had overheard an insult as they went past.

I eventually filed my report on the celebrations and made only passing mention of the riots – it seemed inappropriate to tarnish all my coverage of the Turkish triumph with a report of what, despite its scale and ferocity, seemed a relatively isolated incident. In fact, it was a chilling taste of things to come.

It was only when he heard the screaming that Selahattin realised something was wrong. Until then the young student, who shares a house in a quiet side-street just off Green Lanes, had believed the sounds he had heard were down to some local kids messing about with leftover fireworks.

'I looked out of the window and saw a man crawling across the pavement on his hands and knees, screaming with pain. His clothes were soaked with blood. I knew then that the sounds I'd heard were gunshots. He was moving towards another man who was lying on the ground, not moving. He'd been shot too. It was absolutely terrifying, just like something out of a film. And that was when I called the police.'

What Selahattin had witnessed on 11 November 2002 was the end of a vicious confrontation during which more than a hundred Turkish and Kurdish men, armed with guns, knives, tyre irons and baseball bats, fought a pitched battle in the streets. The fight had started in the Dolstar Lokali social club, close to the Manor House end of Green Lanes, and quickly spread to the surrounding streets as rival gang members pursued one another, often firing indiscriminately. When it was finally over, one man was dead, four had life-threatening gunshot wounds and another twenty or so had been badly injured.

As with the battle I had witnessed five months earlier, the bloodshed was initially dismissed as the result of simmering tensions between the area's Turks and members of the fast-growing Kurdish community, who have been campaigning, sometimes violently, for an independent homeland on the edge of the Turkish state.

The truth is far more complex and disturbing. The fighting was actually part of an ongoing struggle for control of protection rackets, business interests and, most importantly, the international trade in heroin. It is a miniature war that has seen dozens of murders and shootings in the past decade. Furthermore, it is all being orchestrated, funded and controlled by one of the world's wealthiest and most powerful figures in organised crime – a man who, despite being virtually unknown outside Turkish circles, has become to heroin what Pablo Escobar was to cocaine.

He is known as the Emperor. A drug-smuggler for more than thirty years, the forty-six-year-old Turk has amassed a fortune of more than £10 billion.

Born in the small Turkish district of Lice, his criminal life began humbly enough when he started selling black-market cigarettes in Istanbul. From there he moved first into hashish-trafficking before finally getting involved with the drug that would ultimately make his fortune.

From 1970 onwards he purchased vast quantities of raw opium from India, Pakistan and Iran and converted it into high-quality heroin at a series of secret factories close to his home town, selling the drug first to the Turkish and then to the international market. Modelling his empire on that of the Italian Mafia, the Emperor employed only members of his direct family or close relatives. Some remained in Turkey but others were sent out across Europe to establish distribution and sales networks wherever there was an expatriate Turkish or Kurdish community. The Emperor himself set up home in Green Lanes.

As his business grew and the money rolled in, the Emperor invested heavily. He bought a string of business and property interests in Britain including a seaside hotel in Brighton and several foreign-exchange bureaux. He also owns dozens of beach resorts, electrical shops and car-hire businesses along Turkey's southern coast, many of which are used by thousands of British holiday-makers each year.

In 1984 he was arrested in London with a large consignment of heroin and sentenced to twelve years imprisonment. But after just three years behind bars he was transferred to Turkey and immediately released, prompting allegations of corruption at the highest levels of Turkish government.

Following his release he went on a media offensive. He admitted that his wealth came from heroin, but said he became head of one of the world's biggest drugs syndicates only with the full support and approval of Turkish politicians, police officials and the Turkish security service. (Although the Emperor's view that he was acting on behalf of the government is generally dismissed, there have long been concerns that Turkish drugs gangs are being protected by the Turkish state. In 1996 a car crash near Istanbul sparked scandal when it emerged that the passengers were a top crime boss, a senior police commander, a beauty queen and an MP.)

In 1998 the Turkish government, stung by Turkey's international reputation as a haven for drugs barons, orchestrated a round-up of the Emperor's family members across Europe. In January 2001, the Emperor stood trial and was jailed for twenty years.

Yet despite this, the Emperor and his criminal network continue to dominate the streets of north London. At least a dozen of his close relatives and extended family live in the area and their grip on the heroin trade and local protection rackets remains as firm as ever. Massive heroin seizures involving members of the Turkish community are now so common that they rarely make the news. In 2003 alone, more than £150 million pounds' worth of the drug was seized in raids linked to Green Lanes.

The drug usually arrives in specially converted lorries and shipping containers direct from Turkey. The value of an Emperor load is rarely less than £10 million. Once safely inside the country the drug is stored in safe houses, watched over by specially hired couples. For a fee of around £300 per week, their job is to live as normal a life as possible while ensuring that at least one member of the family is always at home to guard the heroin.

Every few days or so members of the gang drop by to check the stock or pick up a few kilos for resale. They also employ couriers (often working for mini-cab companies) to ferry packets of heroin around the country as needed.

'The fact that he is in prison has changed nothing,' says Selahattin. 'His soldiers are everywhere. There are three street gangs – the Bombacillars [Kurdish for bomb-makers], the Tottenham Boys and the Kurdish Bulldogs – all directly controlled by him. Some of them are just kids, even younger than me, but they have guns and everyone is terrified of them. The kids in the gangs consider themselves to be untouchable. They think they are above the law. They think they can do whatever they want because they know the Emperor's family is behind them. It's anarchy out there.'

The young gunmen are paid up to £200 to oversee a drug delivery, or ensure that protection money is paid. The guns and money are supplied directly by the Emperor's relatives, and the members of the Bombers (Bombacillars) in particular are said to be supremely loyal to him. Clashes between the Bombers and other gangs fighting for control of the heroin trade have pushed the number of murders in the Turkish community to an all-time high.

In May 2001 twenty-six-year-old suspected dealer, Oguzhan Ozdemir, from Enfield, was shot dead. Two months earlier Hasan Mamali, twenty-three, and his friend Sama Mustafa, twenty-six, were gunned down in Hoxton, east London. Mamali was shot in the head as he sat in the back of a convertible BMW car. Mustafa tried to run, but was brought down with a volley of shots. His killer then hovered over his body and finished him off with another shot to the head.

In July that same year gangs of gunmen fought outside Wood Green police station one afternoon, firing twenty shots in a busy street. Police arrived at the scene to find bullets in briefcases and three guns left smoking on the ground. One, a .45 magnum, had been loaded with 'dum dum' bullets, outlawed under the Geneva Convention because of the devastating damage they cause. Several of the gangsters are known to possess AK47 assault rifles and other military hardware.

In November 2002 Murat Over, a twenty-nine-year-old heroin dealer, was found guilty of the murder of Mehmet Adiguzel, who had been shot dead six times as he sat at the wheel of his car on Upper Clapton Road. Adiguzel used the cover of working as a property developer to mask his own drug-dealing activities but he was also a police informer and had many enemies. Although Over and Adiguzal had clashed in the past – Over has been stabbed by one of the dead man's bodyguards – many believe he was paid a fee to carry out the killing so that a rival gang could take over Adiguzal's patch.

The most recent murder took place in November 2003 when a twenty-three-year-old Turkish man was found in a canal in east London. He had been shot in the head at point-blank range. Since the dawn of the new millennium, at least ten murders have been attributed to the activities of the heroin gangs, and if this trend continues, they will soon be responsible for more gang-related deaths than any other criminal faction.

And all the signs point to the situation getting far worse. Detectives are also alarmed at signs that the heroin market is expanding rapidly. The key indication of a growing drug market is falling price and rising purity, both of which have been witnessed since 2000. The street price of a kilo of heroin has fallen by more than £2000 to an all-time low of £13,000. The purity of street-level heroin is also at an all-time high – around 40 per cent, compared with 15 per cent during the 1980s.

But the trade in heroin is not the only cause of violence within the Turkish community. In 2003 a survey of 200 Turkish and Kurdish shopkeepers in the area found that 65 per cent of them said they were paying protection money, some up to £10,000 per year.

Historically, the protection money went to fund the Kurdistan Workers Party (PKK), a paramilitary group, which was fighting for a recognised homeland for the Kurdish people. But in April 2002 the PKK abandoned the military struggle and restyled itself as the Kurdistan Freedom and Democracy Congress (KADEK). The Emperor, a long-time supporter of the PKK, decided to move in on its business. Shop-owners were happy to pay the PKK or KADEK but not the Emperor who, they realised, simply wanted to line his own pockets with the money.

The fighting at a café on Green Lanes, owned by a close relative of the Emperor's, was in response to an attack earlier that day on the same greengrocer's that had been the scene of fighting during the World Cup celebrations. At about four p.m. a group of men armed with baseball bats and snooker cues attacked a member of staff at a grocery store run by men loyal to KADEK. Two hours later a mob of around 150 turned up at the café and blocked all the exits. They were armed with a variety of knives, sticks, baseball bats and poles. A few members of the Bombers were initially trapped inside but, because they had their guns on them, were quickly able to fight their way out. Alisar Dogan was not so lucky. The forty-three-year-old father of two was desperately short of money and had taken a weekend job in the café scrubbing carpets. When the mob attacked he was caught in the middle of the battle and brutally beaten before being stabbed in the heart. He was rushed to hospital but died the next day.

Soon after the murder, eager to find out more about the influence of the Emperor's family in the area, I worked up the courage and called at the £1 million house in the beautiful tree-lined avenue in Edgware where some fourteen members of his extended family live. The door was eventually answered by a demure woman, who listened to my request for information and possibly a brief chat, then told me in perfect English that she did not speak English. She promptly shut the door.

In January 2003 police launched their biggest ever action against the Emperor's organisation. More than 550 police officers, some of them armed, raided a series of homes and businesses in north

London. Over the course of three weeks, more than three hundred people were arrested, including those thought to be responsible for Dogan's death.

But while the raids went some way towards easing tension in the area, they had little effect on the Turkish Mafia's core business. Seven months later, Customs officers seized the second largest consignment of heroin ever recovered in Britain. Hidden among 160 tonnes of cat litter they found 368 kilos of Turkish heroin worth more than £50 million.

More raids followed in December 2003 and this time police discovered a makeshift torture chamber inside a scruffy bed-sit just off Green Lanes. Two large metal hooks, hung from the ceiling by lengths of cable, had been used to suspend victims as they were beaten until they agreed to pay protection money.

In the twelve weeks before the December raid there had been three murders, five kidnappings and twenty-seven reported cases of extortion, eight of which involved firearms. Police concede that dozens more incidents would have gone unreported because the victims were fearful of retaliation.

Despite fighting what appears to be a losing battle, the police are determined to smash the Turkish Mafia's hold over the British heroin market. But the truth is that, for some time, that hold has been slipping. In the past few years a new, equally brutal Mafia has emerged and those behind it are now bringing in so much high-quality heroin that the price looks set to drop even further.

CHAPTER NINETEEN

The heavily bearded man standing beside me straightens his turban before passing a small wad of rupees to the barman. Like me he has come inside to escape from the stifling heat and we both lick our lips in anticipation as his frosted bottle of Cobra beer is placed on a mat before him. I shift along the bar so that I'm standing directly beneath the large fan and wait for the barman, who looks serene in his pale blue *dhoti*, to take my order. On the wall behind me, on either side of a giant map of the Punjab, pictures of popular Sikh singers smile down while peering over the tops of their sunglasses. A dozen or so men – there are no women to be seen – are scattered at the various tables. Some are drinking pints or bottles of beer, others soft drinks or fruit juice. A few are tucking into huge platefuls of rice and curry, courtesy of a small counter adjacent to the bar.

Every time the doors to the main road open the air becomes thick with the scent of exotic spices, and the warbling beat of Bhangra music can be heard. It's all such a feast for the senses and so powerfully evocative that, as my beer arrives, I can almost believe that I'm in the heart of Delhi or Bombay rather than a shabby side-street in west London.

Welcome to Southall Broadway, the heart of Britain's Sikh community and an area where around 90 per cent of the residents are of Indian origin, mostly from the Punjab.

With its numerous temples and colourful bazaars, its bustling streets, specialist Indian shops and lively atmosphere, Southall is a prime example of the benefits of multi-cultural society – a chance for everyone to experience life in another country without ever stepping on to a plane. Take the Glassy Junction public house, for example – it's the only pub in Britain that accepts rupees as well as sterling.

But there is also a dark side. Southall is the centre of the fastest-growing branch of the heroin trade and its associated gangland culture. Sporadic violence has been exploding off and on for the past few years and many believe it is only a matter of time before the area explodes into full-scale urban warfare.

Traditionally the perception of Asian culture was that the strong family links and rigid parental control – particularly among Sikhs – helped isolate the youth from drugs and the associated crime. Historically, Asian crime was mostly low-level and non-violent. But criminal intelligence reports from detectives based in Southall have revealed that two Asian-led gangs have grown into powerful criminal organisations by deluging the area with heroin. They control a network of dealers spread all over west London and have amassed wealth and weapons. And now they are at each other's throats.

The current battles are a chilling fulfilment of a prophecy first made in 1995 in a highly controversial Home Office research paper: it warned of a demographic time bomb of Pakistani, Bangladeshi and Indian youths that threatened to shatter the long-held belief that Asians were the most law-abiding community in the United Kingdom. Citing a notable increase in the number of Asians being jailed in young offenders' institutions, the report predicted that many of the groups that started out aiming to protect the community from racist attacks would soon evolve into full-blown criminal syndicates.

And so they did. The gangs started out dabbling in credit-card fraud and low-level protection rackets but have since moved into drug-trafficking. In so doing, they have vastly increased the number of addicts within the Asian community. In 2002 a study in the south of England estimated that more than half of new heroin smokers in the area were from the Asian community, and experts say the figures are echoed across the country. A few months after the study was released the MP Oona King described the East End as the 'heroin capital' of the country after seeing young Bangladeshi boys passed out on the stairs of tower blocks as a result of injecting the drug.

Asian community leaders from Bradford and Tower Hamlets in east London have spoken publicly in recent years about their concerns over the spread of drugs and youth gangs. Tower Hamlets has long been the centre for drug abuse and is also linked to petty street crime led by Bangladeshi gangs of youths with names like the Brick Lane Massive and the Stepney Posse.

More recently it has been associated with large-scale drug-smuggling and distribution. In 2002 a gang of five Bangladeshi men who generated £12 million in six years were jailed after operating a heroin ring in east London. The operation was highly sophisticated. Members of the street teams had their own expense accounts and were reimbursed for meals, mobile phones, hire cars and petrol by people higher up the hierarchy.

Although the majority of Britain's heroin trade remains in the hands of Turkish gangs, customs investigators have of late noticed an increasing number of Asian couriers bringing the drug into the country, often on direct flights from India and Pakistan.

The syndicates often make use of family members to assist in their enterprise. This is partly for added security and partly because relatives can be more easily 'got at' in the event of a betrayal. In April 2002 a thirteen-year-old Asian girl from Bradford was stopped at Heathrow and found to be carrying heroin worth more than £1 million. In another case, heroin was found sewn into a quilt that was wrapped around a six-month-old baby coming off a flight from Lahore.

In Derbyshire a study of the local drugs scene found not only increasing numbers of Asian gangs and dealers but that they were rapidly expanding their operations to the point of competing with other gangs.

'We have found that a growing number of young Asian men are becoming involved in the heroin business,' says Drugs Squad officer Steve Holmes, who is in charge of the study. 'While once any Asian dealers tended to stick to a limited customer base in their own communities, they are now becoming bolder and are prepared to compete in the wider market. These are mainly British Asians who have lived here all their lives. They have seen white and black dealers and the lifestyle they lead and have thought, Why shouldn't I have some of that?'

Around 75 per cent of heroin supplies on the British market come from the opium-poppy fields of Afghanistan, within easy reach of Asian dealers' Pakistani contacts. Cities like Bradford and Birmingham have major links with Pakistan and Afghanistan, a factor that has promoted them to the top of the Asian drug-dealing division.

For the traffickers, importing direct from Pakistan rather than via Turkey means the potential profits are huge. Refined opium, bought in the lawless tribal lands of Pakistan, costs as little as £150 a kilo. On the streets of Southall it will sell for up to £80,000.

But the days of stopping at Southall are long gone. Rather than confining themselves to a limited customer base, the Asian gangs are taking advantage of their ability to undercut the price of heroin yet still make a profit to rake in thousands of new customers. Such is their power that many Asian gangs now employ black and white youngsters to work on their behalf.

In the back room of the Glassy Junction I meet up with Jas, a twenty-four-year-old Sikh who uses heroin on a regular basis (he insists he is not an addict) but recently retired from dealing to support his habit.

It was here in his very room, Jas explains, that he decided enough was enough and that he had to get out of the gang business. 'I was having a drink with a couple of friends and there was a big group of Sikh men in that corner over there. All of a sudden they started arguing, standing up and pushing one another around, and then I just remember hearing shots. One of them had pulled out a gun and started firing. The whole place just erupted. Everyone got up and ran the hell out of there. I thought I was going to die.' Three men were left injured, one shot in the arm, another in the hip and a third in the back. The argument was later linked to a dispute between rival drugs gangs, and for Jas it was the final straw.

According to Jas, the two gangs behind the heroin trade in Southall are known as the Bhatts and the Kanaks. The Bhatts are controlled by the members of a leading Asian family who have a number of business interests including a hugely popular restaurant in west London. The Kanaks, also based in west London, have strong links with Yardies and other black gangsters, whom they have been known to hire to carry out acts of violence on their behalf.

Both the Bhatts and the Kanaks had been active for some time but the full extent of their operations only emerged in early 2002 following the arrest of a gang who were part of the Bhatt organisation. Nicknamed the 'Fiat Bravo Boys' after the nondescript cars they drove to avoid drawing attention to themselves, the gang, headed up by brothers Sukhdev and Rajinder Bassi, had become one of the most successful and ruthless drug syndicates in British history. While on the surface they deliberately adopted low-key, modest lifestyles, they regularly enjoyed breaks at luxury hotels in west London and on the south coast, including the five-star Grand Hotel in Brighton.

They booked the best suites, lavishing girlfriends with champagne and gifts as well as hiring top-of-the-range BMW convertibles instead of the more humble Fiats they used in London. They also took regular luxury holidays in Europe and America, and while in the latter made a point of visiting dozens of firing ranges to hone their shooting skills.

Behind closed doors, the Bassi brothers, along with Jagdev Kallha and Rajinder's girlfriend Rajvinder Gill, relished the lifestyle their criminal activities afforded them and regularly taped their exploits on a series of camcorders. They filmed themselves snorting cocaine, toasting their successes with bottles of Cristal champagne and even brandishing their many guns.

The Bassi brothers started out small, importing heroin a kilo at a time from Turkish dealers and using a network of family members to distribute it. Although both brothers were born in the UK they had strong family ties to the Punjab and soon made use of these contacts to secure new, cheaper supplies of the drug. Sales and profits soared, but as the gang's business grew, so did the level of violence as they fought the Kanaks for control of the increasingly lucrative trade. Soon, wherever they went, the Bassis got into the habit of carrying loaded pistols because of the risks of a shootout with rival dealers.

They also hired Manjit Sangha, a notorious local thug, to work for them as an enforcer on a salary of £1000 per week. His job was to identify the top dealers in the Kanak organisation and scare them away from Southall to ensure the Bassi brothers and the rest of the Bhatt organisation maintained their premier position.

On 5 October 2002 Sangha and an associate walked into the Lady Margaret pub, north of the centre of Southall and known to be a popular hangout for members of the Kanak gang. Sangha, bursting with Dutch courage thanks to several lines of cocaine, marched up to one of the rival gang's leading figures, pulled a gun from the waistband of his trousers and pushed it hard against the man's temple. 'If you don't keep away from our patch, you're a dead man,' he warned.

But instead of backing off the Kanak men rushed towards Sangha, knocking him off his feet and wrestling the gun from his hand. They then proceeded to beat, kick and pistol-whip him to the edge of consciousness before letting him crawl away in disgrace. The Kanaks had made their position clear. If the Bhatts wanted to challenge them, it would take a good deal more than that.

Two weeks later, just before ten p.m. on 18 October, a twenty-six-year-old key player in the Kanaks' gang was walking along a Southall street when a shotgun blast rang out from a passing car. The bullet missed him by a matter of inches.

An hour later and half a mile away, it was near closing time at the Lady Margaret. Sue Day, the assistant manager, was in the middle of pulling a pint for one of the twenty or so customers milling about in the pub when she was thrown back against the wall by a huge explosion. 'We'd been bombed,' recalls Day. 'The windows went in, the doorway went in and the whole place filled with smoke. It was a mess, and a miracle that no one was hurt.'

It was only a few weeks after 11 September and attacks by Al

Qaeda were first and foremost in everyone's mind. But when the anti-terrorist police arrived they soon realised they were dealing with amateur bomb-makers. The device had been made by packing gunpowder, almost certainly emptied from fireworks, into a plastic container with galvanised nails. It had been placed next to the door in a bid to catch people leaving at closing time but had exploded a few minutes too early.

'Everyone knows the Bhatts were responsible,' says Jas. 'They were trying to stamp their authority on the situation. They believed they were untouchable, that no one would ever give evidence against them. That's why they went too far.'

The following day the Bassi brothers attended a twenty-first birthday party at the Agra Indian restaurant in Hounslow. Among the dozens of guests was Sukhbir Pattowala, twenty-five, who ran his own car dealership and had no criminal connections. He had once sold a vehicle to a Bhatt gangster, who was unhappy with it. Through no fault of his own, Pattowala became the next target for the gang as the Bassis continued to flex their muscles.

The early mood was buoyant, if somewhat menacing, and video-footage shot at the start of the party shows Rajinder larking about and waving a gun around. The mood turned darker with the arrival of the gang's enforcer, Manjit Sangha, who, once again, was high on cocaine.

At some point in the evening, Rajinder told Sangha that Pattowala had ripped him off and ordered him to make an example of the man. Sangha pulled out his revolver and began pointing it at people, pretending to fire it at them. He then pointed it at Pattowala's head and pulled the trigger. There was a loud report and his victim fell to the ground, a bullet lodged in his brain.

When the police arrived, the killer had long gone and no one in the room could remember having seen anything. One man, who had been standing close enough to Pattowala to be spattered with his blood, said he missed the shooting because, at that precise moment, he had bent down to tie his shoelace.

At his trial Sangha claimed the shooting was an accident and that he had had no idea the gun was loaded. He told the judge that he was full of remorse and sorrow for what had happened and wished he could find a way to turn back the clock. The murder charge was reduced to manslaughter and he was sentenced to three years. When the sentence was announced his sorrow evaporated and he punched the air with joy, then waved to friends in the public gallery.

The Bassi brothers' reign of terror ended when police, acting on a tip-off, carried out a dawn raid on the home of the brothers' cousin, Jaspal Bassi. They found a kilo of heroin in his six-year-old son's Power Rangers rucksack. Jaspal, who had no previous convictions, cracked under questioning and told police he was being paid £100 a week by his cousins to store the drugs at his home. Against the odds, he agreed to give evidence against them.

Guided by Jaspal, the police launched an immediate raid on the Bassi stronghold and discovered several guns, hundreds of rounds of ammunition, explosives and seventeen kilos of heroin with a street value of more than £1 million.

For Jaspal the arrests marked the end of a normal life. While on remand other prisoners vowed to kill him and his brother received a phone call from Rajinder saying he would die if Jaspal gave evidence. He persevered and, in February 2003, both Bassi brothers were sentenced to ten years for their part in the drug-dealing network.

But even though the Bassis are behind bars, the rest of the Bhatt gang is still active and now the Kanaks have the upper hand. The tensions are as high as ever.

As evidence of this, Jas points out that the shooting at the Glassy Junction pub that led to him giving up his life of crime took place in June 2003, more than a year after the Bassis were first arrested. 'Nothing has changed. The situation on the streets is as bad as ever. There are places round here where you find syringes on the street all the time. The problem with something like heroin is that it doesn't just go away. When you get a gang who come into town and start selling it, people get addicted. When that gang goes to prison, it does nothing to stop the addicts wanting their next fix. All the police do is create a vacuum for the next gang to fill.'

The Asian-on-Asian violence seen on the streets of Southall is far from unique. Keighley, on the outskirts of Bradford, Yorkshire, where one in five of the population is of Asian origin, has been the scene of a bloody turf war between gangs supplying heroin in the area and beyond.

In parts of the town wraps of heroin sell for as little as two pounds – easily affordable by even the most cash-strapped teenagers. Such low prices have assured healthy sales and huge profits, which the dealers invest in scanners, wireless microphones and automatic guns in a bid to protect themselves from police action. When rival gangs clash, they do so violently.

In February 2002 twenty-four-year-old Qadir Ahmed, a convicted drug-dealer, was beaten and stabbed to death in the street after his killers shunted his car off the road as he drove home from a football match. By the time of his murder the local police were carrying out thirty-four separate investigations into drug-related violence, which included four murders and a full-scale street battle during which several shots were fired.

The most public violence is generally confined to those at the bottom of the ladder in the gang structure. These include the young teenagers who make the drug deliveries, often on specially bought mountain bikes. Above them come street dealers, supplying runners and customers with their fixes. Above them are the murky upper echelons of the gang world, often using family ties with Pakistan to arrange the courier routes that bring the drugs back to Britain where they masquerade as legitimate businessmen.

In nearby Bradford forty-six-year-old Waheed Akhtar was just such a man. Nicknamed 'the Colonel', he used his contacts in London and Pakistan to become one of the area's biggest heroin-traffickers. Akhtar portrayed himself as a respectable businessman who bought and sold cars and imported bottled water from Pakistan, but the businesses were just a front for his drugs empire. With a wide range of contacts in the criminal field, both in the UK and beyond, Akhtar had moved quickly up the ranks of the underworld and soon found himself at the head of a powerful trafficking syndicate.

It was a position he was determined to hold on to, and when five kilos of heroin worth more than £250,000 vanished from the boot of his car, it was clear that someone would have to pay. To allow the thief to go unpunished would make him appear weak and his reign would soon come to an end.

Although the actual theft came as a surprise, Akhtar had been warned that something like it might happen. His associate, Daniel Francis, had warned of a plot to rip him off and all the clues pointed to someone in his own gang being responsible. The car containing the drugs had been parked directly outside Akhtar's home and had not been damaged during the raid. Whoever had stolen the drugs had somehow managed to obtain the key, which meant the culprit was almost certainly someone he knew.

The chief suspects – drug-users Naveed Younis and a woman known as Petra – were summoned to his terraced home where they were quizzed, but then released. The following day, the woman returned to Akhtar's house to clear her name once and for all. But his right-hand man Azhar Mahmood had already assembled an 'interrogation squad' from Manchester who bundled her into a car and drove her to a house in Burnley. There, Petra was stripped, beaten, forced to take heroin and drink alcohol before their brutal questioning began.

Meanwhile Younis, widely known as 'Niddy', was again summoned to Akhtar's house where, the moment he walked through the door, he was attacked with baseball bats and sticks. The gang shoved their bleeding victim into the boot of Akhtar's Mercedes and drove to Niddy's house in nearby Girlington, where a search for the consignment proved fruitless.

Akhtar, now becoming increasingly desperate, ordered that both 'suspects' be brought to a dingy warehouse he rented where they were immediately tied to chairs. One man, Sagir Alam, shouted at Petra, 'Where are the drugs?' and hit her with a heavy wheel brace. When it bent with the force of the blow he burst into laughter. At the same time, the gang began 'working' on Younis with a scaffolding pole, a snooker cue and batons. The interrogation and beatings lasted more than six hours. At one point, the gang even tied a noose around Younis's neck and carried out a mock hanging.

Convinced that either Niddy or Petra knew where his drugs were, Akhtar decided to sit the pair opposite each other and told them to argue out between them to see who was telling the truth.

It was then that the name of Francis, who had been watching proceedings, was first mentioned. He immediately became a suspect and the others began beating him to a pulp. He was knocked unconscious but when he fell to the floor they continued hitting him with a scaffolding pole and whipping him with a length of wire. At one point, a gun was pointed at his head, but when the trigger was pulled, it only clicked.

Francis had all four of his limbs broken, both his hands were smashed and his jaw fractured. Akhtar only stopped the beating when Francis stopped responding. He had suffered kidney failure and passed into a coma.

By seven a.m., Akhtar needed to get rid of the bloodied trio before neighbouring businesses spotted them. They were bundled into cars and dumped at various spots across the district. The woman found herself close to Bradford Royal Infirmary while Younis was left near his family home in Girlington.

Francis, whose huge loss of blood had led to hypothermia, was thrown out behind a mound of earth at a rural spot in Wilsden. Detective Sergeant Walker said: 'It was nine thirty a.m. before a passer-by spotted him totally by chance. He was very close to death at that time and would not have survived much longer.' He was so badly injured that when he was finally taken to hospital, medical staff thought he had been run over.

The missing drugs were never found.

* * *

HEROIN

Back in the pub, Jas and I start talking about heroin, its effects, its addictive qualities and the devastating effect it has on so many of those who take it.

'I always told myself I'd never inject. No matter what. I don't ever want to get to the stage when I'm injecting. Once you do that, you're on the steady slope. That's when all the real problems start,' he tells me. 'You're risking HIV, hepatitis, abscesses and all sorts. But now that I'm not dealing I don't know if I have any choice. When you chase the dragon, you spend a lot more money than you do when you mix it up and inject it straight in your veins.'

The problem, Jas explains, is that the first time you take heroin is always the best. Every subsequent experience with the drug is slightly less intense, less pleasurable. This is because the body rapidly builds up a resistance to heroin and needs more and more to produce the same effects. Once addiction sets in, users rarely feel high but instead need a certain amount of heroin just to feel 'normal' and stave off the first signs of cold turkey – withdrawal. The vast majority of users start off smoking it, then move on to injecting, partly because of the costs involved and also because injecting heroin produces a faster, more intense high, particularly in those who have built up a degree of tolerance.

Having already sampled crack cocaine and come out of the experience relatively unscathed, I decide to try heroin. As with crack, I want to see if I can better empathise with those who become addicted to the drug. They are, after all, the end users for those who smuggle heroin into the country and they are also linked to much of the petty crime like burglary and car theft.

There's no question of me injecting – that would be going a step too far and be completely unnecessary as the vast majority of Asian users shun needles. Instead, like Jas, I will 'chase the dragon'.

We head back to Jas's bedsit, a dingy upstairs room in a road alongside the main railway station. As we sit down he rummages through a box of cereal sitting on the counter of the kitchenette and pulls out a deflated balloon with a knot tied in the end. 'I always like to have one or two wraps around,' he explains. 'I guess this is as good a hiding-place as any but the police have seen it all. They're pretty good at finding stuff.'

Jas opens the paper and shows me the contents. It looks like fine sawdust, the sort of thing you find on the floor of a hamster's cage. There is no smell, so far as I can tell.

I sit on the edge of the bed and Jas squats on the ground in front of me, giving a running commentary on everything that he does. 'I sprinkle some of the powder on some foil, on the dull side so it heats more quickly with a lighter.' With the foil folded into a rough half-tube shape and clasped between his fingers, Jas fires up the lighter with his one free hand and runs the flickering yellow flame along the length of the powder. 'You don't inhale right away. You burn off all the impurities first. Let the powder melt, let it become liquid. And then it's ready.'

He hands me the foil but I'm so distracted by the look of the dirty yellow brown sludge at the bottom of the foil that I hardly hear what Jas is saying. He seems to be asking me if I want to eat anything and I shake my head, wondering how he can be thinking of food at a time like this. I set the lighter under the foil and smoke pours off so quickly that it catches me by surprise. I put the tube into my mouth and suck in the hot air.

At first there's nothing to write home about. A slight fuzziness to the eyes. A feeling of relaxation. I reapply the flame and smoke a little more.

But just as I start, the effects of my first attempt come flooding through. Now I'm feeling it. A sensation of floating. It's that feeling you get just before you drift off to sleep after great sex, and you know that you don't have to be at work the following day. Total bliss.

There's a glow, a feeling of warmth and then – to borrow a description common to heroin users – I feel as if I've been wrapped in cotton wool. It's all as far away from the experience of crack as it is possible to be. The two drugs are complete opposites. With crack, for a short time at least, you feel as though you could conquer the world. When you're on heroin, the world could be about to be conquered and you wouldn't care.

HEROIN

Then there's a feeling of acceleration. It's that feeling you get when you're drunk. It's as though I'm standing still and the world is moving faster and faster. Oh, fuck. I know this feeling.

I start to stand up and ask Jas for directions to the toilet. His stupefied smile beams up at me but he says nothing. I manage to get to the sink and throw up violently. It is only later I realise that Jas was not asking me if I wanted to eat something, he was asking me when I last ate. Nausea is such a common effect of irregular heroin smoking that practised users avoid food for several hours beforehand to lessen the urge to hurl.

The inside of my mouth tastes bitter, the effect of my own bile and the heroin itself. My teeth feel like I've been chewing toffee. I stumble back to the bed and sit down. Jas is still on the floor, now leaning back against the wall, eyes closed, a burnt-out match and the ragged piece of kitchen foil still in his fingers.

Part of me feels like I should be doing something – making notes, asking questions – but the larger part of me wants to do nothing at all. The nausea is passing and, apart from occasionally feeling incredibly itchy all over, only the feelings of gentle bliss are left.

I lean back on the bed and fall asleep.

For those seeking the ultimate 'natural' high, heroin will always be there. For those who seek something more, they need look no further than their friendly neighbourhood lab technician.

SYNTHETIC DRUGS

CHAPTER TWENTY

Kenny takes another swig from his bottle of Bud, then wipes his mouth on the back of his hand. 'I'm telling you,' he says, shaking his head slowly, 'if people knew just how dangerous this stuff was, if they had any fucking idea of the risks involved, they'd give the people behind it a hell of a lot more respect.'

I'm sitting in the upstairs section of a plush wine-bar-cum-nightclub in the centre of Liverpool with Kenny, a long-time drug-dealer. Kenny looks younger than his thirty-four years and his dark eyes dance like candle flames as he speaks, but he insists he's completely clean. We've spent the last fifteen minutes talking about the dangers of the dance-drug ecstasy. Not the potential and highly debated risks of long-term use but the very real risks associated with manufacturing it.

'I just help out every now and then but the guys who really make the stuff are seriously fucking clued-up and they have to be. It's fucking dangerous. You can't fuck about with it. Some of the fumes that come off the stuff are deadly. I'm talking about cyanide, I mean fucking cyanide, and you get shitloads of it. It's a real risk-your-life venture. Some of these guys make fortunes but they're worth every penny in my book.'

While some 80 per cent of the world's ecstasy is made in clandestine laboratories in the Netherlands this figure is declining rapidly as increasing numbers of gangs opt to boost their profits even further by setting up on their own. More lucrative than either heroin or cocaine, and more popular than both drugs combined, the market for ecstasy-type drugs is growing rapidly and shows no signs of slowing down. At any one time there are at least fifty ecstasy and amphetamine labs in the UK, a number of them dotted in and around the Liverpool area.

The set-up sounds far more glamorous than it is. A basic ecstasy lab – consisting of mini electric cookers, distillation flasks, over-sized pasta pots (for steam baths) and funnels with access to running water, electricity and a wastepipe – can easily be built in the average toilet. One recent example was set up in a garden shed. Ideally, the labs like to be close to areas of heavy industry or on remote farmland – somewhere the numerous fumes won't be detected.

Start-up costs are relatively low. Apparatus costing around £4000 can be used to turn out several thousand pills a week, and getting hold of the right gear usually involves little more than bribing a destitute student to lift a few items out of their university storeroom. The labs are highly mobile: they are often packed up in the back of vans and moved from one location to another every few weeks to stay one step ahead of the authorities.

The two main motivations for setting up in the UK are increasing profit and reducing risk. With ecstasy from Holland, the biggest problem is getting it safely across the Channel and, with prices falling, the only way to make it worthwhile is to import in bulk, which greatly increases the risk of being intercepted.

Originally I was hoping Kenny would be able to arrange for me to visit the lab that produces the ecstasy he sells, but the more I learn about what goes on inside, the less keen I am. In places like Noord-Brabant and Limburg in southern Holland, at least twenty out of the estimated five hundred illicit ecstasy laboratories give themselves away to the authorities each year by suddenly exploding, sometimes with fatal results. Kenny, who understands the process inside out, explains why.

'It's simple enough if you know what you're doing, but there are a few stages where, if you fuck up, it can all go horribly wrong. When you add the safrole or the PMK [two precursor chemicals used in the process] it creates huge amounts of heat but if the mixture goes over forty degrees it explodes. But it's not just a question of keeping it cool for a few minutes, the mixing and stirring has to go on for sixteen hours. Then you start mucking about with things like benzene – which they reckon causes cancer – methanol, sulphuric acid and ether, which will explode if you so much as turn on a light switch.

'The fumes are a big problem, you can't get away from them and you end up with this thick layer of vapour on the floor. The ones that don't kill you give you one fuck of a headache and the ones that don't do that will burn your skin like acid. That causes other problems – a lot of the equipment is glass tubes and beakers and it's all really fragile. But you have to work in these thick rubber gloves so you can't feel anything and wearing a mask and goggles so you can't really see anything either. It means you're ten times more likely to drop or spill stuff and when you're trying to get from one end of a room to the other with a load of hot sulphuric acid, that's no joke. Some days I go home covered in burns and blisters.

'And even once you're finished, it ain't over. Some of the leftover chemicals will explode if they're not stored properly and you can't just pour them down the sink or the drain without having the local environment-health or Green Party rep on your back. So you end up dumping it on some wasteland. Fuck knows what it's doing to the water out there.'

Kenny has been selling ecstasy for more than fifteen years, ever since it burst on to the British dance scene, having first discovered it while on holiday first in Amsterdam and then in Ibiza during the 1980s. His move into manufacturing two years before we met came almost by accident when he stumbled across a like-minded group of people who wanted to avoid contact with the worst of the criminals who have now moved into the trade. For Kenny, it's a welcome return to the early days of innocence.

'It's a bit like cannabis. At first the whole trade was run by university students and toffs like Howard Marks and it was all some jolly boys' adventure. Then mobs from London and Essex moved in, and before you knew it, people in Range Rovers are getting their heads blown off.' At first Kenny smuggled his supplies from Amsterdam himself, but as his business grew, he had to rely on others with more sophisticated trafficking operations.

'The problem now is that the people smuggling E are also bringing in heroin and cocaine. There are gangs that specialise in getting stuff across the Channel, charging a set price per kilo, and don't care what it actually is because to them anything Class A is all the same. But these people are always ripping each other off, always fighting over stuff. They're not nice people to be around. We started making our own because we thought we could make more money and get away from the aggro. I know we're breaking the law and making money from illegal drugs, but that doesn't mean we want to be gangsters.'

In the earliest days ecstasy production was being pioneered by men like Dutchman Rob Hollemans, a former electrician who, by the mid-1980s, had become one of the biggest ecstasy producers in Holland. By sneaking into chemistry lectures at his local university, Hollemans learnt enough to make some of the highest quality tablets the market had ever known. Working hand in hand with his brother, Hollemans' sole aim was to provide clubbers with the best possible psychedelic experience; making a profit was the last thing on his mind. To that end, Rob and his brother threw open the doors of their Limburg lab to show everyone and anyone exactly how it was done.

'Back then the quality control was excellent – if a particular batch didn't quite hit the mark there was instant feedback and they'd make sure they fixed it,' says Kenny. 'Of course, it helped that it was legal but even after it was banned that was still the case for the first few years.' But as the knowledge spread, so gangs who had previously trafficked in amphetamine moved in and profit became the primary motivation. Hollemans was so disillusioned by what had happened that he quit the ecstasy business altogether. The last anyone heard, he was working as a carpenter in Hungary.

Just like any other mass-market product, ecstasy is subject to the laws of supply and demand, and prices have tumbled as production of the synthetic drug has moved from a cottage industry to a sophisticated, industrialised global business that is worth billions of pounds.

Kenny has seen the price of pills plunge dramatically as a result. 'In 1990 I was going out and buying around a thousand pills for between six and seven pounds each and flogging them for up to fifteen quid a throw. Today I'm paying between forty and seventy pence a pill and in some areas the price is down as low as two pounds and sometimes even less.'

What the dealers have lost in terms of margins they have more than made up for in volume as clubbers consume the increasingly poor-quality drug in ever greater numbers to achieve the desired effect. In the 1980s most of the tablets in circulation contained pure MDMA. The latest research suggests that half of all tablets on sale contain no MDMA, and those that do have had the dosage reduced to such a level that some clubbers routinely take four or five tablets each night.

'Half the people out there are getting a bit of a speedy buzz from something that has so little ecstasy in it as to be no use whatsoever, but because it's all they've ever known, they don't care. In the big cities it's all the same but out in the sticks you actually get different grades of ecstasy. The prices vary from two pounds to fifteen per pill and, believe me, you get what you pay for.'

Kenny shakes his head, almost mournfully. 'The trouble is no one really cares any more. Every dealer says the tablets they are selling are the best ever so no one believes it any more, not enough to pay more for a premium product. They'd rather take pot luck. We thought we could clean up by making some top-quality stuff but in the end we had to charge exactly the same amount as everyone else, otherwise no one was interested.'

MDMA was first patented in 1912 by German pharmaceutical giant Merck, who developed it as a diet pill but decided it wasn't suitable to put on the market. It resurfaced briefly during the 1950s when the US army tested its potential as a tool in psychological warfare and then a decade later when it was taken up by marriage counsellors, who believed it could help estranged couples to empathise with one another.

But it wasn't until research by the American chemist Dr Alexander Shulgin stumbled upon the compound in the mid-1970s that its journey to the dance-floor really began. Fascinated by psychedelic substances ever since he had experimented with mescaline in the 1960s, Dr Shulgin, who will celebrate his eightieth birthday in 2005, has carried out vast amounts of research on a wide range of substances, famously testing every new compound on himself and meticulously recording the results.

His 1991 book, *PIHKAL (Phenethylamines I Have Known and Loved)*, includes the recipe for ecstasy – the first time it had been widely published – and more than two hundred similar substances, and is found in almost every ecstasy lab on the planet. Age has not slowed him down and he continues to test new substances and publish new papers.

Having found MDMA to be the pick of the bunch from an early stage, Dr Shulgin and his wife, Ann, began sharing it with their friends, who in turn introduced it to an even wider audience. Seen as an enlightening alternative to LSD, the substance was openly sold in nightclubs across America and instantly proved a success. When it hit Dallas, Texas, it was renamed 'ecstasy' by an entrepreneurial drug-dealer who spotted its commercial potential. Thanks to his marketing efforts, the new drug was soon selling 30,000 units per month in that one city alone. By April 1985, the US Drug Enforcement Administration had also spotted its commercial potential and made MDMA a Schedule 1 banned substance, classing it alongside heroin and cocaine.

The journey to Britain took a little longer. Some, like Kenny, discovered ecstasy in Ibiza, or Amsterdam, while others came across it in hippie communities in America. Legend has it that one of the first major importations was carried out by none other than a member of the leading Manchester band the Happy Mondays, who allegedly set off to the Netherlands and returned with a bag containing more than a thousand tablets. Some were sold, others were given away for free, and within the space of a few weeks people were asking for more.

Ecstasy use in Britain really took off in the mid-1980s when it became the drug of choice (along with LSD) at vast outdoor parties, raves, organised by New Age travellers and free-spirited devotees of Acid House music. Rarely had a drug received better press. The reputation that preceded it was that ecstasy kept you up all night like speed but without the comedown, and gave you acid-like experiences of sound and colour but without the possibility of a bad trip. The 'love drug' was part stimulant, part hallucinogen and part aphrodisiac. Above all, ecstasy was said to be 100 per cent safe with no long-term side effects.

'I've tried everything – dope, cocaine, speed – none of them compares to ecstasy at all,' says one regular user. 'It's all the best feelings you've ever had compressed into one night. It's called ecstasy for a reason. With ecstasy, everyone's your brother, everyone's your sister, and everyone's your best friend.'

Use of the drug only heightened what was already an utterly mind-blowing experience. Those first outdoor events would often last days at a time and attract crowds of ten thousand or more. But by 1988 cunning, well-bred entrepreneurs, like the infamous Tony Colston-Hayter, had stepped in and the free events became so-called 'pay parties'.

For thousands of young revellers, just getting to an event was half the thrill. Convoys of cars would disappear into the countryside in the dead of night following last-minute instructions left on numerous answering-machines in a bid to keep the organisers one step ahead of the police and get round the public-entertainment, public-order and noise-pollution laws. Another reason ecstasy took off at the events was that, without a drinks licence, organisers faced serious penalties if any alcohol was found on sale: ecstasy, whose effect is diminished if taken with alcohol, proved the perfect alternative.

At the same time ecstasy became a Class A drug, the police formed the Pay Party Unit and pretty soon the organisation of security at the parties and then the parties themselves fell into the hands of organised crime.

GANGS

If you control who gets into a rave, or who goes in and out of a club, then you can control who deals the drugs and can therefore ensure you get a cut of every pill sold. With this in mind, gangs of modern-day hard men began setting themselves up as security firms, often with alarming results. Strikeforce Surveillance, for example, became notorious on the rave scene before it disbanded in 1990. Its reputation for aggressive tactics was sealed when, during an outdoor party at Reigate, Surrey, in September 1999, the sixty-strong Strikeforce team, ostensibly there to guard the event, attacked police officers who were trying to arrest one of their dealers. Armed with baseball bats, knives and CS gas they left sixteen police officers injured.

At one Kent party drug-taking became almost mandatory as the heavies policing the event with their Rottweiler dogs and shotguns 'encouraged' every participant to purchase an ecstasy tablet for fifteen pounds before allowing them in.

One eyewitness commented: 'What has become increasingly clear is that many of the people who claim to be running these parties are nothing more than front men. Parties are now being taken over by well-organised psychos.'

New laws designed to allow clubs to open twenty-four hours a day and increasing the penalties for pay-party organisers forced the rapidly growing dance culture inside and into a commercial setting where police and government officials believed it could be more easily controlled. In fact, all they did was shift the balance of power to club-owners and the criminals who turned up and offered to become their 'business partners'.

The shift from outdoors to indoors was virtually seamless and the drugs became more of a feature than ever. On certain nights, at major venues up and down the country, up to 90 per cent of the crowd would be on E. Any petty dealers would have their stash confiscated at the door and these would then be resold by the doorman's favoured trader. In odd cases where a dealer managed to slip through the net the doormen would give someone some cash and send them out into the crowd asking all and sundry to 'sort them out' until the hapless dealer was found.

SYNTHETIC DRUGS

A whole new generation of gangsters emerged courtesy of the dance-drugs scene and, never slow to spot an opportunity to make money, the old guard also got in on the action. Among the well-established faces known to have dabbled in the ecstasy scene are the likes of Kenny Noye, former Great Train Robber Tommy Wisbey and members of the notorious north London firm, the A team.

Dr Shulgin, often referred to as the grandad of the E-generation, is understandably alarmed at the way ecstasy has become a global phenomenon, let alone such a money-spinner for organised crime. Speaking from his home in Lafayette, California, he told me that the use of the drug in the club scene is overshadowing its higher purpose. 'Psychedelics are a means for adults to gain an insight into themselves. They're research tools. Using them only in the context of music and dance means that whole element of the experience is being completely wasted.'

Early hours in a popular men-only gay club in central London finds the dance-floor heaving with sweat-drenched bodies. All ages, walks of life and looks are represented – the uniting factor is the widespread use of ecstasy. Nowhere is the phenomenal rise of the drug more apparent than on the gay scene where it is considered an almost essential part of any night out. 'Basically, pretty much everyone here is on it,' says Patrick, thirty-two, a regular at the club. 'Some people are going off it and getting into ketamine instead, but that's a completely different kind of buzz. If you've been out the night before and you want to carry on here, then E is what you need. I've only been taking it for the last year. I used to be a bit scared but when you see that everyone else is doing it and having a good time, you think, Why not? I usually club together with friends to buy a batch so we know we're all taking the same stuff, having the same experience.

'When I started it was just half a tablet or maybe one. Then as I got braver I started taking more and more. Now I've realised there's no point in taking more than four tablets in a night – partly because I can't really afford it and partly because you don't get any extra benefit from it, especially if you're in a bad mood to start off with – all it does is make you feel normal. I try not to get too carried away, though: I know I'm basically putting a poison in my brain and I worry about the long-term effects.

'The short-term ones are worrying too. I don't like the hangover. If I have a big weekend I can get really tearful on the Tuesday or Wednesday for no reason, or I get really snappy. But not everyone thinks like that. It's so cheap now that some people are downing them like there's no tomorrow.'

Some experts say the rise in ecstasy production and fall in price is directly responsible for an increase in fatalities. Experts at St George's Hospital Medical School in London linked the rise in the number of UK ecstasy deaths to the falling price of the drug, which in turn has led to increased consumption. There were twelve deaths in 1996. By 2001 this number had climbed to seventy-two and the annual death toll continues to rise.

Some of the deaths have been linked to tablets containing toxic ingredients of higher than normal concentrations of MDMA leading to accidental 'overdose' when the user's body can't cope with the effects going on for far longer than expected. In Amsterdam, users are able to have their pills tested outside clubs, a scheme said to prevent several deaths each year.

There is pressure to introduce pill testing in the UK but there are concerns that this might be seen as encouraging some to take more drugs. 'Say you have a situation where a first-time clubber is offered a tablet by a friend,' says one drugs officer. 'He refuses because he doesn't know what it contains. So the friend offers to accompany him to the testing line where they find out the tablet is pure MDMA. The whole testing process assumes that somehow pure MDMA is safer than any of the variants, but no one knows for certain if that is the case and some people are always going to be predisposed to suffering a bad reaction.'

The number of deaths is still tiny compared to the number of pills in circulation – according to the National Criminal Intelligence Service at least two million ecstasy tablets are consumed each week but this is thought to be an underestimate. Figures from the UN Office on Drugs and Crime suggest that at the start of the 1990s, one per cent of the UK population consumed ecstasy. Within little more than a decade this figure had doubled to 2.2 per cent.

But when deaths do occur they are so shocking that they always receive massive media coverage. An overheating body goes through epilepsy-like seizures, slips into a coma and bleeds through every major organ. It is, by anyone's standards, a terrible way to die.

In July 2002 ten-year-old Jade Slack approached a friend at a house-party in Galgate near Lancaster and explained she was feeling unwell. Kim Speak rushed over. 'She just looked different. Her pupils were massive. Her lips started to change colour to, like, a purple colour. She sat down for a few minutes but when she got up she began banging into things. She was really hot and we tried to cool her down by putting her in the shower and running her head under cold water.' It was then that Jade admitted taking a couple of tablets. Kim asked her what they were and she replied, 'Ecstasy.'

The ordeal continued. 'She started slapping herself and then saying, "Stop slapping me."' As the horrified adults looked on, her body temperature rose from the normal 37.9°C to 42°C. Jade's brain swelled, she suffered a heart-attack, and within a few hours had become the youngest person in the world to die from taking ecstasy.

The United Nations report published in 2003 paints an astonishing picture of just how big the industry, now producing 125 tonnes of ecstasy a year, has become in only a decade. The UN estimates that eight million people in the world now take ecstasy, a rise of 70 per cent on five years ago. The combined ecstasy and amphetamines market is worth $65 billion a year, and more people consume so-called designer drugs than heroin and cocaine combined. And the trend shows no sign of slowing down: the report found that ecstasy use was growing by 27 per cent each year. This compares to a growth rate of 8 per cent for heroin and just 1.5 per cent for cocaine.

'The danger posed by synthetic drugs is advancing relentlessly,' the report noted. 'Access to chemicals, growing demand, corrupt officials, poor law enforcement, lack of extradition and/or light sentencing . . . has led to a greater involvement of criminal groups with ruthless forms of marketing.'

Which means that for men like Kenny, who have a hand in the manufacturing process, the future is looking brighter than ever. Dr Shulgin is continuing his research into psychedelics, and tens of thousands of devotees are eagerly awaiting his findings. At the same time, dozens of other researchers are attempting to synthesise ever more potent stimulants, many of which will ultimately find their way on to the street.

'Some people are always going to be looking for a buzz and the great thing about synthetic drugs is that they can be designed to give specific effects,' says Kenny. 'They design the individual molecules just like architects design houses. They reckon synthetic cocaine is about forty times stronger than the real thing. I heard about five people died the first time they tried it because they didn't realise how powerful it was going to be. It's not big now because there's no need for it, but who knows what's going to happen in the future? This is where the future is. Even if they manage to get rid of every poppy field in Afghanistan, torch every coca plantation in Bolivia, we'll still be here and our market will be bigger than ever.'

PEOPLE-SMUGGLING

CHAPTER TWENTY-ONE

As soon as David Bell pulled open the heavy metal doors, he knew that something was terribly wrong.

The Dover-based Customs officer was carrying out a routine inspection of an articulated lorry that had just disembarked a ferry from Zeebrugge. The manifest said the vehicle was transporting fresh produce so the interior should have been chilled, but as the doors swung open Bell was hit by a blast of intense, fetid heat.

At first the interior of the fifty-foot long container offered no explanation. Boxes of tomatoes on wooden pallets were piled ceiling high and nothing more could be seen. Bell climbed a ladder and tried to see what lay beyond, but when that failed, he called on two freight supervisors, Barry Betts and Darren Bailey, to help unload the lorry's cargo.

And that was when they found the body.

The Chinese teenager was sprawled across the corrugated metal floor, half naked and half buried by the scattered crates and boxes. It looked as though he had been trying to reach the main doors by squeezing through a gap under the pallets, but they had collapsed on top of him.

As Betts climbed in and began clearing crates from around the man's body, he saw another, that of a young girl, lying on her back with her mouth open and eyes closed. He pulled out his torch and pointed it into the darkness. At first he thought the floor was covered with more crates. Then, as his eyes adjusted to the gloom, he realised he was staring at a sea of bodies.

Some looked as though they had died peacefully, holding hands and lying down as if they were simply going to sleep. Others had spent their last moments in agony, their fingers torn and bloody as they had tried desperately to claw their way out of what had become their tomb.

As his torch beam picked out the individual figures, Betts caught a movement. One man was weakly tapping on the side of the container, trying to attract his attention: he was barely conscious and gasping, '*Bang wo, bang wo*' – 'Help me'. Then another young man, bare-chested and dripping with sweat, moved towards the open doors, climbing over the bodies to get there.

Within an hour the team had removed a total of fifty-eight corpses – fifty-four men and four women. The two men they had seen moving were the only ones left alive.

In the words of the head of the National Crime Squad: 'People-smuggling is not *a* crime, it is *the* crime, the crime of the future.'

At present at least six hundred thousand people enter the EU illegally each year and around 80 per cent of them are brought in by criminal gangs. With conservative estimates putting the value of the business at around £20 billion, people-smuggling is easily as lucrative as the drugs trade, but even with recent increases in sentences, the penalties for those who are caught remain far lower. And it's a business experiencing rapid growth. In 1991 a mere sixty-one people were discovered trying to enter Britain clandestinely. In 2002, 21,000 were caught. Despite millions spent on additional security measures, thousands still slip through undetected.

At the turn of the millennium the world population stood at around 6.5 billion. By the year 2025 it will be 8.5 billion. In forty-two countries, twenty-four in Africa, ten in the Middle East, the population doubles every twenty-five years. India increases its population by the size of the population of Iceland every four days, and by the size of Norway's every three months.

What all this means is that the greatest growth in world population is set to come from the poorest countries. This in turn means that in the future, as now, the people-trafficking gangs will have a never-ending supply of 'clients' who, for purely economic reasons, will pay them handsomely to be smuggled from one country to another.

The vast sums to be made mean the gangs are able to invest heavily in the latest technology to stay one step ahead of the authorities. 'The gangs have infrastructures, communications and surveillance capabilities far in excess of anything that the law-enforcement agencies in transit and source countries can muster,' Stephen Boys Smith, head of the UK Immigration Service, said in a written submission to Parliament in 2002. 'The ease with which they operate across international boundaries means that the chances of their activities diminishing are negligible.'

The tragedy at Dover alerted many to the scale of the problem, but it wasn't the first time lives had been lost. In 1995, eighteen Chinese suffocated in a sealed trailer as it crossed Hungary. A year later, five bodies were found in a truck crossing the Austrian border, and in January 2002, a container ship docked in Seattle with eighteen Chinese in the hold. Three were dead and had sunk down into the filth at the bottom of the container, while the remainder were only hours from starvation.

In each of these cases, responsibility for the deaths falls to members of one of the largest, most sophisticated and most powerful criminal organisations anywhere in the world: the Triads.

In 1985 the House of Commons Home Affairs Committee on the Chinese Community in Britain reported the total absence of Triads in the UK. 'The myth flourishes despite the absence of any evidence whatever to sustain it,' their report concluded. 'It is true, of course, that any Chinese criminals in Britain are likely to have contacts in Hong Kong but no one was able to provide us with any evidence or even reasonable suspicion of links between criminal activities or organisations in Britain and Hong Kong and Macao.'

The Triads have been a presence in Britain since the beginning of the twentieth century and, as one of the oldest of all the criminal gangs, they are undoubtedly the best established of all the international groups currently operating in the UK.

Triads were originally established as secret societies set up to overthrow the unpopular Han dynasty in China that ruled from 206 BC to AD 220. As with many other organised-crime groups, in time the Triads went from being protectors of the people to running protection rackets within their midst. Today they are a significant presence in every city with a sizeable Chinese population. Traditionally their main criminal activities have been extortion, loan-sharking, credit-card fraud and video piracy. The vast majority of the extortion takes place within the Chinese community, the victims being restaurants and other businesses. Even though the practice is widespread and occasionally, when payment is not forthcoming, results in violence or acts of criminal damage, only a handful of cases are ever reported to the police.

In recent years the Triads have become heavily involved in the far more profitable business of people-smuggling, bringing tens of thousands of Chinese into the UK, some of whom claim asylum but most of whom simply vanish into the tight-knit community, working in the back rooms of restaurants, sweat-shops and food-processing plants. It is estimated that more than four hundred thousand people have paid the gangs up to £20,000 for a ticket to the UK in the last ten years.

Full members of the Triads undergo an elaborate initiation ceremony where they swear thirty-six oaths of allegiance to the organisation and pledge to accept death 'by myriad swords' should they ever betray their Triad brothers.

It is for this reason that acts of violence carried out by Triad 'soldiers' usually involve the victim being 'chopped' – attacked with meat cleavers or melon knives – to maintain the ancient symbolism. Such attacks are rarely intended to be fatal: the principal targets are the main muscles, including the calves, thighs, forearms and biceps, though the scalp is often slashed too. The hideously scarred amputees who survive are a living warning to others in the community that the Triads are not to be crossed. But knives have also been the weapon of choice for murder.

According to the National Criminal Intelligence Service there are four main Triad gangs operating in Britain: the Wo Shing Wo, the Sui Fong (also known as the Wo On Lok), the 14K and the San Yee On. For the most part they manage to live in reasonable harmony, but every now and then violence flares up, sometimes for the most unlikely reasons.

In June 2002 alleged Triad leader Mann Chung Li, also known as Michael Lee, head chef at the Tin Tin Cantonese restaurant in Wolverhampton, was brutally murdered during a mass brawl between his own men and a rival gang. The battle, which took place in a crowded casino in the heart of Birmingham's Chinatown, had been arranged because Li was accused of ignoring another alleged Triad leader, Phillip Hung Chan, at a wedding earlier in the year.

With his smart tailored suits, dapper moustache and slicked-back hair, Phillip Hung Chan looks every inch the successful businessman. As manager of the popular Happy Gathering restaurant in Northampton, the softly spoken fifty-six-year-old had built a reputation for being polite and attentive. He played host to visiting dignitaries and local VIPs, ensuring his high standing in Britain's tightly knit Chinese community.

'Face' is a key notion in Chinese society. Loss of face, which usually comes about as the result of being embarrassed or humiliated in public, brings shame not only to the person concerned but to the whole family, including its ancestors. At the wedding Li refused to talk to Chan, who lost face as a result. What to Western eyes appeared a trivial dispute quickly escalated into something far more serious, and over the next few weeks the tensions between the two men grew to the point at which it was agreed that their differences could be sorted out only with extreme violence.

On the afternoon of 25 June 2002, after a bout of heavy drinking, Chan made a number of calls to London and put together a group of fighters who were to travel up to Birmingham as quickly as possible. Within two hours a two-car convoy of nine heavily armed thugs was racing up the M1. Chan called Li to tell him what he had done and set up a meeting. Li immediately began to assemble a team of his own, and more than a dozen hardened fighters from Birmingham's Chinatown collected weapons and made their way to the casino.

Just before midnight Chan and nine others entered the China Palace and immediately sought out Li, who was waiting in the bar area. Violence erupted almost instantly. Terrified gamblers ran for cover as around thirty men from the two gangs pulled out their weapons and rushed at each other.

The members of both gangs had clearly been told to target those at the heart of the dispute. Within ninety seconds Li had been stabbed and slashed at least sixteen times. As he collapsed near the casino entrance in a mass of blood, Chan screamed and staggered back, the handle of a ceremonial dagger sticking out of his stomach. The fighting continued. Another member of Chan's gang, Feng-Ching Lim, was stabbed five times, three others were stabbed and one man was badly injured after being bludgeoned with an ashtray.

One man tried to flee, but was set upon by two men with machetes who hacked into his body again and again. One blow penetrated his skull. Witnesses saw several men running out of the casino, hiding bloody knives and swords in their clothes as they climbed into cars to make their escape.

Police arrived within minutes and saw a scene of mayhem. 'There was blood everywhere, and a full box of chef's knives that were to have been used as weapons,' said Detective Sergeant Dominic Kennedy.

During a three-month trial, the dock at Birmingham Crown Court was crammed with defendants, interpreters – translating into Vietnamese, Mandarin, Cantonese and Hakka – and security guards.

In his defence, Chan, who made a full recovery from his injuries, claimed that Li was far more than a chef. 'He was a very dangerous man. He had many men under his control. He was involved in running prostitution, illegal gambling clubs and in bringing illegal immigrants to the UK. He was a leader of the Triads. I was very frightened of him,' he told the court.

PEOPLE-SMUGGLING

Police uncovered evidence that Li was linked to a Triad human-trafficking gang and regularly provided accommodation and work to illegal immigrants who had been smuggled into the country. Other defendants said the exact opposite was true and that it was Chan who was the Triad leader. This, they explained, was the reason that his restaurant was so favoured by dignitaries and why he was able to recruit a band of fighters within the space of a few hours. They said Li's murder was part of an attempt by one gang to take over the people-smuggling operation of the other.

Where once drug-trafficking and extortion were the big money-spinners, the trade in human cargo is now just as lucrative. And whenever there is money to be made, there is potential for conflict. At first it seemed as though all the fighting was confined to the long-established Triad gangs in the UK whose roots are in Hong Kong. But now there is a new, far more deadly enemy.

New criminal gangs from mainland China, particularly the Fujian province, whose members include former soldiers from the People's Liberation Army, all of them highly trained in weaponry and hand-to-hand combat, are muscling in on the old-style gangs. Although they are essentially Triads, they focus entirely on the smuggling of immigrants and are more commonly referred to as Snakeheads – a name that refers to the way their clients need to twist and turn to find ways round border controls and immigration laws. The Snakeheads place far less emphasis on the historical and ceremonial aspects of Chinese organised crime and as a consequence have little hesitation in using firearms if they are available. And all the signs are that, in London, they are.

In June 2003, exactly a year after Li's death, a gunman walked into the BRB bar in the heart of London's Chinatown and shot dead thirty-seven-year-old businessman You Yi He. His death was immediately linked to the Snakehead gangs – he was said to be involved in helping to find work for the new immigrants – but what detectives found most disturbing was the escalation in gang violence: it was the first time in history that a gun, rather than a knife, had been used in a killing in Chinatown. Moreover, a month earlier a terrifying arsenal of weapons had been found hidden in a Chinatown restaurant. The haul included several AK47 assault rifles and a number of handguns as well as more traditional weapons, like serrated knives and sharpened throwing stars.

While the Triads work in relative isolation, the Snakeheads have formed strong alliances with criminal gangs from across the world and, as a result, have become far more powerful. On the streets of Chinatown no one will talk about the Snakeheads for fear of reprisals: both the murder of You Yi He and the deaths of the fifty-eight Chinese at Dover show that the gangs will stop at nothing to achieve their goals. Those who risk the journey from mainland China to the UK often find themselves treated little better than cattle.

At the tender age of twenty, Ke Su De found it hard to escape the feeling that, in many ways, his life was already over. As a delivery boy in Changle, a city in the heart of China's Fujian province, De earned just fifty pounds per month, the same as his father. With no prospects for promotion and no chance of a pay increase in his lifetime, De felt he had no option but leave. 'In China my life was not too good,' he says. 'I didn't have a good life at home or at work and so I wanted to go to Britain because you can earn good money there. Life can be good.'

The Fujian province borders the Taiwan Strait so it is no surprise to find that people from the area have a long history of restless seafaring – and of involvement with organised crime. The first ever Triad gang originated near the capital, Fuzhou, and soon applied the skills they had learnt from the smuggling of illegal goods to the smuggling of people out of China.

In many of the towns within Changle's jurisdiction, up to three-quarters of all the residents are now living abroad. The population of many of the villages has been crippled by this emigration, but for many of those left behind the benefits far outweigh the difficulties.

To take a walk through Changle is to go on an astonishing journey. Alongside the traditional brick huts, windowless shacks and rusty bicycles are fantastically ostentatious mansions replete with huge statues of dragons and warriors, and ornate ponds teeming with goldfish and brightly coloured koi carp. Gleaming new cars sit in the driveways.

Changle and nearby Fuching are, the locals say, 'widows' villages', but such is the admiration given to those who send money back from abroad that poverty is now considered shameful, a disgrace. Those who receive money from relatives working abroad are considered the beautiful people.

It was this peer pressure and the constant view of these symbols of wealth that finally convinced Ke Su De to go to a Snakehead. 'I met him through a friend. He told me that the people he had sent away had sent back enough money to build big houses. The Snakehead told me he'd helped many people go abroad. He said he had good connections with officials everywhere, even in the central government in Beijing. The Snakehead said, "Don't worry, I've been doing this for a decade, it's no big deal. There is no risk."'

De's parents paid a Snakehead £4000, the first instalment of a £20,000 fee to get him to the UK. The balance would be payable on arrival in the West – with massive interest.

Yet despite this, and that De would face years of backbreaking labour and living like a pauper to repay the debt, even a small proportion of his earnings sent back to China would make the rest of his family incredibly wealthy. On average the Chinese migrants make £1000 per month in the UK – considerably more than the fifty pounds they would earn at home. The US offers richer pickings still at about £1300 per month. But travelling to the USA is twice the cost of the trip to the UK.

Ke Su De left his home on 7 June, meeting up with another villager, twenty-two-year-old Ke Shi Guang, as they made their way to the pick-up point for the first leg of their long journey to Beijing. There was to be little luxury. The Snakeheads allowed no luggage, meaning that any clothes the travellers wished to take must be worn day and night. The only food came in the form of small bowls of nuts and rice, handed out by agents who met the travellers at preappointed rest stops. De and Guang were told that, as they neared their final destination, they would be given cheap Western clothes to ensure they fitted in in their new homeland.

Travelling with a group of around fifteen others as well as a Snakehead minder, it took only a few hours for De and Guang to realise they had been cheated. The Snakeheads had given them the impression that they would be flying all the way to England. Instead they boarded a plane and flew only as far as Belgrade.

From Yugoslavia, the group of migrants, now numbering sixty, were moved in separate parties of fifteen or fewer through Hungary, Austria and France to the Netherlands. Others traversed Russia, Poland, the Czech Republic and Germany, often travelling at night, by train, truck, even horse and cart, and sometimes on foot over remote border crossings.

(Such horrific journeys are not at all uncommon. Beng Chew, a London-based solicitor whose firm represents scores of Chinese asylum-seekers, has heard, first hand, many of their stories. 'They walk for days through the mountains, sleep rough and swim across rivers before they finally reach a safe place to cross a border illegally,' she explains. 'It is arduous and taxing. Many don't make it. Often they travel in winter. Last year I heard of one woman in her early thirties who died from exhaustion in the mountains. Some of the others didn't want to leave her but the agent insisted that they carry on.')

As De and Guang passed through Hungary the travellers had their first hitch. Hungarian border police kicked open the doors of the van in which they were travelling, discovered the migrants and turned them back towards Yugoslavia.

It was a minor setback. Within days they tried again and this time succeeded. At this point both men had their Chinese passports confiscated by their Snakehead minder, and were given fake Korean documents. With these they passed quickly through Hungary before crossing into Austria in a van with darkened windows.

They proceeded to Vienna where, on their forged Korean passports, they caught a plane to Charles de Gaulle airport in Paris.

From there they took a train to Belgium and then on to the Netherlands, arriving on 15 June.

A week before the group arrived in Rotterdam, preparations were being made for the final leg of their journey. A local Turkish mafia gang, under the leadership of thirty-six-year-old Gurbel Ozcan, had been subcontracted to take responsibility for the group once they arrived in the Dutch city. All the arrangements for getting them to Britain would be made by him. Ozcan was an old hand at the business: in 1998 he had served six months for people-trafficking offences and the shipment that included De and Guang would be the third he had made that year.

Ozcan and his gang had met to discuss the operation in the bar of the New York Hotel, Rotterdam, on Monday 12 June, six days before the transport. Unknown to Ozcan, his car had been bugged by Dutch police and his every move was monitored. But although they had witnessed Ozcan leaving for the meeting, the police decided that the gang leader had no imminent operations planned and lifted the surveillance.

At the meeting Ozcan expressed concerns about a backlog of migrants building up in Rotterdam. As he was responsible for the cost of feeding and housing them it made sound economic sense for him to get rid of them as soon as possible. For this reason he decided to send all sixty in a single shipment. He was only too aware of the risks. On 5 April one of his drivers, Leo Nijveen, had driven a lorry with fifty Chinese on board, hidden by a pallet of yoghurt, on to the three thirty a.m. Zeebrugge–Dover ferry. Half-way through the journey the human cargo ran out of air and started screaming and banging on the sides of the lorry.

Nijveen threw open the doors and let them out. He was fined £2000 per head for having illegal immigrants on board but allowed to return to Holland. The fine was later dropped when police said there was insufficient evidence to show that he knew the Chinese were on his lorry.

Despite the 5 April incident, Ozcan was determined to clear the backlog. A number of petty crooks were hired to do the dirty work, thus shielding him from any investigation. Hubertus van Keulen was paid £1200 to rent a warehouse at Waalhaven, part of Rotterdam's harbour, while Willem Jansen was paid £2000 to buy the tomatoes, the dummy cargo, which Nijveen later collected. Nijveen also bought the tractor unit of the truck from a garage near his home, and later purchased the trailer.

Knowing that he could no longer risk the journey himself, Nijveen also recruited Perry Wacker, a lorry driver from the city's eastern suburbs. Nijveen and Wacker had previously worked together and Nijveen was well aware that his friend was desperate for cash. The previous year while travelling through Spain, Wacker had fallen in love with a Moroccan girl called Nora. He had quickly proposed and they were due to be married on 17 July. But because Nora was not an EU national the marriage would not go ahead unless Wacker could satisfy the Dutch authorities that he had enough money to support them both. For driving the gang's lorry across the Channel Wacker had been promised a fee of £300 per person – a grand total of £18,000 for just a few hours' work. His money problems, it seemed, were all behind him.

With a driver engaged, the final stage in the preparations was to set up a cover company to protect Ozcan and the Snakeheads in the event that the consignment was discovered by Customs. For this they needed a *katvanger*, a front man paid to provide a cover identity for criminal operations. They chose Arien van der Speck, a petty criminal from the eastern suburb of Terbregge. Days before the transport, van der Speck visited the Rotterdam chamber of commerce and founded a haulage firm, Van Der Speck Transport. Ozcan's carefully constructed plan was ready to execute.

At around two-thirty in the afternoon of 18 June the fifty-six men and four women who made up Ozcan's shipment were brought to the warehouse at Waalhaven. They had arrived in two separate vans, one disguised to look as though it contained building materi-als, the other dressed up to look like an ambulance. Inside the warehouse was a 1995 Mercedes truck hooked up to an eighteen-metre container. Aided by half a dozen members of the smuggling gang, along with a chain-smoking Perry Wacker, the group was slowly loaded on to the lorry.

The third weekend of June was the hottest of 2000, and in three layers of clothing Ke Shi Guang was already sweaty and uncomfortable when his turn came to climb aboard. 'I walked towards the back and squatted on the floor alongside the others. It was dark but there was a small window up on the left almost near the ceiling and I remember that I could see light coming through it.'

Four buckets of water were passed up, along with a handful of plastic bags for excrement. 'They pushed one box of tomatoes towards the back and said we could eat those but that if we ate any more we would be fined,' remembers Guang. 'Then a man in a black T-shirt pointed to the small window and said that if it was open we can speak in low voice. He said if it closed, we not speak at all.'

Then Wacker and the rest of the gang stacked the remaining boxes of tomatoes around the group, hiding them from view and taking up so much space that they were forced to huddle together. The heavy swing doors were slammed shut.

It was shortly before three p.m. when Wacker climbed into the cab and set out for Zeebrugge with his human freight. Just outside the ferry terminal he stopped off for diesel. This was the riskiest part of the journey and the need for total secrecy was at its highest. Having ensured that no one was watching too closely, Wacker climbed up the front wheel arch and reached for the vent. Inside the container, Ke Su De saw a hand reach up, then blackness.

Wacker drove through the gates of the terminal at six p.m. and had to wait around an hour before he was waved forward to board the European Pathway, a P&O freight-only ferry that would be leaving for Dover half an hour later. Once he had parked, Wacker went up into the ship's canteen and dined on shrimp salad, roast lamb and rice, then made his way to the cinema room to while away the five-hour crossing by watching the adventure film *The Mummy*.

By the time the end credits rolled, the sixty Chinese had been inside the container for more than four hours. The single tray of tomatoes had lasted barely an hour but the group had far more pressing concerns than food. The temperature had soared and many felt as though they were being roasted alive. They ripped off their outer layer of clothes and gulped down the water until that, too, was gone.

The air around them became so saturated with moisture that they were no longer able to sweat. Their body temperature rose and some of the weaker members of the group collapsed with exhaustion.

And then the air started to run out.

The vent that Wacker had closed had been the only source of fresh oxygen for the whole container. With sixty, hot sweaty bodies gasping away, the air soon turned dank and fetid as the oxygen levels plummed.

'People began to panic,' recalls Ke Su De. 'Some people passed out in the darkness. I wanted to breathe air so I got close to the tomatoes but I do not think they were any use. Then people started screaming and shouting for help. We tried to move the tomatoes and kick open the doors but it was no use. I did what I could to try to make one fellow passenger comfortable. People were having greater and greater difficulty in breathing. We all banged on the side, hit the walls with our shoes. We shouted and called for help. No help came.'

High above them in the video room, Perry Wacker glanced at his watch. There were still two hours to go before the ship reached Dover. He settled back in his seat and began watching *Austin Powers*.

Back in the container the group were dying one by one. Eventually they resigned themselves to their fate. They held hands and ate tomatoes partly for moisture but also because the Chinese believe no one should die on an empty stomach and 'become a hungry ghost'.

Ke Su De held on for as long as he could, thinking of his family back home and how much he longed to see them again. With the last of his strength he tried to pry open the air vent, ripping off a wooden panel on the inside of the truck. But it was no use. As his fellow passengers lay dying around him, he felt powerless to help. Then he, too, succumbed and fell unconscious.

Across the water a British member of the Snakehead gang was preparing for the group's arrival. Before getting on to the truck at Rotterdam each migrant had been told to either memorise or write down a mobile-telephone number and call it as soon as they arrived in the UK.

It belonged to a Chinese interpreter called Ying Guo, known to her friends as Jenny. A key member of the gang, her task was to organise asylum application and to arrange for any final fees to be paid. Originally from north-eastern China, Guo had worked in a car factory but arrived in England in the summer of 1996 to pursue her own dream of a better life. Having been granted a student visa, she enrolled on a course at Edgware College in north London studying English, accounting and computing.

But before her studies were complete, a chance encounter with a friend led to her finding work as an interpreter at the Home Office immigration centre in Croydon, south London. What began on an *ad-hoc* basis soon turned into a full-time job with Guo spending up to forty hours each week interpreting for asylum applicants at Home Office screenings and interviews with solicitors.

Exactly how she came to work for the Snakehead gangs is not known, but it is clear that once she did she was soon on her way to becoming a wealthy woman. She bought herself a plush flat in South Woodford, Essex, and had so much cash to spare that she even managed to send back £37,000 to her family in China in three months. By agreeing to be the first point of contact for immigrants smuggled in by the gang, Guo would be in a position to refer these new 'clients' to solicitors. Because of her language abilities, the solicitors gave Guo the work of translating the applications.

In the eighteen months before the Dover tragedy, Guo dealt with more than 366 asylum applicants, nearly one in ten of all the Chinese applicants dealt with by the Home Office during that period. Although the work involved a great deal of duplication and took up little of her time, she would earn on average £125 per case plus an additional £100 per person from the Snakeheads. With the arrival of this latest group of immigrants Guo was anticipating a bumper £13,500 payday.

The red flag had been raised over Wacker's lorry long before it arrived in Dover. For one thing Wacker had paid the £412 fare in cash. As the vast bulk of commercial freight traffic is paid on account, Customs agents automatically forward the details of any vehicle paying in cash to the destination port. He had also brought attention to himself because no one at Dover had heard of Van Der Speck Transporten – hardly surprising as it had been registered just three days before.

As the lorry rolled into view David Bell, the Customs officer, picked up the manifest and noted that the lorry was carrying a cargo of tomatoes bound for Bristol. 'I didn't believe it. I just knew it had to be smuggling. My immediate thought was that it was booze or fags, probably both.'

At first Wacker seemed relaxed, smoking a cigarette, chatting and joking with the Customs officers. But when they asked him more about the company he was supposedly working for, he became nervous and evasive, promising to send more details later. But by then it was too late. David Bell was already making his way to the rear of the container and opening the heavy swing doors.

At around eight a.m. on the morning of Monday 19 June, seven hours after the bodies had been discovered but before the news had been made public, Ying Guo telephoned solicitor Chandika Walpita, who knew nothing about her illegal activities, and asked if he could deal with some asylum matters on behalf of a large number of Chinese people.

'She told me that she had been instructed to ask about some Chinese asylum-seekers who had arrived in the country. She said that there were sixty of them and asked whether I wanted to represent them. It was a lot of people. I said I wouldn't be able to take the whole lot but I said I might be able to take half.'

Fourteen minutes later Guo called back to say she was unsure what was happening with the immigrants. Although she did not let on, Guo was starting to worry and Walpita picked up on the anxiety in her voice. She knew that Wacker's lorry should have disembarked hours earlier but none of the immigrants had called her and Wacker's mobile phone had been switched off.

Walpita did not hear from her again until just after midnight on 20 June. 'She was hysterical. She said that they had found her mobile-phone number on one of the persons who had been found dead in the container,' he explains. 'She asked me what to do and I said I had no idea about criminal matters but that I could ask somebody who did. She said she had thrown her phone away, that she had destroyed it.'

In fact, Guo's number had been found on twenty-seven of the bodies, either on scraps of paper or stitched into their clothing, and on a further sixteen items discarded on the floor of the lorry. As well as destroying her mobile phone she had also deleted a number of incriminating files on her computer including records of the bank account where she kept the vast sums of money she had made by working for the Snakehead gangs.

But although hers was a crucial role in the operation, Guo knew she was all too expendable and that the rest of the gang would do nothing to protect her. The following day, she turned herself in to the police.

A few weeks after the Dover tragedy I travelled down to the Kent port to meet with Lin, an illegal Chinese immigrant who worked in a nearby town, having been brought into Britain illegally by a Snakehead gang a few months earlier.

Speaking with the aid of an interpreter, as we sit in the corner of a quiet Chinese restaurant on Dover's high street, Lin tells me his journey was fraught with difficulty. His family had paid a small deposit and promised to pay more when he arrived in Europe so that he could complete his journey. But the person who had promised to loan the rest was unable to help so Lin found himself stuck in Rotterdam for nearly four weeks. It was a desperate situation. 'If the money was not paid then I'm in the hands of the Snakeheads. I would be the one in real danger. They told me I could earn some money if I worked for them, helping with the other immigrants. I had no choice, I had to do it.'

Lin helped maintain the safe-houses in which the immigrants were made to wait before being loaded on the lorries for the journey across the Channel. 'Conditions were very bad. One small house with more than fifty people. Everywhere was dirty and everywhere was like a bedroom – blankets, mattresses, pillows – even in the kitchen. The people were not allowed to leave in case they were seen – they had given me a false Dutch passport so I could pick up their supplies but the rest of them had to remain inside all the time.

'There is a woman there. She is the one who is in charge of everything. She is the one who gave me the job. Everyone is scared of her. I was glad to get away. The Chinese community is very closed in the Netherlands so she could do a lot of things without a lot of people in Dutch society knowing about it.'

A month later, Lin was finally allowed to travel to Britain, loaded on board a lorry with around thirty others for the crossing to the UK. 'We had no papers – they took them all from us – but they told us that if we were stopped we should tell them we wanted to claim asylum. We had to say either that we were Christians and that we were being persecuted for wanting to practise our religion or that we had parents who had broken the rule about having only one child and we were fleeing for our lives.'

But they were not discovered and Lin was let out of the lorry at a quiet layby on the outskirts of Ashford. Brought in by the same organisation that subsequently smuggled in the Dover sixty, he travelled to London soon after arriving and met none other than Jenny Guo at London's Victoria station: 'There were several other Chinese – four or five, all male,' he explains. 'I did not know if she was a solicitor. She asked us to wait, then there was a foreign woman who took us to apply for asylum. She took us to collect the forms they said we needed to fill in to be able to stay in Britain. I took the form but I did not understand it so I called Guo. She met me and filled in the form for me. All I did was sign it.'

Since then Lin has been working in the kitchen of a Chinese restaurant. The hours are long, he tells me, and the work is hard, but he is grateful to be in England and enjoys it much more than the time he spent in Holland.

As our conversation draws to a close, I ask if he will give me the name of the woman in Rotterdam who was in charge of everything.

Lin looks at his translator, perhaps wondering if he can trust her. Then he glances about the room to ensure no one is listening to our conversation. Then he leans towards me, his mouth close to my right ear and hisses a single word: 'Ping.'

Barely five feet tall and slightly built, Jing Ping Chen has mastered the art of looking frail and demure. It is a talent that has served her well: few who have met her can believe that she is capable of harsh language, let alone acts of violence.

The thirty-seven-year-old, better known as Sister Ping, is one of the most ruthless gang leaders in Europe. Her origins are obscure, but it seems she was herself smuggled to Holland from Fukien in south-east China in the mid-1980s. In six short years, she made millions by trafficking human beings from her native China into the UK.

Using a combination of violence and intimidation, Sister Ping swept aside all her rivals and cornered the people-smuggling market between Holland and Britain soon after arriving in Rotterdam in 1997. Through her connections to the Triads – her boyfriend is the head of the Triad gang 14K in Rotterdam – she was able to hire muscle to do her dirty work whenever necessary. In one case a man was beaten so badly he was left with punctured intestines. In another Lam Chee Ming, with whom she had fallen out, was brutally assaulted. Five men attacked him while he was eating dinner, beating him with hammers, an axe and a pistol. Sister Ping directed the assault, listening in on her mobile phone. Her instruction was to place the barrel of the pistol in his mouth, right to the back of his throat and 'rattle it around with vigour'. Eyewitnesses later told police they would never be able to forget the sound of Lam's teeth breaking. He was unable to eat solid food for weeks.

When a rival mobster tried to muscle in on Sister Ping's territory, she made a big show of inviting him to the Orient restaurant in Rotterdam's Chinatown, the headquarters of her operation, ostensibly to discuss ways of dividing the territory between them. As soon as he was inside, he was dragged up to the first floor, beaten with a hammer, then shot in both legs.

According to police, Ping's smuggling operation was a well-oiled machine. With more than a dozen people on the payroll, a fleet of eight cars, several other vehicles and at least eight safe-houses, the overheads alone were £35,000 per month.

Ping's earnings are unknown, but in one recorded telephone conversation a key member of her organisation was heard boasting that he had earned £300,000 in two months. The best estimates suggest that she had accumulated at least £15 million from her criminal activities.

Long before Lin had given me her name, Dutch police had already picked up Sister Ping's trail. Although Turkish gangster Gurbel Ozcan seemed to be the head of the smuggling operation, police had long suspected that he had been taking orders from above. He refused to name anyone when he was arrested following the Dover tragedy, but his ex-girlfriend later called the authorities and pointed them in Ping's direction, telling them, 'You must look for the woman. She is the Snakehead. She is the highest in Holland. She has contacts in China who fix things. She is very dangerous.'

Within hours of the deaths at Dover, Ping had gone into hiding but, convinced she was above the law, she soon went back to work. 'The Dover transport was a financial setback that had to be recuperated,' noted a report by the Dutch prosecutors' office. 'This organisation wasn't put off by the police or the Chinese deaths. After the incident, the gang simply went back to business as usual.

'Up to five hundred people per week went from France to England; the number depended on how many lorries were available. Following Dover there was a maximum of thirty people per vehicle.'

She was arrested following a massive police operation. In August 2003 a Dutch court sentenced Sister Ping to three years in jail and fined her £8000 for offences related to human-trafficking. Despite evidence that her gang was involved, Ping was cleared of any personal involvement in the Dover tragedy.

But despite Ping's conviction, the trade in human cargo shows no sign of slowing down.

As big and as slick as her operation was, it pales alongside those who have stepped in to take the mantle. Whereas once the Chinese Snakeheads reigned supreme over the human-trafficking business, they now face stiff competition from a gang said to be the most ruthless and dangerous criminal organisation in the world.

And this time I will do more than simply hear about their operation: I plan to see it with my own eyes.

CHAPTER TWENTY-TWO

It is only minutes before I am offered a place.

I'm sitting in the corner of a tiny café just off the Place d'Armes in the centre of Calais, unwashed, unshaven and wearing a shabby jacket I should have thrown out years ago. There's a mug of coffee cupped between my hands and I'm staring into it intently between sips, doing my best to look like someone desperate for a new life in the Promised Land.

A short, stocky man dressed all in black with wavy dark hair and a cigarette hanging from his lips suddenly appears and sits down beside me. I feel his eyes boring into the side of my head and I'm so intimidated it takes me a second or two to work up the courage to meet his gaze. He smiles with tobacco-stained teeth and points a gnarled knuckle northwards, the direction of the Channel. '*Vous allez en Angleterre?*'

I shake my head as if I don't understand. I've never been much good at fake foreign accents and the one I've spent most of the morning practising is barely believable in pidgin English, let alone French.

The man cocks his head to one side and furrows his brow as he thinks about what language to try next. Eventually he speaks: 'England, you want to go to England?' The accent is strong and East European. I nod enthusiastically.

'You can pay?'

'How much?' I ask.

He shrugs. 'Depends. To ride on truck . . .' He shrugs again, then holds up his right hand and extends all five fingers.

'Dollars?'

He shakes his head. 'Euros.'

I gesticulate and roll my eyes as if I'm searching for the right words. 'Er . . . how?'

'You give me the money. I take you to truck, ten, twenty others, and load you on. Then I put cardboard on top of you so you look like a box. In a cage. No move. You have a bottle of water and a plastic bag for your shit and maybe some chocolate. Three hours – England.'

I nod slowly. It sounds appalling and instantly makes me think of the fifty-eight dead Chinese at Dover.

The man soon picks up on my lack of enthusiasm. 'But this way not good. Many police, many guards to check the trucks. They catch you, they beat you, lock you up, then back here and have to pay again to try again. You go to claim asylum?' I nod once more. 'Yes. Then better to have guarantee, be able to walk around on boat, not sit in back of dark truck covered in boxes.'

'How much for guarantee?'

'More, much more. Maybe one thousand, maybe two, we can fix a good price. Depends. But good price to you and better. With guarantee we give you passport. Your picture inside but different name. You buy ticket, you walk on to boat. Not difficult. No problems. You give passport to man on boat. In England, at Immigration you claim asylum. Is guaranteed, you see? And also we give you a number to call so you can find work. Is good, yes? I was there, London, two years before here.'

'What kind of work?'

'Whatever you want. In restaurant, in factory, in hotel. Inside, outside. Whatever you want. Good money. No tax.'

I tell the man I need time to think about it, that I may need to get relatives to send me more money in order to pay. I finish my coffee and make for the door, leaving him to sidle up alongside two Sudanese men sitting on the other side of the room. He barely misses a beat as he launches into his sales pitch once more.

Although I am left surprised by just how blatant the offer is, it was anything but unexpected. According to my source, a little-league bootlegger and white-van driver called Barry, the café is just one of a number of well-known haunts for the 'agents' who tout for business among the illegal immigrants on behalf of the smuggling gangs.

Although the agents are wary of being caught by the police and face stiff penalties if they are arrested, they have little choice but to work openly if they are to attract potential clients. Some of the more sophisticated gangs have Internet sites and place advertisements in local newspapers to promote their services under the guise of 'employment agencies' and 'travel consultants'. Others base themselves in cheap hotels and pay scouts to bring customers to their door.

That said, I am only too aware that I am dealing with a group that cares little about human life. In the people-smuggling business there have been numerous cases of paying passengers being thrown overboard so that the boat-owners can escape prosecution.

These agents belong to an organisation that adheres to a culture where the belief persists that you are only a man if you own a gun, a society where blood feuds dating back hundreds of years are still fought out with astonishing brutality, sometimes in the UK. It is an organisation that took on the best that Italian organised crime had to offer. And won. It is an organisation that took on the Turks and the Triads and emerged victorious.

It is an organisation that, according to every police agency in Europe and beyond, represents the greatest threat to law and order to emerge in the last hundred years.

It is the Albanian Mafia.

It wasn't always that way.

Like every country in the world Albania has always had a criminal element, but for years they were confined to within their own borders by the actions of a government that made it almost as hard for natives to leave the country as it was for outsiders to enter.

Occupied by Italy during the second World War, Albania emerged under the iron rule of Enver Hoxha who decided the nation should turn its back on a wide range of Communist influences. By the end of the 1960s Hoxha's campaign had included a violent battle to extinguish all religious life in Albania. More than two thousand religious buildings were closed or converted to other uses while religious leaders were imprisoned and executed. When the work was completed, Albania was declared the world's first atheist country. Foreign doctrine of any kind was banned. Journalists and Americans were forbidden to enter. There were no private cars, no inflation, no priests or mullahs. Albania didn't even have private taxation.

Caught in a virtual time warp, Hoxha ensured that Albania remained one of the least economically developed and most isolated countries in Europe. In 1985, the year Hoxha died, just three thousand tourists were allowed into the country, all of them in small, strictly controlled groups. By contrast, neighbouring Yugoslavia played host to more than 1.5 million visitors, most of whom had the freedom to roam around at their leisure.

With its harsh mountain landscapes, unforgiving climate and lifestyle that relied far more on physical labour than modern machinery, the men who would go on to form the Albanian Mafia became hardier than most for the same reason that the Russian Mafia rose to the ascendancy in the early 1990s. Macho pride reigned supreme, within a family and within a village. Mass brawls and sometimes brutal murders over issues like loss of face or village pride became commonplace. Law enforcement was at best rudimentary.

Albanians currently form the majority not just in their own country but also in Kosovo, a region heavily disputed between Albania and Serbia (one of the six republics that made up the former Yugoslavia.) While the Albanians claim that they are the area's original inhabitants, the Serbs say that Kosovo lay at the heart of its medieval kingdoms and that during the Middle Ages few, if any, Albanians lived among them. Kosovo had been under the control of Italy and part of Greater Albania during the war years, and in 1974 a new Yugoslav constitution granted Kosovo autonomy (but not independence).

These were the glory years of the Albanian Mafia who, like the Sicilian Mafia, originated as a protection network for the poor. The Albanian networks inherited the same protective instincts. The family and its codes are everything. The Besa, or Oath of Trust, puts deep obligations on every family member. The fledgling Mafia swore to uphold the notion that Kosovo was part of Albania.

From this time on, Serbs in Kosovo began to complain of harassment by Albanians who were demanding the status of a full republic for the province. The Serbs were particularly worried because, thanks to Serb emigration and a high Albanian birth rate, the proportion of Serbs in the province had now fallen to a mere one for every nine Albanians.

It was through the subtle manipulation of these grievances that Slobodan Milosevic, the head of the Serbian Communist Party, rose to supreme power. In 1989 he stripped Kosovo of its autonomy, a move that sparked a frantic round of war, ethnic-cleansing and land-grabbing across the whole of Yugoslavia which would eventually lead to its collapse. The conflicts continued throughout the 1990s until NATO intervened. But by then it was too late to prevent the Mafia expanding.

Before the war, heroin from Turkey had travelled to Western Europe via Serbia, Croatia and Slovenia. During the conflict this traditional 'Balkan' route closed and the Albanian gangs with their local knowledge found they were perfectly placed to take over the trade, guaranteeing safe routes through the conflict zones. At first they only assisted other gangs, but once they had the ability to expand their horizons, they were perfectly poised to take over completely. They based themselves in Veliki Trnovac in southern Serbia, which was quickly dubbed the 'Medellín of the Balkans'.

As the war reached Kosovo proper, so ethnic Albanians were added to the list of nationals that qualified for 'refugee' status. The only problem was that there was no way to tell the Kosovo Albanians from other Albanians and the Mafia's barons took advantage of the situation to spread across Europe like wildfire. They went first to Albanian communities in Germany and Switzerland where they quickly took over the heroin trade. Within a few months their tentacles had reached out as far as the east coast of the United States, and the Albanian drug syndicates had become among the most powerful on the European continent.

According to Professor Ernesto Savona, the director of Italy's Transcrime research institute, the Albanian Mafia has now grown so powerful that it has already chased the Italian Mafia, once its patron and big brother, right out of the lucrative business of trafficking migrants. 'Albanian organised crime has its foot in the door, which is Italy, and this means people, prostitution and drugs,' he warns.

By the spring of 1998, alarm bells were ringing in British government buildings about increasing numbers of Albanian im-migrants arriving hidden on the backs of lorries at UK ports. One internal Home Office report noted, 'Albanian Mafia gangs are very vicious and make the Italian Mafia look like crowd-control officers at a local whist drive. Concern has been expressed in the Immigra-tion Service and the police at the involvement of Kosovans in organised crime in the UK and Europe.'

By the end of 2003 at least a dozen gangland murders in Britain had been attributed to the Albanian Mafia and police were warning of a massive potential for an all-out turf war between Albanian, Turkish and Pakistani gangs.

It failed to emerge, but experts believe the Albanians are simply biding their time and building their numbers. They are believed to be concentrating on building wealth through people-trafficking and other allied activities before moving on.

All of which means that, despite the large numbers of Albanians operating in the UK, there are at present even more to be found on the other side of the Channel.

I arrived in Calais little more than a year after the closure of a controversial refugee camp just outside the port town. Opened by the Red Cross in November 1999, the centre quickly transformed Sangatte from a tiny village with a population of around eight hundred into a frantic staging post for those attempting to reach the UK. With more than sixty-eight thousand asylum-seekers and illegal immigrants housed at the camp during its three-year existence, Calais soon became a firm base for the Albanian Mafia gangs making a profit out of helping them on their way.

The problems came to a head on Christmas Day of 2001, when 550-odd illegal immigrants tried to invade the Channel Tunnel in an attempt to walk to Britain. More than 150 overwhelmed police and guards, and got seven miles into the tunnel on Christmas Day before finally being turned back.

But within hours of the first group being brought back, a second wave of 400 made their own attempt. This time the French called in the riot police, who fired tear gas and made more than fifty arrests.

The incidents were enough for the company behind the Channel Tunnel, Eurotunnel, to win a legal challenge to have the camp closed. (Ironically the site was owned by Eurotunnel and was used as storage space before it was leased to the Red Cross.)

Yet despite the closure migrants are still flooding into northern France hoping to reach Britain with the aid of the smuggling gangs. Calais is still their preferred port because it is incredibly busy – more than 30 million people pass through it each year – and because it has the most crossings and offers the shortest route to the UK. But a tightening of security and the introduction of new high-tech equipment to detect migrants hiding in vehicles has forced them to travel further afield.

By the end of 2003 the number of people attempting to sneak on to ships at Calais had fallen by more than two-thirds, but other ports along the coast had experienced a sharp increase. The once-quiet ferry terminal at Caen, close to the beaches made famous by the Normandy landings in 1944, experienced a 400 per cent increase in the numbers detained while trying to board vehicles. Similar increases have been detected elsewhere in France, as well as in Ostend and Zeebrugge in Belgium. Initially hit hard by the new measures, the smuggling networks are rebuilding and are said by some to be stronger than ever.

As Barry, my bootlegger guide, and I travelled east along the coast, through Boulogne, Dieppe and Le Havre, then across to Cherbourg and St Malo, agents and the small groups of illegal immigrants they had taken on were easy to find. Some were camped in squalor beneath bridges or in abandoned buildings; others had made temporary homes in disused factories. For those who had been smuggled by the more organised gangs the conditions were often worse. They would find themselves in stinking squats, twenty to a room, with no running water and few provisions.

In Ouistreham we met twenty-two-year-old Iraqi Amal Abbas, who along with a small group of friends had spent weeks travelling across Europe before stumbling at the last hurdle. 'We are desperate to get to Britain. We have friends there who say the Government is good and that there is work. I thought we would be able to get on a truck but the gangs control everything.

'The Albanians have their guards everywhere. If you try to go past them they ask for the name of your contact. It is like a code. If you do not give the right name they beat you up and send you back. It is too difficult to go on our own so we will have to go with an agent. Our families are trying to borrow money to send us so that we can pay. It is the only way. They are like a Mafia. They try to pretend they are your friends, that they want to help you to have a new life, but the only thing they care about is the money.'

Further along the coast in Cherbourg, France's second largest port and said by some law-enforcement officials to be in danger of becoming the new Sangatte, dozens of migrants are escorted into the town each night to be smuggled through the ferry-terminal perimeter fence on to lorries at dawn for the journey across the water to Poole in Dorset or Rosslare in Ireland.

It's not only at the ports that attempts to board the lorries are made. Back in Calais, Barry and I waited until night had fallen to make our way to an infamous petrol station close to the ferry terminal. Hidden from view by bushes, we watched as a British-registered lorry pulled up for the driver to fill up with diesel. As soon as the pump began working, three men dashed out of the shadows and, keeping out of sight of the driver, tried to open the rear doors. After a few seconds of fumbling they sprang open and one of the men climbed up. It soon became clear that the lorry had been filled to capacity – there was no space for anything or anyone. The men shut the doors and retreated into the shadows to wait for another try.

'Once the pump's going,' Barry explains, 'the driver can't hear a thing. One of those guys will be working for the gang, the other two will be the clients. I've got quite a few mates who drive lorries across Europe. They're vulnerable, but you just can't be on your guard twenty-four/seven. It's worse for the guys driving the curtain-sided trucks. All someone needs is a Stanley knife and they're inside quick as a flash. A few of them have ended up completely paranoid – sometimes even missing their ferries – because they've found a slash in the side of the tarp but they can't find anyone inside. It usually means someone's had a go and either switched vehicles or just not had time to get inside. Not only do they face fines for having illegals but they have to pay for the damage to the tarp too.'

Within a few months of my visit to France increased security measures were announced at Cherbourg and other ports on the coast but, according to Barry, the only effect this will have is to change the way the gangs operate: 'There's no way they're ever going to put a stop to it. There is too much money at stake and too many people who want to travel from one country to another but don't have the right. Drugs gangs don't stop smuggling cocaine just because they think they might get caught, they look at the money they're going to make and think, Fuck it, it's worth the risk. This is exactly the same. All this extra security, all it's going to do is put the price up.'

And Barry knows better than most the mindset of the gangs involved in the people-smuggling trade. In the five years since he became a full-time bootlegger, shuttling back and forth across the Channel with huge loads of spirits and tobacco, he has seen his income drop to the extent that bootlegging alone is no longer worth his while. Now, like many others in his profession, he supplements his income with small-scale people-smuggling, working hand in hand with the trafficking gangs.

Away from the crowds of booze-cruisers and day-trippers in the bar of a small hotel in a quiet street close to the railway station, Barry tells me more: 'A lot of the bootleggers are doing it now. In fact, I think they're all at it to some degree because it makes sense. If you get stopped by Customs with beer and fags, they take the lot and you lose all the money you were going to make. With people you're laughing because you always get paid up front.

'It's not at all difficult to find people. They're coming out of the woodwork at every port you can think of. Half the time you don't have to do anything. As soon as they see that the van has UK licence plates they come up and ask you how much it is to go to England.

'Sometimes it's the people who want to travel who approach you but most of the time it's the agents, the people from the gangs. They hang out in all the same places you find the immigrants and the bootleggers, round the bars and in the car parks of the big cash-and-carry warehouses.

'They don't want people to be able to cut out the middleman and approach you direct. They'd rather do the deal for you and that suits me fine because that's how you get regular work.

'Sometimes, when the agents approach you, they offer to adapt your van. They say they can put in a false floor, fake panels or a suspended roof so you can get a few people in there. I've never gone in for any of that. I've been lucky so far but I'm bound to get stopped one day, and when I do, my only out is going to be that they must have slipped in when I wasn't looking. The more work you do on your van, the less chance you have of getting away with it.'

I ask Barry to explain the precautions he does take and he ushers me out into the street to see his van. It's a plain, fairly battered Ford Luton van and we walk round to the rear door where Barry points to the lock. 'You see this? It's busted. I broke it myself. If I ever get stopped all I need to do is claim that I locked the van and that the people inside must have broken into it some time during the crossing. There is no way they can prove that I let them on deliberately. I always make them climb in and out themselves and open the door. Then you get them to move some of the boxes around so that they're hidden from view. More fingerprints. That way their fingerprints are all over it.

'Another thing, I only ever take families. No way in the world will I take a bunch of young blokes because you never really know who these people are, and for all I know they might beat the shit out of me and steal the van. Families are a much safer option. You know they're not going to try anything when they've got their kids with them. You don't want them too young, mind – you don't want the little bastards making any noise as you're coming down the ramp.'

Working with the agents and on the fringes of the smuggling gangs, Barry has seen a shift in the way the business operates since the closure of Sangatte: 'It used to be that everything in Calais was being run by the Turks and the Kurds along with a handful of Chinese. I got to know a few of them and they're a real mixed bag. Some of them are illegal themselves and others have got full British citizenship but they spend all their time in France because that's where the money is.

'It used to be a bit of a laugh and only a few people were getting involved but now everyone's doing it and the authorities have started paying a lot more attention to the vans. People are getting caught.

'Also, the people behind it have changed. Now that the Albanians have moved in it's getting nasty. It's a problem. It's scary, more violent. They don't care about anyone apart from themselves. They've pulled out of the port towns and moved their operations into Brussels and Amsterdam. That means that, unless the people you're dealing with are connected to the gangs, they're probably gonna be idiots. It used to be split. You had Indians dealing with Indians, Iraqis dealing with Iraqis, and Chinese with the Chinese. Now the Albanians run the whole lot and deal with everyone.'

According to Barry, the new gangs have brought a higher level of sophistication to the smuggling industry: 'What a lot of the bigger gangs are doing now is bringing people in with loads that naturally emit carbon dioxide to fool the machines that they use to detect human breath. Cut flowers and potted plants are two that I've heard of. It's not perfect, though, and they've had to reduce the number of people on each trip. If you have sixty people in the back of a lorry there's no way you can get away with it. Now they're lucky if they put more than ten people through at a time. They make them sit in boxes with carbon paper stuck to the inside so they can't be seen by X-ray machines.'

Barry is far from being the only Briton involved. Drawn by the large and seemingly easy profits, small gangs of British Snakeheads are setting up in business and often going out of their way to find clients. In August 2003 two Britons were arrested in Romania after trying to find clients who wanted to pay thousands of pounds to be smuggled all the way to Britain.

Little wonder, then, that by the end of 2003 ferry operators were warning that the number of asylum-seekers trying to reach the UK was once again on the rise, doubling during the course of the year.

Barry heads off towards the EastEnders cash and carry and I decide to make my way to Brussels.

I am on the trail of a man called Mhill Sokoli, a fearsome Albanian gangster now behind bars for smuggling more than twelve thousand of his countrymen into the UK in the space of just two years. I meet up with his Belgian prosecutor.

'Every night we watched, they tried to bring at least twenty people across the Channel hidden on lorries aboard ferries,' says Anne-Marie De Hondt. 'It was brilliantly run, with a sliding scale of tariffs. The top rate – two thousand one hundred and fifty pounds – was for a guaranteed successful passage on a lorry with a bribed driver. There were lower fees for clients who took their chance by scrambling aboard parked lorries on motorway laybys near Zeebrugge while the driver snatched some sleep.

'Clients were enticed with the promise that Britain was the "promised land" and that it was easy to find well-paid work in London. Sokoli ran his gang with military precision. Each member had a specific task – some were drivers, others ran safe-houses while others were in charge of meeting and greeting the new arrivals. Then, every morning, the gang's "bookkeeper" made a call to a mobile-phone number in Britain belonging to yet another member of the gang in order to check how many had made it through Dover.'

Belgian police spent months on the trail of Sokoli and his twenty-four-strong gang, following their trail from tiny Albanian villages to Italy, then to Zeebrugge and across the Channel. The gang not only provided transport for those seeking it but actively recruited people by infiltrating the refugee centres to drum up more business. Sokoli was estimated to have made £6 million, which he invested in blocks of flats and businesses in his home area of northern Albania. But he never flaunted his wealth in Belgium, living in a small flat and planning his operations from back-street cafés.

'Sokoli's case was the biggest of its kind so far,' says De Hondt. 'But we know there are other big fish still active.'

I find this out for myself when I head off to the district where Sokoli used to live. In the modest apartment block on the rue Emile Feron I find few people willing to talk openly. One neighbour tells me: 'He kept himself to himself. He was quiet. It was like he had a regular job. He would leave in the morning and come back in the early evening. There was nothing about him that suggested he had money. We were shocked when we found out the truth.'

It's the same story in the Wittamer tea room where Sokoli would often while away the time. Staff remember him as a quiet customer but not one who drew any attention to himself. 'He was a nice man,' says a young girl, behind the bar. 'He was always reading, always going through the paper. I simply thought he was a businessman who didn't like to spend too much time in the office.'

But while catching Sokoli was a real coup for the police, those who work to try to combat the gangs remain sceptical about the impact this will have on the trade. 'Every time someone is caught, the others look at the mistakes they made,' a Belgian police officer confides to me. 'The gangs are like a herd of animals and the police are like the big cats. They kill off the sick, weak ones and leave only the strongest.

'The gangs are now more sophisticated. They have worked hard to establish contacts with the legal profession and law enforcement. Thanks to the vast amounts of money they make, they are able to offer huge bribes to border guards, police and Customs officers in order to let people through.'

Some gangs get homeless people or others to apply for passports, then pass them on. That way they get genuine documents that can be altered. A common method is to obtain a student visa by signing up for a course. In some cases, the courses are genuine, but the student does not attend, sometimes with the complicity of the college. Other gangs go further and set up entirely bogus colleges expressly to provide migrants with the documentation to obtain a visa.

A lot of the gangs are taking advantage of low-cost airlines and the fact that they operate from smaller airports with less sophisticated security, and staff who often have little time to check documents prior to boarding. They will use false documents to embark on the flights, then pass their papers to the facilitator for recycling.

Such sophistication is not the sole province of the Albanians, though it has almost certainly been copied from them. In September 2003 Sarwan Deo was jailed for seven years after being found guilty of running a gang responsible for bringing more than six thousand people into the UK. Deo doctored passports that had been stolen and replaced the photographs with those of the illegal immigrants. Each immigrant was charged around eight thousand pounds for the journey from the Punjab to the UK and Deo's gang is believed to have earned more than £50 million from the scheme.

Deo, a forty-two-year-old father of four, bribed Indian diplomats and African immigration officials to provide his clients with a complete entry service. It included everything from documentation and rudimentary English lessons to advice on what clothing to wear and accommodation in a succession of safe-houses *en route*. For those who were caught there was free legal representation, and for those who were deported a second attempt to enter the UK was provided at no extra cost.

The numbers entering the UK illegally are now so large that traditional areas where they could mix in and vanish into the black market are fast becoming saturated. New destinations are being found, sometimes in the most unlikely locations.

When a small three-bedroom house on the Fairstead Estate in west Norfolk burst into flames in the early hours on a Tuesday morning in June 2003, firemen were shocked to discover eighteen Chinese workers sleeping there. All escaped alive. In the weeks before the fire the local council had received thirty-one complaints about overcrowded houses and flats, some containing as many as forty people.

It has since emerged that at least two thousand Chinese workers moved into the King's Lynn area during 2003, most working in food-processing or farming, often for as little as two pounds per hour. They hang about King's Lynn bus station in groups, smoking and talking among themselves. If not there or working twelve-hour shifts in the Fens, they can invariably be seen at any of the cut-price supermarkets in the town.

There are also growing numbers from Portugal, Eastern Europe and Albania. PC Tony Lombari, the police minority liaison officer for West Norfolk, said the plentiful supply of land-based or food-processing work makes the area all the more appealing. 'Some arrive here with nothing more than a phone number on a piece of paper that they've carried from home. They will be met by whoever and set up in a home and that's where it starts to get cloudy. Some come legitimately and some are illegal, but once they are here they can move around and it's also very difficult to return them without the proper documentation.'

Landlords have been quick to cash in on the boom. They charge the migrants up to forty pounds per person per week. By packing in as many people as possible, properties that would normally rent for perhaps £500 a month can generate almost ten times as much income.

Work is provided by local 'gangmasters', who employ people on a day-to-day basis for cash in hand, regardless of their immigration status. In King's Lynn, dozens of minibuses arrive at the Fairstead Estate each morning to collect hundreds of workers.

Some of the workers are legal, others are illegal and in the middle are those who are claiming asylum. While their claims are being processed they get accommodation but they are not allowed to work, and may have to spend up to six months without any income. It means they are virtually forced to go into the underworld.

Luckily for them the people-smuggling industry is directly linked to an increasingly lucrative black market in illegal workers. Some industries – most notably agriculture and food-processing – have a reputation for turning a blind eye in exchange for being able to pay lower salaries and flout health and safety regulations. In February 2004 gangmasters were blamed for the deaths of nineteen Chinese cockle-pickers who drowned after being caught in fast-moving tides at Morecambe Bay in Lancashire. Locals spoke of hundreds of illegal Chinese workers being moved into the area in the weeks before the tragedy to take advantage of rising cockle prices. The desire to maximise profits and collect the shellfish without the proper permits had led to the Chinese being told to work at dead of night when the incoming tides and stretches of quicksand could not be seen. It later emerged that some of the dead workers were being paid as little as a pound for a full nine-hour shift of backbreaking labour.

Although some of the new arrivals have work lined up or a good idea of the kind of employment they are likely to find, others find themselves forced into virtual slavery. And for increasing numbers of young women brought to this country in search of a better life, the work turns out to be anything but what they expected.

CHAPTER TWENTY-THREE

When Mei first arrived in Britain from Thailand on a six-month student visa, she could not speak a word of English. Now, just six weeks later and without attending a single lesson, she has picked up several key phrases – 'massage', 'blow job', 'condom' – and she can count up to fifty in five-pound increments.

Each morning she reports for work at a small sauna in Glasgow's Charing Cross, where she 'services' up to twenty clients a day, charging them fifty pounds for full sexual intercourse. Of this, she hands over forty-five to the sauna's boss to cover her rent, security and contraceptive pills. Any money left over goes towards repayment of the £17,000 debt she owes the Triad gang who arranged her passage. Mei is just one of hundreds of foreign women being trafficked into Britain by major criminal gangs – including the Triads and the Russian Mafia – to work in the UK sex trade.

I learn of her plight not from Mei herself – her English is not good enough and, following a series of exposés by television and print journalists, Mei has been warned by her bosses to report anyone who arrives at the sauna, declines anything more intimate than a massage and proceeds to interview her about her background.

Instead I speak to Sandra, a girl who works in the same sauna to whom I am assigned when I enter. Sandra is short and dyed-blonde. After I have handed over my fee she gives me a small towel and directs me to the shower, then asks if I prefer talc or baby oil for my massage. We walk up a single flight of stairs to a small booth on the top floor, containing a single bed and a small television screen showing pornographic movies on an endless loop.

Sandra pulls off her tight-fitting T-shirt to reveal her naked breasts. She leaves her short skirt in place as she kneels on the edge of the bed and nods towards it, inviting me to join her. Keeping my towel strategically placed, I lie down on my front and immediately feel her oiled hands working up and down my back. Being careful not to sound too much like I'm interviewing her I begin to ask about her life.

She tells me she has been working in brothels for the past five years, since she was nineteen, that she has a young daughter and that she lives with her boyfriend, who is fully aware of what she does but somehow doesn't mind. 'It's weird. In many ways it's great to have someone to help look after my little girl and to be there, but then at the same time you think if someone really cares for you they wouldn't want you to be doing this,' she says sadly.

We begin talking about the morality of the world's oldest profession and before I know it, before I've even had a chance to turn over, my fifteen minutes are up. I tell Sandra how much I've enjoyed chatting to her and ask if it is possible to extend it – not so that we can have sex but simply to continue talking.

She reaches for an intercom by the door and buzzes down to Reception, informing them of what is going on. 'I have to do that,' she tells me, returning to the bed and slipping her T-shirt on as I scramble to put on my boxer shorts without dropping the towel. 'Otherwise, if I don't come out on time, they'd think you'd attacked me and come up here with the knives.'

We talk for another fifteen minutes and I tell her – honestly – that I find her really interesting. I wonder if it would be possible to meet her away from the brothel for a drink.

Sandra eyes me suspiciously. She explains that she gets this kind of offer at least a dozen times a day. 'My theory is that the ultimate fantasy for any bloke is to sleep with a prostitute and not have to pay for it. I think they like the idea of being so good in bed that the girl just says, "Nah, mate, you keep the money, I really enjoyed that."' But then she gives me her mobile-phone number anyway.

The following morning I call and explain the truth – that I am a writer looking to expose the trade in sex slaves. There is a pause, then Sandra agrees to meet me. She says that it is about time someone knew the truth of what is going on and that many of the women are being treated in the most appalling way.

We arrange to meet in a coffee bar close to Glasgow railway station that same afternoon.

The trade in sex-slave women first hit the headlines in early 2000 when three Russian gangsters linked to a top Lithuanian crime syndicate were jailed for smuggling women into Britain and forcing them to work as prostitutes in brothels in north and west London. Zilvis Paulauskas, Tomas Kazemekaitis and Alenas Ciapas lured four poverty-stricken women from Lithuania, promising that they would be able to earn thousands of pounds after they had paid back the cost of their air fare. On arrival the women were kept prisoner, charged hundreds of pounds a week in 'rent', and told that their families would be attacked if they tried to escape.

The racket – which generated tens of thousands of pounds for the trio – was broken when police launched an undercover investigation after spotting a card in a telephone box advertising a 'blonde Russian kitten'. The investigation threw up alarming information about the numbers of trafficked women involved in the capital's sex trade. A police survey of flats used by Soho prostitutes found that 60 per cent were occupied by women of Eastern European origin.

But the criminal gangs behind the multi-million-pound industry now believe the capital is too well policed to be viable and in recent months have begun establishing new operations in the regions, where profits are almost as high but the risk of detection is minimal. Despite the massive growth in the number of massage parlours offering foreign girls, police forces outside the capital seem ill-equipped to deal with the problem: neither Liverpool, Manchester nor Glasgow have a dedicated Vice Squad, and all admit they do not consider the field a priority because they receive few complaints from the public.

In the heart of Manchester's Chinatown, one newly launched massage parlour offers a selection of British and Oriental women. The brothel is run by a Vietnamese man who obtains his Thai women via Triad gangs in London. Close by is another new brothel, situated above a popular restaurant, which caters exclusively for Oriental customers and is run by the man reputed to be the head of Manchester's Wo Sing Wo Triad.

In Glasgow, the sauna where Sandra and Mei work is registered to the name of a prominent Chinese businessman. Local law-enforcement sources say that the man is known to be a pawn of the Triad gangs. One of his business contacts, 'Dan', is in charge of bringing the women from Bangkok. Dan recently returned from the Thai capital, having travelled out to find a batch of new recruits, whom he intends to establish in a series of new properties across Glasgow.

According to Sandra the girls are 'bought' from the gangs for £15,000 each, then charged £17,000 for their passage once they arrive. 'The reality is that they make that money back in a few weeks, but because of all the expenses they have to pay, their debt stays the same, no matter how hard they work,' she says. 'The Thai girls are popular when they first arrive – all the customers want something different. But after the clients have been with them once, few go back. The problem is that they don't speak English, so they can't talk to them. They start off making loads of money but it soon slows down, and they end up with a huge debt that they can never pay back.

'The Scottish girls have a choice about working, but the Thai girls can get trapped. If they don't pay off their debts within six months, they're left with nothing. They become sex slaves. It's appalling.'

It's a problem that is repeated all across the country. In June 2003 Thai sisters Bupba Savada and Monporn Hughes were jailed for running a suburban prostitution ring that brought in more than £1 million per year. The pair ran a network of brothels operating in Wimbledon, Surbiton, Harrow and other London suburbs. They paid traffickers just £6000 for each young woman lured from Thailand on the promise of earning a substantial sum as a domestic servant in Britain. Once in London, as illegal immigrants, the women were told they owed Savada and her colleagues £22,000 and were coerced into working as prostitutes. They were taken to a flat in Wimbledon and kept under close supervision as they were 'trained'. The women were then 'sold' to other prostitution rings or sent to work at a string of brothels in the suburbs. Many women had to earn £44,000 before they were allowed their freedom.

The sex-slavery trade is also emerging within the Asian community, another group associated with heroin. Gangs operating under the cover of the Bollywood film and music business are forcing teenage girls to work as prostitutes. The business revolves around a traditional form of Indian dance called *mujra*. Publicised almost entirely by word of mouth, performances take places after normal closing hours at a small number of venues in the heart of the Asian community.

A typical show will involve up to sixteen women, all wearing traditional costume, dancing one at a time on a stage area to the soundtracks of hit Bollywood films. The audience is exclusively male. Threats of violence are used to force the women to co-operate. As the evening progresses, they come down from the stage and perform private dances for the men and offer them sexual services for between £75 and £100. All the money earned has to be passed back to the organisers and the top promoters are said to make profits of up to £10,000 per night. The women are usually smuggled into the country on the pretext that they are involved in promotional work. Many have been lured away from their homes on the promise of well-paid jobs as dancers or actresses and only learn the truth about what they are required to do when it is too late.

One regular attendee who spoke to me anonymously said, 'There was always an element of suggestiveness in the *mujra* tradition – like all dance to some extent – but nowadays it's all sex and no art. Today going to a *mujra* is basically just like going to a brothel. Sometimes they do away with the dancing altogether. The girls wear tight clothes, lots of makeup and are very friendly. You are served drinks first, then the madam comes over and asks you to pick out a girl that you like. She is then introduced to you and that's when you start to negotiate over the price.'

A police source who has studied the trend in trafficking foreign women said he believes that, unless action is taken, the problem – and the violence associated with it – will get even worse, because the profits are enormous compared with the risks. 'If you get caught smuggling cocaine, you're looking at twenty years,' he said. 'If you smuggle women, the profits can be just as high, and if you get caught the only thing you're looking at is living off immoral earnings. The most you'll get is three years. If you're a criminal, the choice about which to go for is pretty simple.'

Little wonder the fastest growing and most brutal Mafia in Europe has moved in on the act.

Her real name was Ileana but by the time she was rescued it had been so long since anyone had used it that she had nearly forgotten it.

At the age of twelve she was sold for £600 by a relative to a gang of criminals in Skopje, the capital of Macedonia in the former Yugoslavia, who forced her to work as a prostitute. She was taken to a strip club and made to have sex with dozens of customers each day as well as dance. A few months later another gang bought her for £2300. She was taken to Albania and then by speedboat to Naples where she was again forced to work as a prostitute. She was just fifteen.

It was then that she met Albanian Mustapha Kadiu. At first he seemed different from the men who had used and abused her all her life. He took her to Rome, then said that she should come with him to the UK and start a new life away from prostitution. He gave her a false passport and paid for a trip that took her via Brussels and Ostend to Harwich, Essex, and then by train to Victoria station in London. Kadiu travelled independently to ensure that if Ileana was stopped he would not be caught with her. He took Ileana to his house in Harlesden, where he lived with his cousin, Edmond Ethemi, and a twenty-two-year-old woman who was Ethemi's girlfriend; she was also a prostitute.

But the promise of a new life away from the world of vice was nothing but a lie. After four weeks Kadiu made Ileana work in saunas in Tottenham, King's Cross, Camden, West Hampstead and Chalk Farm. He would drop her off in the morning and pick her up in the evening, at least twelve hours later and often more. She was to charge thirty pounds a time and had to earn at least £400 a day. She worked seven days a week, week in, week out. Kadiu, police later noted, was making as much money from pimping just one girl as he would from drug-dealing.

Leaving was not an option. She had no money, no papers and little idea of where she was. She knew that if Kadiu caught her she would be beaten severely. Kadiu convinced Ileana that if she went to the police they would simply hand her straight back to him. Having spent all her life in countries where police corruption was rife, and having been abused by one man after another, she knew no better.

Eventually she plucked up the courage to tell one of her regular clients of her plight and he tipped off Scotland Yard that a girl was 'in difficulty and needed help'. Police took her to a safe-house then launched a surveillance operation against Kadiu and Ethemi before arresting them.

During his trial at Southwark Crown Court Kadiu claimed Ileana willingly went into prostitution and denied harming her. After hearing Ileana's evidence the jury decided he was lying. He was convicted of raping and indecently assaulting her, and of living off immoral earnings. He was sentenced in December 2002 to a total of ten years in prison. Ethemi, twenty-one, was jailed for six and a half years for living off immoral earnings and possessing cocaine. Ileana is now rebuilding her life and studying at college under a new identity.

The plight of Ileana is an example of the growing power of Albanian vice gangs in London and beyond, and of the booming sex trade involving girls and women from Eastern Europe smuggled to the West. Most of those who end up in the vice industry are victims of some form of deception. The gangsters advertise in local newspapers abroad offering jobs as maids, nannies, bar and catering staff, receptionists, clerical staff, dancers and entertainers. Even the women who knowingly get involved in vice are told they will be able to keep their profits. Some gangs even pay women to return to their home countries to tempt others with false tales of wealth and happiness.

The gangs use extreme violence to control their victims. In some instances, women have been killed and their bodies dumped in public places as an example to others.

The number of Albanian vice barons in London is rising fast and they now control 75 per cent of all prostitution in Soho. Walking along Baker Street early one Monday morning, I noticed that three men in front of me were acting oddly. Two were looking this way and that, making sure the coast was clear, while the third quickly nipped into a nearby telephone-box, then emerged without having had time to make even the briefest of calls.

It was only when I reached the box myself that I realised what had been going on. A small card had been stuck beside the telephone with a picture of a naked young woman holding her breasts, a mobile-phone number and the words 'New 18-year-old blonde'. The men were 'carders', working on behalf of the vice gangs to advertise the services of the prostitutes they control.

I moved closer and it soon became clear the trio were Albanian. When they noticed me staring they approached, worried that I was a police officer. I assured them that I was far more interested in the girls they were advertising and was waiting to see if they had any more cards. They did not and I made good my exit. When I called the number the following day I discovered it had been blocked by British Telecom — an increasingly common tactic to disrupt the activities of the carding gangs.

In Europe, Albanian gangs have first established themselves in the vice trade, then moved into other areas of criminality, including heroin-trafficking. They have a fearsome reputation for violence, and police fear that unless they can nip the gangs in the bud, there will be bloody clashes with the Turkish and Pakistani gangsters who currently control the UK heroin market.

There are signs that another Albanian criminal speciality – kidnap – is also on the rise in the UK. Many of the girls who are brought to work as prostitutes are literally snatched off the streets. In some rural areas of the Balkans, the fear of kidnap is such that families keep adolescent girls at home rather than send them to school or work.

But when it comes to Britain, women are not the only targets.

KIDNAP

CHAPTER TWENTY-FOUR

At first he thought he had left one of the downstairs windows open and that a cat had sneaked into the house. Then, his heart sinking fast, he realised the sounds of movement coming from downstairs were people. Had they been burglars that would have been bad enough but as Clive Hobbs, a manager at a Lincoln Sainsbury's store was about to discover, they were something far worse.

It was just after three a.m. on 19 April 2000 when the gang of four hooded men, led by convicted drug-dealer Gary Skinner, burst into the Hobbs home forcing Clive, his wife Suzanne and their two-year-old daughter from their beds.

'We went to sleep after a normal, quiet day together and the next thing I remembered was being woken up with a hand clamped around my mouth,' Suzanne said later. 'There were dark figures moving around the bedroom. I tried to struggle but I could not move my arms. I was being held down, I was panicking, it was difficult to breathe. I looked at Clive and he seemed paralysed. I was absolutely terrified.'

Suzanne was gagged and tied, then she and her daughter were forced to lie down in the back of a car and driven the ten miles to a derelict farmhouse near the village of Bardney where the gang had prepared a makeshift 'cell'. The tiny cupboard under the main stairs had been soundproofed and kitted out with two mattresses, cushions and a bucket for a toilet.

'They pushed us inside and bolted the door. Eleanor didn't understand anything so I put on a smiling face for her. I don't know how I did it but I decided if it was going to be our last few hours together, we were going to enjoy ourselves. Eleanor was just a little baby and didn't know what was going on, except that she was with her mother. So her mummy had to be normal.'

Meanwhile Clive was kept at his home until eleven a.m. the following morning, then driven to the Sainsbury's branch where he worked. On the way Skinner produced a revolver and told him, 'If the police turn up I'll fire shots all over the place. I'm not going to do life.'

On arrival Clive was told to empty money from the three cash machines inside the branch. At first he refused but then Skinner asked him, 'Who do you love more, your wife and child or Sainsbury's?' As Clive collected the money he told the bemused staff what was happening but begged them not to call the police, fearing the kidnappers would kill his family. The machines had been freshly stocked that morning and Clive soon removed £326,000.

The gang, who had given him a mobile phone, instructed him to deliver the cash – £326,000 in all – to a local pub where another member of the gang was waiting. 'At this stage I felt so frightened, not knowing what the outcome would be. I didn't know if I would see my wife and daughter again. I thought I was going to be killed because I had now fulfilled my part of the operation.'

Clive was then told to go to a second pub and to wait for the gang to contact him again. After waiting anxiously for more than an hour, he received a call at the bar telling him, 'Thank you, Clive, for your co-operation.' He was told where to find his wife and daughter, and immediately rang the police.

Twelve hours after she had been abducted armed officers found the farmhouse at Bardney. Huddled in the darkness, Suzanne thought the footsteps she could hear were those of her captors returning to kill her. 'There was banging on the door and it was eventually opened by a policeman who told me that Clive was still alive. The sense of relief I felt was overwhelming. It was a wonderful feeling.'

Despite the gang's careful planning it took only four weeks for the police to track them down. All four men had criminal records so all four were on the forensic databases. They found one man's fingerprints on a bucket at the farmhouse in Bardney and another's saliva on a bottle at the Hobbs home. They also matched mud from the farmhouse to the mud on Skinner's car.

Police raided Skinner's home and found £80,000 stuffed under his bed and a further £30,000 hidden in his sofa. At the home of Donald Pleasants they found more than £8000 buried in the garden.

Once the sole domain of Mafia gangs, Colombian cartels and hoodlums in Chechnya, kidnapping has now become one of Britain's fastest-growing crimes with incidents rising by more than 2000 per cent in the past decade. Home Office figures show that the number of kidnap cases in England and Wales has risen from 403 in 1988 to more than 2700 in 2003.

Tighter security, video surveillance and the increasing move towards a cashless society has made traditional robbery harder and less rewarding than ever before. For this reason the gangs are now targeting the weakest links in the security chain: the employees themselves.

But although they are increasingly common, such incidents form only a small proportion of the total. Although the crime has but one name, kidnap comes in many different forms. Incidents like those involving the Hobbs are known as 'tiger kidnaps'. These are distinguished by the fact that they are as much a form of extortion as they are kidnap. The victim is seized in order to force another person to do something.

By contrast the express kidnap is like an extended robbery or mugging. The gang involved lays a trap and the victim is whoever happens to come along first. A typical express kidnap will involve a victim being briefly held against their will, threatened and then taken to a cashpoint machine or bank to pay the ransom to secure their own release.

Then there are the so-called barricade kidnaps, which tend to be largely domestic, when someone holds a former partner hostage, or, less commonly, bank robbers seizing hostages when a raid has gone wrong. They are distinguished by lack of planning and usually take place in the heat of the moment. Rather than money, those who carry out such crimes usually want to convince a former loved one to return or secure themselves safe passage.

Traditional kidnappings can generate hundreds of thousands or even millions of pounds. These require a great deal more sophistication and planning, particularly in the early stages when the gang watch their victim to build up a picture of their day-to-day movements. Typical victims include celebrities, entrepreneurs or their relatives.

In April 2002 businessman Arap Mytak was kidnapped by two Albanian teenagers and spent three days tied to a tree in Epping Forest without food or water. He was kicked and punched and his family were forced to listen to his cries of pain as the gangsters phoned demands for a £50,000 ransom. Despite warnings that Mytak, who owned a successful car business in Romford, Essex, would be decapitated if they told police, his relatives felt they had no choice but to raise the alarm. Detectives tracked his captors to the forest and arrested them when they went to collect the ransom. Mytak was found bound and blindfolded in the boot of a nearby car.

The father of four – unaware that a massive hunt had been launched for him – repeatedly tried to escape his tormentors. During one attempt he snatched a screwdriver and stabbed one in the hand, only to be quickly overpowered and severely beaten. After a second attempt, when he tried wriggling free from the tree to which he was tied, he was warned he would be shot if there was further trouble.

In August 2003 the body of wealthy mother of two Yuk Ying Phuah was found near a layby in Sidcup, Kent. She was found partly clothed and wrapped in a sleeping-bag. A post-mortem showed she had been suffocated.

Phuah, originally from Vietnam, had moved to Britain twenty years earlier and she and her husband, Boon, owned several restaurants and food-delivery businesses in Middlesex and Wilt-shire. The forty-three-year-old had gone missing from her Wembley home the previous day. Her daughter came home late at night to find the house had been ransacked, her mother's possessions were all over the place, but her purse and mobile phone were still there and a vacuum-cleaner had been left switched on. Little attempt had been made to hide the body, suggesting it had been dumped in a hurry. Detectives believe she was the victim of a kidnap attempt that had gone wrong before the gang were able to send a ransom demand to her husband.

The police response to kidnapping is becoming increasingly sophisticated and the vast majority of cases end with arrests. Where possible, undercover officers carry out the exchange of money – their main opportunity to catch those responsible. The cash is fitted with a tracking device and often leads the police right to the kidnappers' hideout. 'You can't do anything to alarm the kidnappers, especially as you know many of them are armed,' says one officer. 'When the victim's family contact you, you can't just send a squad car round in case the place is being watched. You have to sneak someone in around the back or do everything on the phone.'

Kidnappers, too, are becoming more sophisticated. When George Fraghistas, a wealthy Greek shipping agent, was kidnapped at gunpoint, he was drugged and locked in a cupboard for nine days. His captors used voice distorters during phone calls and had their mobile phones registered in France to prevent them being traced. They were caught when police traced a car that had been used in the snatch. Despite regular successes and a high clear-up rate, police fear the majority of such kidnap cases go unreported, with the families choosing to pay the ransom rather than go to the police.

Traditional kidnaps are rising fastest among certain ethnic com-munities – 80 per cent of all British kidnaps involve a foreign national, with Albanians and Chinese being the most likely victims. The latest twist to the crime is that those targeted are often illegal immigrants who have just arrived in the UK courtesy of Snakehead gangs or people-traffickers.

These incidents are often characterised by their extreme violence and indifference to life. One case involved the abduction of five Chinese nationals, who were successfully freed following days of negotiations. Later it emerged that, during the stand-off, the kidnappers had realised they stood no chance of getting money for one of the victims so had drawn lots to decide who would kill him.

Another of their victims was forced to act as their slave, cooking and cleaning for his kidnappers while yet another had his fingers sliced to the bone for refusing to rape a fellow captive.

Chef Xiao Ming Cao, twenty-five, was kidnapped in north London, as he walked home from work, and forced to telephone his family in China, telling them that if they wanted to see him alive they must pay £40,000. Over the course of twelve days – one of the longest kidnaps in British legal history – Cao was kept handcuffed to a radiator and only allowed to move to go the lavatory. He was given a cup of boiled rice once every two days and humiliated by being made to crawl around the floor and bark like a dog while his tormentors kicked him.

Another typical case was that of Chen Cun Laing, who left China after a freak typhoon destroyed his fishing-boat and left him penniless. Convinced the only way he could earn enough money to support his family would be by finding his way to the UK, Laing approached a local Snakehead gang and agreed to pay more than sixteen thousand pounds to be smuggled into England.

The journey took several months and, after arriving in London and applying for asylum, Laing eventually found work at a restaurant in Wigan. After only a few weeks he was suddenly kidnapped by members of a Triad gang, linked to the Snakeheads, who had travelled up from London to track him down. The gang explained that he still owed more than seven thousand pounds, then took him to a secluded house in Manchester and began systematically to torture him. He was repeatedly beaten and cut with a machete and on several occasions telephone calls were made to his family in China so that they could hear his screams.

He was released only after signing a Triad 'debt of honour' certificate, which is considered as good as currency. By signing, the victim agrees that he or she will be executed if they do not pay. Alerted by Laing's family in China, police tracked down the five-strong gang of kidnappers who were jailed for a total of forty-two years.

The problem is particularly acute in Dublin where, instead of illegal immigrants or asylum seekers, the Triad kidnap gangs are targeting the student population, which has exploded in the city in recent years. In February 2002 four self-confessed members of the Wo Shing Wo Triad gang were deported from Dublin for kidnapping, assaulting and extorting money from Chinese students.

Between 2000 and 2002 the number of Chinese living in Dublin more than doubled, thanks to the growth in student numbers, and in 2003 the Irish government issued a record nine thousand study visas to Chinese students. It is a popular destination because, unlike most other student visas, the ones issued to Chinese allow them to work as well as study. The move came about after intense pressure from Ireland's Chinese community who were finding it difficult to fill unskilled jobs. Many believe the situation has since got out of control with more students than there is work. This, along with the fact that arriving students have to bring at least three thousand euros in cash to show they are capable of supporting themselves, has made them extremely vulnerable to express kidnaps.

The viciousness surrounding this type of kidnap became apparent when police were called to one incident. By the time they arrived and kicked open the door, the screams could be heard across the street. The scene in the flat in the Rathmines district of Dublin was horrific: two battered students were tied up in a corner while a group of men were viciously kicking and punching a third on the floor in front of them.

As the officers stepped forward the attackers turned on them, lashing out with meat cleavers. One blow almost severed a policeman's arm.

So lucrative is the market that the Triad gangs are now fighting among themselves to take control of the kidnap racket. This first came to the fore in the summer of 2001 when twenty-two-year-old Hong Xiang Qui was murdered during a fight involving up to fifty Chinese men in central Dublin armed with a variety of knives and cleavers with ten-inch blades. A similar brawl had taken place that April, leaving two men injured. Since then there have been at least four more murders as the gangs continue to clash.

Some Triad members are so eager to come to Dublin that the language schools are being offered bribes of up to five thousand euros to falsify letters of enrolment. On arrival, the Triads use their contacts within the community to identify likely targets.

There was a time when every kidnap case produced at least two innocent victims: the person who had been kidnapped and the partner or family member left behind. This is no longer the case.

One of the largest rises in the field has been attributed to a relatively new phenomenon – the retribution kidnap. Described as 'bad on bad', these involve criminals who imprison one another either for revenge, to cover an unpaid drugs debt, or to make some quick money. The trend is most noticeable in London where retribution kidnaps occur at the rate of two or three each month.

In one case, an Asian man told police that his son had been kidnapped. He had been played a recording down the phone of his son being tortured and had been asked to pay a ransom of £40,000 within five days. Police inquiries quickly revealed that the father was a major heroin dealer and the ransom was equal to a payment the man had failed to make for his latest shipment. A gang working for his suppliers had kidnapped his son to secure payment.

Liverpool-based restaurateur Charles Seiga was kidnapped a month after he was cleared of murdering a thirty-six-year-old nightclub bouncer. He was abducted by armed men and had boiling water poured over his face and body in a thirty-six-hour ordeal. He telephoned his brother to say that the price of his release would be

£100,000. He was eventually released after £17,000 raised from friends and family had been handed over.

Increasingly the families of criminals are also finding themselves the target of kidnap gangs. In July 2002 the wife and son of drug-smuggler Robert Garlick were abducted after visiting him at Manchester prison. Denise Garlick and her son David were thrown into the back of a Transit van and taken to an address in the Cheetham Hill district of the city, where they were handcuffed and blindfolded. Members of the kidnap gang then arranged for Denise to call her husband and tell him to arrange to pay a ransom of £250,000 if he wanted to see them alive again.

Garlick informed the police who arranged for part of the ransom to be paid in order to be able to track those responsible. After more than a week in captivity, Denise and David were released unharmed. The gang, led by André Burke and Tunde Adiodun, were watched by a surveillance team as they spent more than £10,000 before they were arrested.

By the time of the Garlick incident Greater Manchester Police were well versed in the art of dealing with kidnaps. But just three short years earlier, the force had never dealt with a single case of the crime. Then, over the course of one fateful weekend in May 1999, following a pattern usually seen with buses and bad luck, three came along at once.

CHAPTER TWENTY-FIVE

Ten minutes into the second half, the crowd watching the big-screen coverage of Manchester United v. Leeds at the Ship public house in Salford suddenly fell silent. A lone voice had cut through the boozy cheers and asked for Stephen Lydiate, one of the pub's regulars, who was sitting at the bar with his teenage son. The thirty-two-year-old demolition worker turned towards the door just in time to see a masked man in combat gear fire a volley of shots from a submachine-gun. At least eight bullets found their target and Lydiate fell to the floor in a mass of blood and mangled flesh.

'I was at home getting ready to go out when the phone went,' Lydiate's sister, Louise, recalls. 'It was a mate of mine at the Ship. She was in a complete state, yelling down the phone again and again, "Stephen's been shot, Stephen's been shot." I got there as fast as I could. There was blood everywhere, total chaos, horrible. People had been hit by ricochets – I had to step over their bodies to get to him. Right away I was sick, physically sick, then I passed out three times. Stephen was a mess, he looked dead, he honestly did. I couldn't believe he was still alive. I kept running outside, looking up and down the road. "Where's the fucking ambulance, where's the fucking ambulance?" But there was nothing. The police wouldn't let the paramedics anywhere near him until they got an armed team over there. It took more than half an hour.'

Lydiate had been hit in the chest, abdomen, left arm, elbow and upper thigh. One bullet had torn through a kidney, almost ripping it in half, while others had broken several of his ribs. As the doctors fought desperately to save his life they noticed that his heart and lungs were curiously unscathed – the bullets had only penetrated the outer edges of his body. Lydiate, they concluded, had been wearing a bullet-proof jacket, though someone in the pub had seen fit to remove it long before help arrived. Despite this, his injuries were so severe that he was not expected to survive, and on each of the six nights that followed his family were told that he would not last until the morning. That he finally made it off the critical list was seen as no less than miraculous.

The moment Lydiate regained consciousness the police were at his bedside eager to hear the full story. They suspected Lydiate of running a drugs gang and that the attempt on his life had been made by a rival firm. Lydiate stunned the officers by refusing to make a statement, file a complaint or assist them in any way. On Thursday 6 May 1999, less than two weeks after he was shot, barely able to walk, in constant pain and with one bullet still lodged in his groin, Lydiate discharged himself and went home.

The streets of Salford have long been associated with violence, a legacy of the seventy-five thousand dockers who worked there during the heyday of the Manchester Ship Canal. Once the very heart of commerce in the North-west, the city has spent the last fifty years fighting rising unemployment and the ravages of industrial decline. When the last of the docks finally closed down, the densely built, poor-quality housing that once fuelled Salford's rapid expansion provided the perfect breeding-ground for a generation that excelled at little other than petty crime and drunken brawling.

In the summer of 1992, following a week-long orgy of rioting, robbery and arson attacks, which included two incidents of shots being fired at the police, a local councillor declared that organised crime in Salford was being run by one man, Paul Massey. Describing himself as a 'security consultant', Massey allegedly controlled protection rackets for contracts for nightclub doormen worth millions. He also commanded so much respect that virtually nothing moved in the city without his approval.

'People used to look up to him, listen to what he had to say,' says Lydiate's sister Louise, who also happens to be Paul Massey's wife. 'They called him a Mr Big but it wasn't like that, he was never a criminal. When he was around, people felt safe. Nowadays, the old folk round here won't even come out of their homes, that's how bad it is.'

Massey was fiercely anti-drugs, and while he was around the amount of heroin and cocaine sold in Salford was kept to a minimum, often to the chagrin of others on the underworld scene. But then Massey was jailed for fourteen years after a man was stabbed at a stag party, and suddenly it was open season.

Within weeks dozens of drug-dealers and couriers had been kneecapped, stabbed and bludgeoned as rival factions fought for control of the trade. There were attacks with samurai swords and machetes; one man was shot in the leg and had to have it amputated, another's hand was almost completely severed. 'The first we would hear about it was when we got a call from the hospital,' says Detective Superintendent Dave Brown, the man in charge of the Salford patch. 'By the time Stephen Lydiate was shot the situation was rapidly getting out of hand. Some of the attacks were very nasty but no one was willing to say anything. The climate of fear running through the city was like nothing we had ever known. And just when we thought things couldn't possibly get any worse, they did.'

It was in the early hours of Saturday morning, little more than a week after Lydiate had come out of hospital, that petty criminal James Kent, who had fallen asleep on the sofa in his living room, woke to find himself surrounded. There were four armed men, all wearing Balaclavas, dark camouflage trousers and bullet-proof jackets with 'POLICE' printed in large white letters on one side. The man nearest him was carrying two handguns, both fitted with silencers.

Kent made a dash for a nearby open window but was grabbed from behind and hit on the back of the head with the butt of a machine-gun. Again Kent tried to get away and the man with the two pistols lined one up and shot Kent through his left leg. Reeling in pain and with blood spurting from the wound, Kent fought on, desperate to reach the window. He was then shot in the other leg and collapsed to the ground.

At that point his girlfriend, who had been asleep upstairs, appeared bleary-eyed on the landing. 'What the fuck is going on?' she asked.

'Armed police,' came the reply. 'Get back in your room right now.'

Kent knew they were lying. From their voices he recognised two of the men as Norman Shawcross and Jason Gregson, both associates of Stephen Lydiate. Once more he attempted to fight off his captors. The man with the two pistols then leant forward and hissed in Kent's ear, one hand pointing up the stairs, 'If you don't stop fucking about, I'll put the next one in her.' Kent ceased struggling, a pair of police-issue handcuffs was snapped on his wrists and, clad only in a T-shirt and boxer shorts, he was dragged outside to a waiting van.

Detective Superintendent Brown hadn't been due to work that weekend but had agreed to cover for a colleague. He arrived shortly before nine a.m. and began looking through the overnight incident logs. At four a.m. a burnt-out bloodstained van had been found in the Lowton area; at eight a.m. a call had come through from a woman claiming her boyfriend had been shot and driven away in a van at three thirty a.m. It was while Detective Superintendent Brown was at the scene that police were first told Kent's abduction was directly linked to the shooting of Lydiate. The information came from a reliable underworld source but it made little sense: Kent and Lydiate barely knew each other and were not thought to have fallen out. Brown spent all day and most of the following night searching for Kent's body – it seemed a good bet that he had been killed – but made little progress. 'To be honest, we didn't really know what was going on, we were at a bit of a loss.'

In fact Kent was still alive, but only just. He had been taken to Hickey Farm, an isolated area of land close to Wigan, shown a hole in the ground and told that it was where he would be buried, then thrown into a nearby cabin. Gregson and Shawcross wrapped him in a plastic sheet 'to prevent any evidence being left behind', then put the barrels of their guns into his mouth and pulled the trigger. Kent shut his eyes and prepared to die. When the empty guns clicked harmlessly, Gregson and Shawcross burst out laughing.

It wasn't until midday that Kent finally found out the reason he was being held – Shawcross explained that they wanted him to provide the whereabouts of the Jamma gang, the men behind the shooting of Lydiate. When Kent told them he did not know, the torture began in earnest. Another member of the gang, Michael Boyle, appeared and hit Kent over the head with a machete telling him, 'You'd better start talking.'

A man in a Balaclava appeared. 'You see this man?' Shawcross said. 'He's going to rape you. He's going to fuck you up the arse unless you talk.' The masked man moved forward but as he got closer he declined: Kent's legs were bleeding too much, it was putting him off.

Instead Gregson left the cabin and returned with the branch of a tree. As Shawcross and Boyle held Kent's legs together, Gregson forced the end of the branch three or four inches into the bullet wound, first in Kent's left leg and then in the right leg. Kent screamed in agony as fresh blood spurted out. Shawcross began pistol-whipping him once more, telling him to shut up. Gregson reached for a nearby packet of salt and poured the contents over Kent's open wounds. His screams became louder and more frantic. At that point Shawcross reached for a mobile phone, dialled a number and held it out so the person at the other end could hear Kent screaming.

As the ordeal continued throughout the day, Kent still refused to give the gang the information they wanted, but only because he did not have it. Crazed by the power they had over their captive, Gregson and Shawcross decided to make some money on the side. They made Kent call his brother and ask him to pay a ransom of £50,000 to ensure his safe release. It wasn't until Sunday morning that Kent's brother called the police. Incredibly, although Greater Manchester Police is one of Britain's largest forces, it had never had to deal with a single case of kidnap. Every force in the country has a set procedure for dealing with the crime, based on a blueprint first devised by the Metropolitan Police. Once the news that Kent had been kidnapped came through, Detective Superintendent Brown pulled his dusty procedure manuals from the shelf and began to read. Soon, calls to Kent's brother were being redirected to police headquarters and specialist surveillance equipment had been brought in to attempt to track down the kidnappers. The family had managed to collect £10,000 and a drop was arranged for early Monday morning. With any luck, detectives hoped, the outbreak of Manchester's newest crime could be nipped in the bud.

Just after midnight, another of Salford's petty criminals, Anthony Shenton, was woken by the sound of his front door being blown off its hinges by two 12-bore shotguns. He was still half asleep when five men, led by Shawcross and Gregson, burst into his bedroom. A brief struggle ended when Shenton was shot in the leg. He was then dragged into a waiting car and driven away at high speed. He was taken to a former council house in the Lower Kersal district of the city. Placed in a room upstairs, he was held briefly with James Kent, who had been moved from the farm. Kent noticed that Shenton was losing a huge amount of blood from his leg – the bullet had ripped open an artery – and implored him to tell the gang the whereabouts of the Jammas. 'Just tell them where they are, they don't want us, just tell them,' he pleaded. Gregson decided further encouragement was needed. He told Shenton that his wife and son had been kidnapped and that his wife would be raped unless he helped them. He then poured salt into Shenton's wounds, forcing him to bite down on a pair of handcuffs to prevent him crying out.

News of Shenton's abduction came through to police headquarters just as the team were hoping to pounce on Kent's captives. 'No one knew what the hell was going on,' says Detective Superintendent Brown. 'One minute we'd never had a kidnapping before, the next minute we have two at the same time. But was it the work of one gang or did we have two rival gangs battling each other? No one had a clue.'

The only lead was Kent's brother and the money drop. At three twenty a.m., the kidnappers called and gave an address for the drop. Kent's brother returned a little later without the money and without his brother. The trail had gone cold again.

By eleven fifteen on Monday morning, Detective Superintendent Brown had been working more than twenty-six hours without a break but was still no closer to finding Kent or Shenton. For all he knew either or both could have been dead. It was at this time that Michael Davidson, another Salford 'face', who was in his BMW with his girlfriend, Joanne, and their two young children, popped into a shop to get some cigarettes. Seconds later he ran back to the car, panic etched into his face.

'Drive, just fucking drive,' he gasped. Joanne put her foot down and sped off. A red Rover loomed large in her rear-view mirror and several shots whistled past the car. The Rover overtook the BMW and skidded across its bonnet, forcing it to stop. As the gunshots echoed around her, Joanne fought with the gearstick and put the car into reverse, leaving a trail of smouldering rubber behind her. Once more the Rover overtook and blocked the BMW and more shots were fired. Desperate to save his family, Davidson jumped out of the car and rushed towards his attackers, dropping to the ground in agony as a bullet tore through his body. By then police sirens were wailing in the background and the occupants of the Rover made good their escape.

The police arrived to find Davidson badly wounded, his girl-friend and children traumatised. When officers asked if they had any idea who had done this, it was Davidson's eight-year-old daughter who screamed out the name Jason Gregson.

Back at police headquarters, Detective Superintendent Brown was tearing his hair out. 'When was it going to stop? Who was going to be next? And on top of that, while we were slowly building up a picture, we still didn't really know what was going on.'

Half an hour after the attempted abduction of Michael Davidson, the red Rover was found abandoned and set alight in Ordsall. Inside the footwell was a magazine from an automatic handgun and a mobile telephone. Checks quickly revealed it was the same phone that had been used to make the ransom demands to James Kent's brother. At last, the picture was becoming clearer.

Gregson and Shawcross returned from shooting Davidson to find Shenton in an even worse condition. It was clear that he was going to die and, deciding that he was of no more use to them, they packed him into a van, drove him to the car park of a nearby Children's Hospital and made an anonymous call to the police telling them where he could be found. The move had nothing to do with mercy. Shenton had been told to tell the police that he had been abducted by the Jamma gang. The idea was that the Jammas would be arrested and, at last, Gregson and Shawcross would know where they were. Arranging to have them killed in custody would be a relatively simple matter.

What happened next was like something out of a James Bond film. The gang's sole remaining captive, James Kent, was being given sleeping pills to help him deal with the pain of his wounds. Kent had saved several and managed to slip them into a cup of tea the guard was drinking. Early on Tuesday morning the guard was fast asleep and Kent managed to slip out of an insecure window. Still in agony and bleeding profusely from both legs – one of which was fractured – he ran until he came across a group of workmen. He hid in their tent until the police were called.

Gregson, Shawcross, Boyle and another member of their gang, Jason Danson, returned to the house later that morning to find Kent gone. In desperate need of a new safe-house they went to the home of Sylvia Roberts, the warden of a block of flats that provided sheltered accommodation for the elderly. Gregson knew Sylvia because he had gone to school with her son. Having threatened her with death if she gave them away, Roberts was forced to allow the gang to stay at her home. She was sent out to buy hair-clippers and dye, wigs, sunglasses and various forms of disguise so that the gang could blend in among the elderly residents.

Despite the setback, Gregson and Shawcross were determined to proceed with the execution of the Jamma gang. They bought a motorbike and two sets of leathers, planning a classic drive-by shooting using a powerful machine-gun they had acquired. 'I can't see how this is going to work,' Gregson told Shawcross, as they planned the crime.

'It's easy,' came the reply. 'You just point this end towards the person you want to kill and pull the trigger.'

Gregson laughed. 'I know that, but I'll never be able to pull the trigger with the bike gloves on.' To prove his point, he tried to force his gloved finger into the trigger space. The loaded gun went off immediately. After realising no one had been hurt, the two men burst out laughing.

By now the police were hot on the gang's trail, with both Shenton and Kent having identified their captors and the places they had been held. A lengthy surveillance operation had tracked them down to a flat in Redmires Court where they had moved after leaving Roberts's flat. When they were finally arrested, detectives recovered dozens of guns, body armour, machetes, false beards and police scanners. The reign of Salford's most notorious gang was finally over.

Tying Gregson and Shawcross to the crimes was relatively easy – they were identified by Kent and Shenton, their prints were found at the places the men had been held and the guns they were found with matched the wounds. What was more difficult was tying Lydiate into the crime. A man taken captive before Kent – the gang tortured him to get Kent's address – claimed he saw Lydiate at the farm. Dozens of phone calls were also made to Lydiate during the course of the kidnappings. During the trial that followed, Lydiate insisted that Shawcross, Gregson and the others had been acting independently of him, that he had no idea what they were up to. He claimed he was being picked on by the police because in 1993 he had been convicted of kidnapping and torturing two drug-dealers in order to find the whereabouts of a third. On that occasion he had pleaded guilty, but he insisted he was innocent this time.

The jury, however, chose to believe the prosecution's account: that Lydiate had instigated and directed the kidnappings as part of a plan to seek revenge of 'biblical proportions' against those who had shot him. In all, six members of his gang were jailed for a total of sixty-three years, Lydiate receiving twenty-two, Gregson sixteen and Shawcross and Boyle fifteen.

GUNS

CHAPTER TWENTY-SIX

He wears a baggy white collarless shirt that seems to glow against his black skin and black jeans. There's a rope-thick gold chain around his neck and his hair is a mass of tightly bunched locks – I can see them at the sides of the baseball cap that he wears pulled down low over his yellow-tinged eyes. When he talks, his voice low and surly, I can see that one of his bottom front teeth is missing.

Although I do not know his name, this is the kid – he is at most twenty years old and probably a good deal younger – who has promised to help me to get in touch with one of London's most notorious gangsters, a twenty-two-year-old known as G-man who walked free from court a few days earlier after being cleared of involvement in a shooting for the second time in six months.

G-man first came to prominence in 1998 when a fourteen-year-old mugger who tried to sell him a stolen watch was shot in the back by two of G-man's friends. G-man was sentenced to five years for conspiracy to rob, reduced on appeal to three years. In September 2002 he appeared at the Old Bailey in connection with the murder of a DJ who was shot dead at a fast-food restaurant in west London. The victim was carrying a gun but by the time he got it into his hand, he had already been hit in the chest by his opponent's bullet. Eyewitnesses likened the incident to a Wild West shootout.

I covered the case for my newspaper and for the first time I saw G-man in person. I arrived in the court's press box just in time to see his brooding face and stocky form, flanked by three security guards, standing impassively as the indictments were read out: murder, wounding, possession of an 8mm pistol, a Webley .455 calibre revolver and an Uzi submachine-gun. Ever the showman, each and every time he was taken back to the cells, G-man blew a kiss to the public gallery.

The prosecution case was built around CCTV footage from the restaurant, which showed a figure, with a startling similarity to G-man, pulling out his gun and firing as other terrified diners dived for cover. A nearby waitress caught in the crossfire was wounded in the hand. The trial was hampered by violent clashes in the public gallery between supporters of G-man and friends of Bobb, the victim, but ultimately G-man's claims that he was not the man on the film were upheld by the jury and he was allowed to go free.

Six months later he was back at the Old Bailey, accused of driving a car that sprayed bullets at police and partygoers outside a Croydon nightclub. One man was injured when he was hit by bullets from an Uzi. Police appeared on the scene and gave chase, dodging bullets from at least three weapons. By the time they caught up with the vehicle – which had crashed into a wall – the occupants were long gone.

G-man's fingerprints were found both inside and outside the vehicle but the jury accepted his claim that he had had nothing to do with the shooting and, once again, he was allowed to go free.

Eager to secure an interview with G-man about guns and their role in gang culture, I have ventured to the edge of his Notting Hill turf in a bid to see if I can track him down. The man in the white shirt, who I first approached tentatively immediately after G-man's acquittal, seemed friendly enough and told me to return a day or two later. Now he is asking me to follow him into an alleyway on the edge of a large council estate in the shadows of the flyover known as the Westway.

'Come,' he says, motioning with his hand and walking ahead. For a second I hesitate, but then I remember that in the world of street gangs, image is everything and to show weakness is to invite others to treat you with no respect. I take a deep breath, puff myself up to my maximum height and follow.

We stand there in silence for a few seconds, so I break the ice by asking if he has managed to talk to G-man. 'What's in it for me? Are you gonna give me a little something?

I wonder if he is simply stringing me along but subconsciously my hand gently touches my wallet, which is tucked into the right pocket of my jeans. That same moment the man in the white shirt is on me. He pushes me back with the flat of his palm, knocking the wind out of me as I hit the wall behind me. Then his hand delves into my pocket and grabs my wallet.

I am in shock. I can't believe this youngster thinks he's going to get away with this. The wallet is nearing the top of my pocket when my own hands land on top of his and clamp it tight against my body. We start to struggle, grunting and pushing and heaving against one another, moving away from the wall never uttering a word.

And then it happens.

The man in the white shirt twists his body and, with one free hand, moves around to the small of his back, lifting the material. For a split second I see something in the half-light. At first it looks like the misshapen head of a hammer, carved out of wood. But then I spot the telltale screw in the centre and the two subtle peaks carved on the inside. I know exactly what it is: the handle of a gun.

I release my grip on him and jump back what feels like fifty feet. My heart is pounding in my chest; I can hardly speak because there's so much tension and adrenaline flowing through my body. He doesn't reach for the gun again but he knows I've seen it. He has my wallet. He stands there calmly, flicking through its contents but his voice is pure rage.

'Who the fuck are you? You ain't no Babylon. Why you looking for G-man? Where you from? Peckham?'

'No, no, I'm a journalist. A writer. Really. I'm just a writer. You can see my press card, business cards, everything.'

He pulls out the cash and looks through my credit cards. I curse myself for not having carried a 'dummy' wallet – one with just a few pounds and some old storecards that are no longer valid. Something you can hand over and act concerned about. I've done it in the past and I kick myself mentally for not having done it this time.

He examines the cards, takes the cash and tosses the wallet on to the ground behind him. 'Fuck off. You hear me. Just fuck off. No one is going to talk to you about anything. Not now, not ever.' He vanishes into the shadows. I try to pull myself together and get out of the area as fast as I can.

It isn't until the following day that I found out why everyone in the area is so jumpy. G-man had been acquitted on the Friday afternoon and spent most of the weekend celebrating. On Monday evening, while walking along Kingsdown Close with a friend, someone had run out and shot him in the chest and arms at least five times. He was hit in the liver, spleen and kidney. One of his lungs had collapsed. At the time I was trying to track him down he was in hospital under armed guard, fighting for his life.

The fact that I, a stranger to the area, had been asking after him, trying to find out where he lived just a few days earlier did not look good, even though the streets were alive with rumours of who had been responsible. Believing he was literally minutes from death, G-man had gasped the name of his attacker to passers-by who came to his aid. By the time the ambulance arrived his steely resolve had returned and he refused to say any more.

While it is difficult to understand how people this young can be using their guns so freely, it is increasingly common among a whole new generation.

'Children come out of school talking about guns,' says Paul Simpson, a church youth worker on the Stonebridge estate in north London. 'The mentality is so much more vicious now. They don't talk about beating each other up; they talk about killing each other. The simple fact is that with a gun, you are someone, you can hold your own. Without one, you are a dead man.'

Nowhere is this phenomenon more apparent than in Birmingham, where in January 2002 gang warfare claimed the lives of two girls, eighteen-year-old Charlene Ellis and her seventeen-year-old cousin Latisha Shakespeare. Charlene's twin sister, Sophie, and her other cousin, Cheryl Shaw, were also hit but survived. The four had spent the night seeing in the New Year at a party at the Unisevens hairdresser's on Birmingham's Birchfield Road and had gone outside for some air when a car rolled past and sprayed dozens of bullets from at least three weapons.

Originally portrayed as innocent victims, it has since emerged that at least one of the dead girls might have had links to local street gangs and that the group may have been targeted deliberately. (Surveys suggest at least half of all teenage crime gangs have female members. The week before the two girls were murdered, two women were charged with the murder of a male gang member who had been shot dead three months earlier.)

The girls were shot in an area known locally as 'Checkpoint Charlie': cross it at the wrong time and you may end up dead. The area is the undisputed frontline between Birmingham's two main gangs, the Johnson Crew and the Burger Bar Boys, which are made up of predominantly young men with guns.

Both Burger Bar and Johnson Crew gangs formed in the mid-1980s. Burger Bar took their name from a local burger joint in Lozells while Johnson Crew used to meet regularly at Johnson Street Café in Nechells. Ostensibly the two gangs were created as a home defence against the growing right-wing element, which was terrorising the city's black community. But when the threat died down they evolved into crime syndicates.

In a pub in the heart of Handsworth, another notoriously violent area of the city, I tracked down a nineteen-year-old Burger Bar boy who goes by the street name of TC.

'The Johnson Crew were our rivals from day one and that rivalry has just escalated and escalated. As crack cocaine came on the scene the firearms became more and more openly available so the levels of violence increased.

'In the drugs trade ten out of ten people either carry guns or have access to them. If I'm rolling with a Rolex I am up in the money. That means I have to carry a gun because I have to watch my back. My gun brings fear to people. So now everybody has to have a gun.

Since I got my gun nobody fucks with me. Fucking with me is like fucking with death because I will put you down for good.

'It's a way of life now. Once you get into the gang culture it is very difficult to get out. Your gang is your family and people are willing to die for their families. You are pressurised to continue doing what you are doing and your own pals will shoot you down if you cross them. It's not something you can just walk away from. You become a liability. If you're not in then you're an outsider like anybody else.

'We grow up this way, we don't know anything else. How can you teach people not to be violent if they see people getting stabbed, people getting shot every night? Everyone I know has been to a funeral of someone they knew. I know death in a way even my parents can't understand.'

The situation is also repeated in parts of Manchester where one of the fastest-selling T-shirts at the main city flea market features a picture of a chalk outline drawn round a dead body accompanied by the words: 'Welcome To Longsight'.

Just three miles south of the city centre, Longsight, with Moss Side and Hulme, forms a 'gang triangle' where violent death has become an all-too-familiar occurrence. In July 2002 a dozen members of one of the most notorious gangs – the Pitt Bull Crew – were jailed for their part in a turf war that saw fourteen young men shot in the space of three years.

The Pitt Bull Crew was founded by Thomas Pitt soon after he was released from a young offenders' institution after a drugs conviction. He dedicated the enterprise to the memory of his brother, Ray, who had been shot dead outside a nightclub on New Year's Eve in 1995. Ray Pitt had been the leader of the Doddington gang, which had made millions by selling drugs in the city, and Thomas and another Pitt brother, Ken, had been members. The scale of their operation became clear when police filmed a dealer making 219 sales in a few days.

Thomas decided to pick up where his brother had left off. He recruited boys as young as fourteen to sell drugs on his behalf.

Using mountain bikes, they could cruise around the city in pairs with at least one carrying a gun for protection. Those who impressed Pitt were rewarded with gems, gold chains and bullet-proof jackets. The gang used police scanners to evade capture and always wore gloves so police would not be able to get fingerprints.

The gang had access to an array of guns, but Pitt was the only one allowed to use the deadliest weapon in the arsenal, a MAC10 submachine-gun fitted with a silencer and capable of firing up to 300 rounds per minute.

They regularly sold more than three thousand pounds' worth of drugs each day. The money being made soon attracted interest from all quarters. Members of the rival Longsight crew tried to install their own dealers in the same patches, so Pitt declared war on his rivals.

The two gangs fought at least seventeen gun battles, including drive-by shootings, which left four people injured and two dead. In September 2000, Pitt tried to shoot two rival dealers with his MAC10 but it jammed. By the time he had cleared the blockage the two men had gone, so he searched for another victim. Within minutes he had found Marcus Greenidge, twenty-one, a drugs courier with the Longsight Crew. Greenidge had a loaded automatic pistol in his pocket but had no time to reach it. Later Pitt boasted, 'I've just whacked one of the Longsight Crew boys. I struck with five bullets out of seven.'

Pitt was equally ruthless with members of his own gang. On the night Greenidge was shot, Pitt asked his friend and fellow crew member, Thomas Ramsay, sixteen, to move a gun that was hidden in a flat in Longsight. Ramsay forgot, and a few days later the police obtained a search warrant to the flat and found the gun. Forensic tests linked it to Pitt, who was furious. A few days later Ramsay was dead. Pitt was charged with the killing but acquitted.

Less than a week later Pitt himself was shot at by a hooded man on a mountain bike. He survived, but was arrested soon afterwards when one of his fellow gang members, alarmed by Pitt's increasingly violent behaviour, agreed to give evidence against him.

While Pitt was awaiting trial the violence being carried out by his gang continued. Taxi driver Mohammed Ahmed, who had been working as a courier for the Longsight Crew, was ambushed while taking Lee Fielding, another Longsight Crew member, to a meeting. Two Pitt Bull Crew members appeared on the scene and shot Ahmed four times in the head as he sat in his cab.

The killers then bundled Fielding into a stolen car and took him to a disused railway line in Longsight. There, he was shot with a sawn-off shotgun, doused with petrol and set alight. Amazingly, he survived, although he suffered horrific burns.

'Twenty or thirty years ago, a gun was just a tool of the trade,' says retired villain Joey Pyle. 'You carried it while you were working, used it only if you were brave enough and felt you had no option, then stashed it when you were finished. These days, the kids stick them down the backs of their trousers just to go out clubbing. The first sign of trouble, they whip it out. And they shoot first because they know that, more than likely, the other guy is going to be tooled up as well.'

It didn't take long for me to discover just how easy it is to buy guns in today's black market.

Chris, an affable thirty-something south Londoner recently retired from a career in armed robbery, comes bounding back from the bar with a cheeky grin on his face. 'It'll be about twenty minutes,' he says. 'Less time than it takes to deliver a pizza and plenty of time for another drink. Same again?'

We are sitting behind a busy pool table in the dingy annexe of a pub on the outskirts of Catford, which, according to Chris, is one of the easiest places in the capital to buy an illegal gun. After spending a few minutes obtaining the phone number of a local underworld armourer from one of the pub's regulars and placing an order, the only thing left to do is wait. It all seems almost too easy.

'I'm known in here so there's no problem with people trusting me. That's why it's going to be so quick. If you came here on your own as a new face, you would be under suspicion, but that just means it would take a bit more time and a few more calls. But at the end of the day, there are people out there who would much rather have the money than the gun, so they're always willing to sell. To get in touch, all you have to do is get friendly with the barmaid or a bouncer and, sooner or later, you'll be put in touch with someone,' he says cheerfully.

Although he officially retired a few months after his last spell of imprisonment, Chris is still fully tuned into the growing gun culture. 'Pricewise, you're looking at around two hundred and fifty quid for a small, newish .22 revolver. You can get .32 automatics for a lot less, around a hundred pounds, but it's almost impossible to get ammunition for them so they're just for show. The older generation like .38 revolvers, good old-fashioned guns. The younger boys all want 9mm automatics and Uzi submachine-guns but they tend to end up with .22 revolvers because there are so many of them around. There are also some .22 automatics but because they're usually converted from blank-firing guns, they tend to jam after each shot. You're better off with a revolver.

'The last gun I had was a Glock,' says Chris. 'It was brand new and cost me nine hundred pounds. Beautiful gun. I also had a .22 Derringer, which was just for my personal protection as it was easy to hide. It's only one shot, but sometimes, up close, that's all you need.'

According to Chris, guns are easy; the hard part is getting hold of the ammunition. Tricks for dealing with the general shortage include wrapping clingfilm around smaller rounds to make them fit into larger calibre guns; converting blanks by adding special metal caps or, most commonly, 'reloading' used cartridges with new gunpowder and bullets.

It's just over half an hour before Matt, the gun-dealer, arrives. He nods at Chris and the three of us make our way to the gents' toilets, squeezing into the cubicle furthest from the door. Anyone looking on would probably think we were buying drugs not guns, but this is how the majority of weapons are bought and sold – in the dark corners and lavatories of dodgy pubs.

With Chris acting as lookout, Matt swiftly pulls a plastic bag from the folds of his jacket, delves inside and shoves a black lump of metal into my palm. The first thing that strikes me about the gun is that it's much heavier than it looks, so heavy, in fact, that it's almost a struggle to hold it with one hand. It's as cold as ice and covered in a thin layer of oil, which stains my hands as I examine it, fascinated.

'It's a Browning Hi Power 9mm,' says Matt. 'Argentinian, someone's souvenir from the Falklands, but it's in good nick. Been well looked after. Guns last for ever, it's only the ammo that gets fucked up. The clip's half full of good stuff, but I can get you more if you need it.'

I'm still turning the gun in my hand, too dumbstruck to speak. Then I start to panic: I'm a writer investigating a story. The last thing I want to do is actually buy the gun but I realise that I'm getting my fingerprints all over it – and, besides, Matt seems to think the sale is a foregone conclusion.

I hand back the weapon and try to think of a way to avoid upsetting him, especially as he now has a loaded gun. Thankfully, Chris is there to smooth things over.

'What's the history?'

'It's been fired,' says Matt, scratching his nose. 'Dunno if anyone got hurt.'

'I need something clean,' says Chris, without missing a beat. 'Sorry, mate, have to pass on this one. Let me buy you a drink for your trouble.'

These days, a 'clean' gun generally means a reactivated one. Top of the gangster shopping list is the Brocock ME38 Magnum air pistol, which fires pellets using a cartridge of compressed air. Manufactured to high standards, gangsters quickly discovered that the air cartridge could be drilled out and used as a sleeve to hold a live .22 round. The simple procedure turned an innocuous air weapon into a lethal firearm.

Within months of the discovery, converted Brococks became the choice of a new generation of wanna be gunmen. There were dozens of murders, shootings linked to the gun, including two separate high-profile incidents where Asher D of the south London music collective, the So Solid Crew, was caught in possession of a converted Brocock.

Banned from general sale in the early part of 2003, the guns are still widely available. In the course of my investigation for this book I was offered three and actually managed to buy one legally, long after the supposed ban had come into place.

After that, it was simply a matter of paying a visit to an under-world source to find out how to make the conversion and obtain some live ammunition. Hundreds of back-bedroom gun factories have been set up in homes across the country and detectives everywhere admit guns are being put on the streets more quickly than they can take them off.

It didn't stop there. I also managed to get hold of a brand new Glock 17, which had been converted to fire steel ball-bearings with all the force of a bullet, numerous canisters of CS gas, and a riot pistol.

Then there was the stun gun. These weapons, which incapacitate victims for up to fifteen minutes, are officially classed as firearms, but have become increasingly popular with muggers and robbers as they are highly effective but cause no permanent damage.

Stun guns are widely available on the Internet. I placed an order with a French company, and within a few days received a 200,000-volt stun gun through the post, even though they are prohibited in the UK. The stun gun I received is four times more powerful than the Taser models being used by British police forces.

There are now as many as thirty thousand gang members across England and Wales and the numbers are rising rapidly. The number of gang members aged under sixteen doubled in 2003, and nearly half of all gang murders committed with firearms now involve victims under the age of eighteen.

For many, it is the rise of these younger gangs that forms the most worrying aspect of modern organised crime. Youth gangs have always existed and, to some degree, have always been associated with violence, but as little as ten years ago, they were still con-sidered a phase that teenagers went through.

Today, however, those in youth gangs find themselves on the

edge of organised crime proper. They have the opportunity to earn vast sums of money through crime and drug-dealing. They can look to older or former members of the gang and see the success and material wealth they have gained and set themselves a goal for achieving the same. Rather than a phase, gang membership now is the first step on the criminal career ladder.

Steve Shropshire, an expert on gangs and youth culture told me: 'Young people are being drawn into the gangs and crews in ever-increasing numbers and the average age of new members is falling dramatically. The gang culture is now inextricably linked with gun violence.'

2002 saw a record 35 per cent jump in gun crimes. During that year there were almost ten thousand incidents involving firearms recorded in England and Wales and, although the largest increases were in metropolitan areas, the figures showed use of handguns was also growing in rural communities.

Handgun crime has soared past levels last seen before the Dunblane massacre of 1996 and the ban on ownership of handguns introduced the year after Thomas Hamilton, an amateur-shooting enthusiast, shot dead sixteen schoolchildren, their teacher and himself in the Perthshire town. It was hoped the measure would reduce the number of handguns available to criminals. Now handgun crime is at its highest since 1993.

New laws that make carrying a firearm an offence with a mandatory five-year sentence have won little favour with officers on the street. 'It changes nothing,' said one Drugs Squad detective, who asked to remain anonymous. 'Most of the kids carry guns in order to protect themselves when they are dealing. They are going around with enough crack or heroin to ensure that they go away for ten years if they get caught. Because of that, they feel they have nothing to lose and everything to gain by carrying a gun. They carry them just for the hell of it.'

Guns, it seems, are here to stay. And, with growing teen gang membership providing a ready supply of new recruits to the upper echelons of organised crime, the gang problem is here to stay too.

INDEX

INDEX

401

INDEX

INDEX